Taught by God

Other books published by the ORTHODOX RESEARCH INSTITUTE include:

St. Cyril of Alexandria. *Against Those Who Are Unwilling to Confess that the Holy Virgin Is Theotokos*. Edited and translated with an introduction by Protopresbyter George Dion. Dragas.

St. Cyril of Alexandria. *Commentary on the Book of Exodus: First Discourse*. Translated and edited by Evie Zachariades-Holmberg.

Metropolitan Bishoy of Damiette, Kafr el-Sheikh, Barrary and the Monastery of Saint Demiana. *The Real Holy Grail: An Orthodox Response to Dan Brown's Deceptions in Angels and Demons and The Da Vinci Code*.

Metropolitan Panteleimon (Rodopoulos) of Tyroloë. *An Overview of Orthodox Canon Law*. Edited by Protopresbyter George Dion. Dragas.

V. Rev. Fr. Sebastian Dabovich. *The Holy Orthodox Church: The Ritual, Services and Sacraments of the Orthodox Church*

Protopresbyter George Dion. Dragas. *Ecclesiasticus I: Introducing Eastern Orthodoxy.*

Protopresbyter George Dion. Dragas. *The Lord's Prayer according to Saint Makarios of Corinth.*

Protopresbyter George Dion. Dragas. *Saint Athanasius of Alexandria: Original Research and New Perspectives.*

Protopresbyter George Dion. Dragas. *St. Cyril of Alexandria's Teaching on the Priesthood.*

Alphonse and Rachel Goettmann. *The Spiritual Wisdom and Practices of Early Christianity.*

Archimandrite Kyprian Kern. *Orthodox Pastoral Service*. Edited by Fr. William C. Mills.

Fr. Stephen Headley. *Christ after Communism: Spiritual Authority and Its Transmission in Moscow Today.*

Mathew the Poor. *The Titles of Christ.*

Taught by God

MAKING SENSE OF THE DIFFICULT SAYINGS OF JESUS

Daniel Fanous

ORTHODOX RESEARCH INSTITUTE
ROLLINSFORD, NEW HAMPSHIRE.

Published 2010 by
ORTHODOX RESEARCH INSTITUTE
20 Silver Lane, Rollinsford, New Hampshire 03869

COVER ICON: *Detail of Christ*, Aidan Hart

Library of Congress Cataloguing-in-Publication Data

Taught by God: Making Sense of the Difficult Sayings of Jesus/ Daniel Fanous.
Includes bibliographical references.
ISBN 978-1-933275-50-5 (paperback)
ISBN 978-1-933275-51-2 (hardcover)

Library of Congress Control Number: 2010942095

www.orthodoxresearchinstitute.org

For my wife Sherry,
an icon of joy and selfless love

A certain sophist of this age came to visit an Elder. Seeing that he had nothing but the Scriptures, he gave the Elder his own commentary on the Scriptures. A year later, he again visited the Elder and asked: "Father, did my book help you better understand the Scriptures?"

"On the contrary," answered the Elder,
"I had to turn to the Scriptures in order to understand your book."

CONTENTS

Taught by God: An Introduction

God, who at various times and in various ways
Spoke in time past to the fathers by the prophets,
Has in these last days spoken to us by His Son...
—HEBREWS 1:1-2

IN THE EARLIEST MORNING, A CRIPPLED MONK limped quietly beside the bed of a sleeping novice. Suddenly, without warning, and without the slightest remorse, the crippled monk grabbed the novice by the shoulders and violently shook him. As the startled novice recoiled in terror, the monk only managed a single saying: "My dearest son, I did not mean to awaken you, but since you are already up... I am in need of a certain drink that may only be found in a little village, which is about one day's journey west."

The novice, still in a fearful stupor, hurriedly jumped out of his bed, grabbed his staff, and immediately ventured westward. After some time he arrived at what looked to be a little village. He then hastily purchased a drink and returned to his master, humbly presenting it to him in a most sincere and pious prostration. Looking intently at the novice, the monk calmly unfastened the cap of the drink. The crippled monk then casually proceeded to empty it out in full upon the head of the novice without saying another word. The novice for a few moments stood still, trying to gather his thoughts so that he could make sense of the perplexing events. But overcome with failure and great regret, he made resolute haste once more in the hope of pleasing his master. Once more he ventured westward; once more he purchased a drink; and once more he returned to his master. This time, however, he was careful to purchase a different drink. But, to his dismay, once more it was emptied out upon his head. The next day was the same. Day after day, no matter what he did differently, he returned with the fruit of his labor, only to have it consistently poured out upon his now accustomed head. Finally, in exasperation, desperation, and, of course, polite irritation, with the remnants of the fluid still flowing down his face, the novice exclaimed: "Why, master, do you ask me for a drink, only to pour it out on my head?"

With the anger on his face slowly turning to the gentlest of smiles, the crippled monk meekly responded: "Child, you have ventured in obedience time after time, and for this you are to be commended. But in all these days, through all these countless journeys, and with all these innumerable rejections, and you did not think to ask the simplest of questions: Which drink?"

The single detail that prompted this most bizarre chain of events was the original saying of the crippled monk. Faced with such a saying a number of thoughts may have crossed the mind of our poor novice. Perhaps he understood the saying to mean that the crippled monk thirsted for water, or that he desired a little wine for the Eucharist. Or that he was in need of a certain cough medicine, or that, conceivably, he was feeling a little sinful and craved some strawberry juice. One may even hazard that he wanted some arbitrary drink, simply for the sake of teaching the novice a painful lesson! But in any event the thing that becomes clear is that the novice was forced to speculate without any further information. And it is this speculation that incited his daily humiliation.

This fictional though not impossible story reveals at least two simple yet vital truths. The first is that trying to fulfill a command is futile (no matter one's strenuous efforts) unless one *understands* that command. The second is that to understand any command or saying, one would need to ask the *right questions*, instead of speculating as to the answers. The same is to be said of the sayings of Jesus.

In the case of our novice, in order to make sense of his master's obscure saying, he possibly could have asked: What drink is it that you desire? Where exactly may it be purchased? And, finally, perhaps most importantly, why do you desire it? This, if we look closely enough, is essentially asking: What was the present *context* of the monk's wish, and more significantly, what was his *purpose*? It is precisely these two questions that are of the utmost importance in understanding the sayings of Jesus (and any other saying for that matter).

But why is all this important?

Because many of the sayings of Jesus are rarely understood; some are difficult at best, others inexplicable at worst. In fact, it is rare to find a single chapter in the Gospels that is without a difficult saying of some sort. And it should not surprise us that this is so; after all, the sayings were spoken two millennia ago in a world so ancient that it is barely comprehendible to the modern mind. On the other hand, some sayings are so conceptually complex that even their initial first-century hearers walked away murmuring: "This is a *hard saying*; who can understand it?"[1]

For instance, what did Jesus really mean by "the kingdom of heaven suffers violence," or, "I did not come to bring peace but a sword"? How can God's kingdom suffer, and how can the king of Peace wield a sword? Or for that matter, did Jesus actually mean "My Father is greater than I," and did He genuinely cry out: "My God, My God, why have You forsaken Me?" Is Jesus, then, admitting that He is less than the Father, or that God really abandoned His Son? To the ordinary (and even scholarly) mind, sayings like these make little sense. Or else if they do make sense, they often do so in ways that radically differ from the meaning that Jesus perhaps intended. It is, of course, no secret that the greatest heretics of the Church were often clergy who for a variety of reasons misunderstood such sayings to tragic and destructive ends. Indeed, not a few wars have been waged, nor a few empires made desolate in the wake of such sayings.

Clearly, then, if we may say anything at all, these sayings, and others with them, have confused many before us. Books, if not libraries, have been written about them. And yet each day young children ask the same questions that their fathers asked before them: *What did Jesus really mean?* And their fathers, centuries after centuries, have stared blankly back at their children. Sadly, it would seem that little has changed over time. But first let me insist that I am not in any way suggesting that two millennia of Christians have been ignorant of what Jesus really said, in fact truth be told, many of the earlier centuries heard Him far clearer than we. Rather what seems to have occurred as time has gone on is that there has been less interest in what Jesus said and why He said it, than in what we wish He had said.

One reason for this looks to the first question we asked of the crippled monk: What was his circumstance? Any saying only makes sense when it is carefully understood in its *particular context*. If its context be removed,

---

[1] John 6:60.

forgotten, or denied, then it can fairly easily come to mean just about anything, if not everything. The problem of context is thus a chief obstruction in making sense of the sayings of Jesus.

In other words, modernity has filled in the blanks with speculation instead of asking the right questions. Rather than understanding what a particular saying of Jesus meant in His own day (and in His own life), the modern mind has often sought to disfigure it so as to make it inapplicable in the present, or worse, a justification of present behavior. Even when a saying is easily understood and applicable but far too offensive to our much practiced sensibilities, it is simply dismissed on account of its "*only* being for them back then." Otherwise, if a saying is too difficult it is innocently relegated to the library of the theologian who as the "un-spiritual academic" is "better" able to appreciate its complexities. But whatever the motive may be, all of these approaches care little for what Jesus actually had to *say*.

At this point, a brief disclaimer need be made. Whilst the subjects of this study are the "difficult sayings" of Jesus, this by no means entails an elevation of the words of Jesus *above* His salvific deeds, namely the crucifixion and the resurrection. That is to say, the aim is not to become engaged in a "red-letter" reading of the Gospels divorced from the actual life and deeds of Jesus. Consequently, many of the sayings of this study are examined not only within the context of Jesus' teachings, but also through the prism of His life and death. It is therefore of little surprise that the final and penultimate saying that we will examine comes from the mouth of Jesus as He is hung crucified—the verbal expression of His mystical deed. The aim, then, is to consider the sayings of Jesus as an intrinsic manifestation of His entire life and mission.

This brings us to the final burning question we asked of the monk: *why*? What was his purpose, and what did he hope to obtain? It is this, above all else, that has been ignored by the modern approach to the sayings of Jesus. Each word uttered from the mouth of Jesus bears an indispensible attachment to His purpose, to His why. Without acknowledging this we run a very real risk of mistaking what Jesus had to say for what we wish He had said. And it is here, I believe, that the Church stands with remarkable solidarity.

In answering this question of purpose let me suggest something at the risk of sounding ridiculous. There was a time not so long ago when humanity was *taught by God*. Not through prophets, nor through ambiguous oracles, nor through the visions of charismatic mystics. Rather, humanity was taught by God Himself.

This is seemingly ridiculous on two accounts. For one, we should not forget that there remains a fairly significant chasm between man and God, and secondly, though humanity was for a time taught by God, few have seen in such teachings anything other than the words of a man. It seems to me that this stems from a singular mistake: God became the man Jesus and now humanity has forgotten (or else has chosen to forget) that this man Jesus, at the same time, really was God.[2] Let me be clear. This is not to deny that Jesus was a human in the very same way that we are human, but it forces us to recall that He was *also*, in a very real way, God. Put differently, if Jesus was not divine, then His sayings cease to be the pure and untainted words of God. It is this that marks the *why* of Jesus!

In every saying (whether we are able to make sense of it or not) Jesus has but one purpose: To reveal the Word of God to humanity. That is to say, that humanity would now be *taught by God*. Men would no longer be taught by judges, kings, wise men, or prophets. Now God would be their only teacher. Here, once more, my initial suggestion becomes all the more ridiculous. For if we truly understood that what we have before us in the sayings of Jesus is a direct and immediate access into the teaching of God—indeed His Word—then we would not hesitate to devote our lives to their meaning. The sayings would not be relegated to only scholars, nor to the past, nor distorted so as to be unrecognizable. Rather we would sit before such words straining as best we may to hear those words as authentically as they were first spoken—for in doing so we would be sitting at the feet of God.

But at the same time, straining as best we may, we cannot possibly or practically deny that many of the sayings evade precise interpretation. Most do not find consensus in their understanding among the Church fathers, and none have found any resemblance of unanimity among modern scholars. It is for this reason that it is near impossible to state the "doctrinal" meaning of many of the difficult sayings of Jesus, given their diverse interpretations among the early theologians of the Church. Then again, there definitely are some sayings that may be said to have singular interpretations; some for what they *do* mean, and others perhaps for what they *do not* mean. For instance, the saying, "My Father is greater than I," may or may not have a singular and concrete interpretation, but the Church would insist on what it *does not mean*—namely the heresy that Jesus was not equal to the Father. And as such there has always been room for personal reflection and opinion within the Church concerning the sayings, albeit within the strict boundaries of Orthodox theology.

In this vein, although I have argued for some specific interpretations of certain sayings, this does not necessarily mean that they are doctrinal

---

[2] This does not, of course, lessen the value of the present study of the sayings for one who does not believe that Jesus is divine. Any reader may benefit from a historical approach to the sayings and thus the study's relevance is the same regardless. But its effect, I expect, is not.

(though at times they are). And it certainly does not mean that what is presented is the *only* meaning of any given saying, indeed to claim otherwise would betray the very diversity of patristic thought. Rather I have argued for the most plausible interpretation among many (sometimes forcefully) given the results of modern scholarship and more significantly the vision of patristic witness. Accordingly, what is presented in this study is an attempted synthesis and analysis of ancient and modern thought, all the while humbly and desperately holding fast to the mind of the Church. Ultimately and undoubtedly other valid explanations may be put forward, and future interpreters have a ripe harvest before them.

Finally it may well be—as pointed out by the likes of Origen and Athanasius—that the enigmatic natures of such sayings are in fact divinely sanctioned obstacles, placed in Scripture as it were in order to urge the reader to more lofty spiritual heights. In search of these heights, this study will proceed with a singular aim: To hear the sayings of Jesus in His first-century Judaic *context*, through His *life* and *purpose*. The first three parts will examine only the most difficult sayings of Jesus by following His attitude to the law, to the other, and to the kingdom. Finally, the fourth part will seek to come close to what Jesus revealed of Himself in the sayings, the very content of what it means to be *taught by God*. But first let us in a few breaths examine the first-century world of Jesus.

CHAPTER ONE

The Galilean Context of the Sayings

Galilee, Galilee, you hate the Torah!
—RABBI YOHANAN BEN ZAKKAI

A STORY IS RELATED IN THE JEWISH WORK OF THE *TALMUD* that goes as such: A Galilean, for some reason or other, left his home town and traveled south to Jerusalem. As he walked through this boisterous city and took in its marketplace, something now lost in the pages of history, caught his eye. He walked up with no hesitation and frankly asked: "Sir, could I please buy an *amar*?" The merchant, looking quite puzzled with a sly smile beginning to dawn upon his lips, responded:

> You stupid Galilean, do you want something to ride on [donkey=*hamār*]?
> Or something to drink [wine=*hamar*]? Or something for clothing
> [wool=*'amar*]? Or something for sacrifice [lamb=*immar*]?[1]

The Galilean not understanding the merchants taunting words, promptly mentioned words in response of which it would be wholly improper to

[1] *Babylonian Talmud Erubin* 53b.

replicate here, and tread heavily away, back to Galilee, cursing Jerusalem with his every step. What our poor friend did not know (or perhaps he did) was that the distinction of certain sounds almost vanished in the Galilean dialect of Aramaic, and as such clothing, 'amar, sounded very much like a donkey, hamār. It was this dialect that identified Peter as he denied his Master three times: "And a little later those who stood by came up and said to Peter, 'Surely you also are one of them, for your *speech* betrays you,'"[2] and in another place: "Surely this fellow also was with Him, for he is a Galilean."[3] It was within this context that the words of *Jesus the Galilean* were spoken. Of this context much has already been said elsewhere, and hence we shall touch only on the most salient points.[4]

THE WORLD OF JESUS

Some time in and around seven or six BC, in the city of Bethlehem, Judea, Jesus son of Joseph was born. He did not, as may be thought, grow up in Judea, but rather spent His childhood in a hill-town called Nazareth, a city of *Galilee*. It was ironically a relatively peaceful and prosperous city, at least for once in its troubled history, under the flustered and anything but peaceful Herod Antipas (39 AD—4 BC). As first-born, Jesus would have followed in the footsteps of His father, training and working as a woodworker, a trade that would ensure a modest standard of living. He grew up sharing in the life of the average peasant, the *amme ha-aretz*, the common people of Israel. Along with carpentry, He would also have been intimately familiar with the fertile slopes and fields of lower Galilee—a familiarity that would indelibly color His sayings in their imagery of nature and agriculture. And thus in short, Jesus was a Jew, and significantly a first-century Jew.

One rabbi famously said of Him: "we behold a Man who is Jewish in every feature and trait of His character."[5] And so in keeping with the Mosaic Law, Jesus commanded lepers to show themselves to the priests to confirm their healing, and mandated fasting and prayer. As a faithful Jew He worshipped in the Temple, and though His disciples were often rebuked by the scribes and Pharisees for transgressing the "tradition of the elders,"

---

[2] Matt 26:73.

[3] Luke 22:59.

[4] See Daniel Fanous, *The Person of the Christ: The Earthly Context of the Savior* (Boston: Regina Orthodox Press, 2008).

[5] Leo Baeck, *Judaism and Christianity*, tr. Walter Kaufman (Philadelphia: Jewish Publication Society, 1958), 101.

Jesus Himself is never accused of such.[6] It was this first-century Judaism that marked the very nature of His speech in its highly stylistic use of parable and wisdom saying. We do well to remember this as we examine the sayings, for a Jew He remained till His last breath.

That Jesus was a *Galilean* Jew is of the greatest consequence. Galilee was a region which was, as we have already alluded to, a relatively insignificant place. It was also a region that was fiercely proud and independent.[7] But its people though proud were often the taunting song of the rest of Israel, their dialect at times making them subjects of mockery. For instance, when some thought that perhaps Jesus was the promised Messiah, others ridiculed: "Will the Messiah come out of Galilee?"[8] Nicodemus, a Pharisee, on calling for reason before judging Jesus was mocked: "Are you also from Galilee?"[9] And later, rabbinic literature, in the mouth of Rabbi Yohanan ben Zakkai, would go on to extend this sarcasm to the theological ineptitude of the Galileans: "Galilee, Galilee, you hate the *Torah*!"[10] But truth be told, their lack of education in no manner indicated a lack of piety. Working the land for their very survival, they "would have had no time for or interest in the theological niceties, the special observances, and the fierce disputes of the Essenes, the Pharisees, or the Sadducees. For these Galilean Jews...fidelity to the Jewish religion meant fidelity to the basics spelled out in the Mosaic Law."[11]

It was this fidelity that was formative in the upbringing of Jesus. In other respects, however, Jesus stood apart from His fellow Galileans. He taught in the synagogues and the Temple, debated superiorly with the scribes and Pharisees, and expounded upon the Scriptures.[12] At the tender age of twelve, in true rabbinic fashion, He was listening, asking, "and all who heard Him were astonished at His understanding and answers."[13]

As Jesus came of age He chose not to marry, an uncharacteristic and yet not unheard of choice of life. That said, it would be "a point that automatically made Him atypical...and to that extent 'marginal' to mainstream Jewish society."[14] As He neared thirty years of age He gave up this modest yet settled

---

[6] Mark 1:44; Matt 6:5-7; Luke 22:53; Matt 15:2, respectively.

[7] For further background on the Galilean context see Geza Vermes, "Jesus the Jew," in *Jesus' Jewishness: Exploring the Place of Jesus within Early Judaism*, ed. James H. Charlesworth (New York: Crossroad Publishing Company, 1996), 112.

[8] John 7:41.

[9] John 7:45-52.

[10] *Jerusalem Talmud Shabbat* 15d.

[11] John P. Meier, *A Marginal Jew: Rethinking the Historical Jesus*, Vol. II (New York: Doubleday, 1994), 1039.

[12] Luke 20:1; John 7:15-31; Luke 4:16, respectively.

[13] Luke 2:42-47.

[14] John P. Meier, *A Marginal Jew*, Vol. II, 1040.

and comfortable life, and began what is known as His public ministry. He announced daringly and with authority the kingdom of God. He spoke mighty words and performed mighty deeds. Exorcisms, healings from illness and even death, along with astonishing control over nature, all served to intensify His words. His words did not simply resound throughout the Galilean and Judean countryside as mere speech of eloquence, rather "His word was with authority."[15]

Jesus thus stood out as a celibate Galilean, who surprisingly for a Galilean, spoke with wisdom and education. Such were His words *and* deeds that at least some of the things He said or did so confronted the ruling elements of His society, both Jewish and Roman, that He was crucified in close proximity to the year thirty AD. But His words did not die with Him. And in the same measure that Jesus still lives, so do they.

[15] Luke 4:32.

PART ONE:

The Righteousness of the Kingdom

CHAPTER TWO

'Whoever divorces his wife'

*...the LORD God of Israel says
That He hates divorce,
For it covers one's garment with violence...*
—MALACHI 2:16

A QUESTION WAS ONCE POSED TO JESUS as He came to the region of Judea beyond the Jordan:

Is it *lawful* for a man to *divorce* his wife for just any reason?[1]

His reply was unmistakably clear: "What God has joined together, let not man separate."[2] Strangely, it is from this saying that we must by necessity begin. Some may, however, query whether this really is a "hard" or enigmatic saying. And even if that is admitted, many would question what bearing this saying has on Jesus' attitude to the law. The answer comes when we consider the next words of His questioners: "Why then did *Moses* command to give a certificate of divorce?"[3]

[1] Matt 19:3.
[2] Matt 19:6.
[3] Matt 19:7.

This incident in the life of Jesus has often been examined only in respect to divorce. Yet what stands at its core is actually a confrontation. Not only between Jesus and the Pharisees, but between the words of Jesus and the words of Moses ("Why then did Moses…"). That is to say, this saying of Jesus on divorce is accused of being *against* the law of Moses, which if we look a little deeper, is the law commanded by God Himself. Is Jesus then against the law of the God of Israel?

We may now appreciate why it is that this saying will be our introduction into the sayings that seemingly run counter to the law given by God. To consider the true meaning and context of this saying, we must first look to the origins of marriage.

HISTORY OF MARRIAGE & DIVORCE

Early Judaic thought lacked clarity as to personal survival after death. It only held some unclear allusions to a hell-like place called *sheol*. Therefore, it is not surprising that the call to procreation in Genesis: "Be fruitful and multiply…,"[4] along with God's blessing of Abraham, takes the form of prosperity through one's children:

> …blessing I will bless you, and multiplying I will multiply your *descendants* as the stars of the heaven and as the sand which is on the seashore…
> In your *seed* all the nations of the earth shall be blessed.[5]

Blessing could not guarantee that one would live longer, or that one would live after death, but instead focused upon the perpetuation of life not through resurrection but through childbirth—one's seed. For the ancients this was an essential dimension of marriage. And thus we hear that when Abraham's wife, Sarah, could not bear him children, he looked to her maidservant Hagar to fulfill the promise of prosperity.[6] Later, this hope in the blessing would lead to the development of the *Levirate* marriage, where a man was obliged to raise seed for his dead brother (with his dead brother's wife).[7] The promise of blessing thus detached from personal survival, became survival *through* one's descendants:

---

[4] Gen 1:28.
[5] Gen 22:17-18.
[6] Gen 16:1-3.
[7] Gen 38:8.

The Old Testament Judaic thought saw the essential meaning and goal of marriage in procreation. The most obvious and necessary sign of God's blessing was seen in the *continuation* of the race.[8]

It is for this reason that on glancing through the pages of the Old Testament texts we find so many examples of polygamy, which to be accurate are *polygyny*.[9] In certain times it was even the norm, with no seeming limit on wives or concubines, that is, as long as they could be "maintained." The first known to take more than one wife was Lamech,[10] the great-grandson of Enoch. Abraham had one wife and two concubines,[11] Jacob had two wives,[12] and Esau had three.[13] Gideon the Judge is remembered as having seventy sons, "for he had many wives."[14] The kings likewise began to multiply wives, David having seven named[15] and one unnamed wife,[16] whilst Solomon seemingly kept a flock (for want of a better word) of wives by his side.[17] It would seem that with an increase in status came a multiplication of wives, bringing, as one may imagine, a multiplication of problems.[18] But by the time of the prophets polygyny was in a variety of ways and degrees discouraged, with Hosea and Isaiah being monogamous, and the books of Proverbs and Ecclesiasticus exalting the place of the wife within the monogamous home.[19]

Within the New Testament, explained in part by the promise of personal survival through resurrection, marriage once more was seen in the light of its original creation. Marriage ceased to be a function, or rather, a servant of procreation. In the words of John Meyendorff: "Not a single New Testament text mentioning marriage points to procreation as its justification or goal."[20] Once conceding to polygyny for the sake of perpetuating the blessing, marriage was now returned to its original state of monogamy.[21]

---

[8] John Meyendorff, *Marriage: An Orthodox Perspective* (New York: SVS Press, 1975), 12.

[9] *Polygyny*: One man, many wives; as opposed to *polygamy*: more than one wife or husband.

[10] Gen 4:23.

[11] Gen 16, 25:1-2.

[12] Gen 29:15-30.

[13] Gen 36:2.

[14] Judg 8:30.

[15] 1 Sam 18:17-30, 25:38-43; 2 Sam 3:2-5.

[16] 2 Sam 5:13.

[17] 1 Kngs 11:3.

[18] For example, David's in-house domestic problems; see 2 Sam 13, 1 Kngs 1-2.

[19] Prov 12:4, Sirach 25:1, 8.

[20] John Meyendorff, *Marriage: An Orthodox Perpective*, 13.

[21] Though "polygamy was allowed in rabbinic Judaism...it was beginning to fall out of favor, and there were groups within Judaism who disapproved of polygamy or even disallowed it." David Instone-Brewer, *Divorce and Remarriage in the Bible: The Social and Literary Context*

But long before the time of the New Testament, the union of men and women unfortunately, at times, led to strife and tension. And thus it was not long before men began to question: When and how may I dismiss my wife? The response of Moses is the law which was placed in opposition to the word of Jesus:

> When a man takes a wife and marries her, and it happens that she finds no favor in his eyes because he has found some *uncleanness in her*, and he writes her a *certificate of divorce*, puts it in her hand, and sends her out of his house, when she has departed from his house, and goes and becomes another man's wife, if the latter husband detests her and writes her a certificate of divorce, puts it in her hand, and sends her out of his house, or if the latter husband dies who took her as his wife, then *her former husband who divorced her must not take her back* to be his wife after she has been defiled; for that is an abomination before the Lord...[22]

What strikes us is that there is *no* actual law of divorce. Take note of this, for it is key to understanding the words of Jesus. First, we see that divorce results because the wife "finds no favor" in her husband's eyes, for he has found "some uncleanness in her." Therefore, the matter discussed here only concerns *when* men divorce. Secondly, to enact the divorce, a certificate of divorce, *git* in Hebrew, must be given to the wife. Thirdly, and most importantly, a man may not remarry a woman that he has previously divorced, for this is an "abomination before the Lord." Let us begin with the third point.

The law here has only and narrowly to do with the specific case prohibiting a man from remarrying a woman he has previously divorced. The reason he divorced her (her "uncleanness") and how he may divorce her (by a "certificate") are only secondarily mentioned in the context of remarrying a previous wife. In other words, the law was not forbidding or permitting divorce, what *was* forbidden was the remarriage to a previous wife.[23] Nowhere was there a law of divorce, only a single specific case of prohibition of remarriage. Simply and succinctly put, there was no law of divorce! Over time, this principal prohibition of a specific case of remarriage was overshadowed by the discussion of when a man may divorce his wife.

(Grand Rapids: Wm. B. Eerdmans, 2002), 137.

[22] Deut 24:1-4.

[23] Also there were two cases when the right to divorce was taken away from a husband. (1) If a man *falsely accused* his wife of prenuptial intercourse (Deut 22:19); and (2) If a man *lies with a virgin before marriage* he must then marry her and may not divorce her for all his days (Deut 22:8).

The point that the law had nothing to do with divorce fell decidedly into the background. Great rabbinic debate, in fact an entire book of the *Mishnah*,[24] would then centre upon the statement "he has found some uncleanness in her." It was this statement which created the confrontation between Jesus and the Pharisees. But before Jesus, it had already caused dispute between the Pharisees themselves, between the School of Rabbi Shammai and the School of Rabbi Hillel, both of whom were contemporary with Jesus. The argument went as such:

> The School of Shammai say a man may not divorce his wife unless he has found unchastity in her, as it is said, "...because he has found in her *indecency* in a matter." But the School of Hillel say he may divorce her even if she burns his food, as it is said, "...because he has found in her indecency *in a matter.*"[25]

For these two bickering schools of Pharisees, what was of primary concern was not whether the law was about divorce, but about whether there was justification within the text of the law—though the law was about something else altogether—for divorcing a wife "for just any reason."[26]

In the text "indecency," in Hebrew *erwat dabar*, literally means "the nakedness or shame of a thing." The School of Shammai turned *erwat dabar* into *debar erwa*, by changing the order of the wording. That is, instead of "shame of a thing," they read it as "thing of *shame*," placing the emphasis on the shame or "indecency." Thus a wife may be divorced if she has done something that is shameful, a "thing of shame." Historically, many scholars have claimed that this restricts divorce to when a woman has committed adultery, when in actual fact it restricts divorce to any case where the wife has done something shameful. On the other hand, the School of Hillel kept the original order of the wording, *erwat dabar*, and therefore understood it as "shame of a *thing*." They thus placed the stress on the thing or "the matter," and hence *anything* was grounds for divorce.[27]

---

[24] *Mishnah Gittin.*

[25] *Mishnah Gittin* 9:10. Also see David Werner Amram, *The Jewish Law of Divorce According to the Bible and Talmud* (Philadelphia: Edward Stern & Co., 1896).

[26] This whole debate is found in the rabbinic work of the *Mishnah*, a work compiled in its final form, centuries after Jesus. Some have claimed that such debates are not applicable to the time of Jesus, and are simply retrojections of post-Jesus Pharisaic discussions. However, it is historically quite likely that controversy over grounds of divorce colored the debate with Jesus, given the similarities in language, "for just any reason," and the words of Josephus who was alive in the same century as Jesus.

[27] I owe this insight to John P. Meier, "The Historical Jesus and the Historical Law: Some Problems with the Problem," *The Catholic Biblical Quarterly* 65, 1 (2003): 75-76.

From this we may then understand that the stricter School of Shammai allowed divorce only if a wife had done something shameful, such as committing adultery, whilst the more lenient School of Hillel permitted divorce for any reason whatsoever if the husband was displeased. In the above case, because "she burns his food," the husband was entitled to a divorce if he so wished. In such vein did Rabbi Akiba of the School of Hillel claim that a man may divorce his wife, "even if he found someone else prettier than she, since it is said, 'And it shall be if she finds no favor in his eyes...'"[28] Josephus, the first-century Jewish historian, further confirms that a man was permitted to divorce for "any cause whatsoever (and many such causes happen among men)..."[29] and in fact did so himself: "I divorced my wife also, as *not pleased* with her behavior, though not till she had been the mother of three children."[30] And thus we may conclude that in first-century Palestine "there was little stigma attached to divorce."[31]

We do well to remember, however, that though the argument in some cases exaggerates the reasons for divorce (for example if another woman is found "prettier") we should not think that divorce was a whimsical and day to day act.[32] Rabbi Eleazer exclaims the gravity of the matter: "When a man divorces his first wife, even the altar sheds tears..."[33] To further the point, later rabbinic developments added three more restrictions to divorce: when the wife was insane, when she was in captivity, and when she was a minor and thus incapable of understanding the bill of divorce.[34] The rabbis also placed obstructions to the process by introducing formalities in ordering, writing, attesting, and delivering the bill of divorce, as well as requiring the husband to consult one learned in the law who was obliged to attempt to reconcile the parties first.[35]

JESUS & DIVORCE

We have seen that the issue of divorce was a trigger of controversy among the Pharisaic schools in first-century Palestine. We also need to deepen this

---

[28] *Mishnah Gittin* 9:10.

[29] Josephus, *Antiquities of the Jews*, IV:253.

[30] Josephus, *Life of Flavius Josephus*, I:426.

[31] David Instone-Brewer, *Divorce and Remarriage in the Bible*, 132.

[32] Gerald Friedlander, *The Jewish Sources of the Sermon on the Mount* (New York: Ktav Publishing House, 1969), 57.

[33] *Babylonian Talmud Gittin* 90b.

[34] *Mishnah Ketubot* 4:9; *Yebamot* 14:1.

[35] *Babylonian Talmud Kiddushin* 6a.

with a political dimension. It was not long before Jesus that another spoke
on the issue of divorce, and correspondingly met his death quite soon after.
John the Baptist had just been decapitated because of his opposition to the
incestuous marriage of Herod Antipas with his brother's wife Herodias.[36]
And therefore the issue of divorce itself was laden with inter-pharisaic
religious controversy as well as being politically charged. But these issues in
themselves stand secondary to the real contention: Does Jesus stand with or
against the law of Moses?

> The Pharisees also came to Him, testing Him, and saying to Him, "Is it
> lawful for a man to *divorce* his wife for just any reason?"
> And He answered and said to them, "Have you not read that He who made
> them at the beginning '*made them male and female*,' and said, 'For this
> reason a man shall leave his father and mother and be joined to his wife,
> and the two shall become *one flesh*'? So then, they are no longer two but
> one flesh. Therefore what God has joined together, let not man separate."
> They said to Him, "Why then did *Moses* command to give a certificate of
> divorce, and to put her away?"
> He said to them, "Moses, because of the hardness of your hearts, permitted
> you to divorce your wives, but *from the beginning it was not so*. And I say
> to you, whoever divorces his wife, *except* for sexual immorality, and mar-
> ries another, commits adultery; and whoever marries her who is divorced
> commits adultery."[37]

Consider the question itself: "Is it lawful for a man to divorce his wife
for just any reason?" Interestingly, the addition "for just any reason," does
not exist in the Markan version of the encounter.[38] And given that Matthew
was writing for the Jews, it follows that "Matthew has brought the question

---

[36] Interestingly, Herodias is claimed to have sent a bill of divorce to her first (or second)
husband. Whilst perhaps done on rare occasion, it was not legal for a woman to divorce
her husband. Some have claimed that the originality of Jesus' teaching on divorce is in His
protection of women. Briefly, the "law" said a man could put away his wife, but the wife could
not put away her husband. Some have thus concluded that Jesus championed women, by
disallowing divorce, and by claiming that adultery could also be committed against a woman.
Yet, we should remember that the bill of divorce was in fact put in place to protect women (a
man renounces his right over a woman, and is unable to remarry her if he changes his mind).
Therefore, *in this case* we must conclude that Jesus abrogated divorce for all—He did not take
away any women's rights, nor did He elevate them. For it was not a matter of rights, but rather
propounding the ideal of creation. For further discussion see C. G. Montefiore, *Some Elements
of the Religious Teaching of Jesus* (The Jowett Lectures for 1910; London: Macmillan, 1910), 44;
John Kloppenborg, "Alms, Debt and Divorce: Jesus' Ethics in their Mediterranean Context,"
Toronto Journal of Theology 6 (1990): 195.

[37] Matt 19:1-10. Also Mark 10:1-12.

[38] Mark 10:2.

of divorce into the realm of strict legal discussion."[39] As we have seen, the Schools of Shammai and Hillel had been disputing the "reason" for divorce, and it was into this dispute that Jesus was invited to respond. The expectation being that He would side with one or other of the Schools. But to their surprise Jesus refused to enter such a debate, and instead referred all present to the institution of marriage, to the original union in Genesis. Immediately following this we have the real controversy: "Why then did *Moses* command to give a certificate of divorce..." (It is of note that the Pharisees claimed Moses had *commanded*, whereas Jesus is quick to correct that Moses *permitted* not commanded.) The Pharisees had thus carefully primed the scene, by contrasting what Jesus prohibited with what Moses had commanded.

We have already seen that the command of Moses was not by any means a law of divorce. In actuality the law was a prohibition of remarriage in a specific case, and therefore Moses never commanded anyone to "give a certificate of divorce." Divorce in the Mosaic law was neither allowed nor disallowed. For Jesus, the law preventing remarriage to a previous wife then was not a justification of divorce. The matter was thus not whether one could divorce in this or that case, it was whether one could divorce at all: "what is subject to debate is not the interpretation of Deut 24:1, but rather the very claim of Deut 24:1 as a legal ground for divorce."[40]

Moses did not command that divorce was legal; he simply permitted it within a particular context. If Jesus *prohibited* what Moses *permitted*, then He is not on any account *permitting* what Moses *prohibited*.[41] This confusing statement may be made clear by an illustration. Imagine I said to a child: "You are not permitted to drink alcohol until you are eighteen," and then my wife came later and said: "You are never to drink alcohol." In this case she has not permitted what I prohibited (alcohol); rather she has prohibited the permission I gave (after the age of eighteen). No one would then accuse her of being against my law for the child; simply she has strengthened my law. In other words: "It is a general principle that greater stringency than the law requires is not illegal."[42] It then stands to reason that Jesus was not speaking against the law, for in the first point, the law never

---

[39] W. D. Davies, *The Setting of the Sermon on the Mount* (Cambridge: Cambridge University Press, 1964), 104. Also for an examination of the exception clause see B. Witherington. "Matthew 5:32 and 19:9—Exception or Exceptional Situation?" *New Testament Studies* 31 (1985): 571–76.

[40] Herman Hendrickx, *The Sermon on the Mount* (London: Geoffrey Chapman, 1984), 72.

[41] E. P. Sanders, *Jesus and Judaism* (London, SCM Press, 1985), 256.

[42] E. P. Sanders, *Jesus and Judaism*, 256.

allowed divorce, and in the second, he who chose not to divorce his wife cannot have been said to transgress the law. First-century Judaic thought took a Mosaic prohibition and transformed it into a law allowing divorce. Jesus on the other hand, took the very same prohibition, highlighted and elevated it, and thus created a law prohibiting divorce! To prevent divorce was simply to take away the need for Moses' prohibition against remarriage in the beginning. Ironically, "to forbid the divorce was not to annul the law of divorce but to intensify it."[43]

At this point Jesus' argument changes direction. If they wish to put Him at opposition to the law of Moses, then Jesus shall meet them with another part of the law. If the Pharisees will refer to Moses, then so shall He. The entire Pentateuch or *Torah*, the first five books of the Old Testament, was the work of Moses' pen. Therefore, for Jesus, to cite the book of Genesis in this legal debate was just as valid as citing from the law in Deuteronomy, given that Moses wrote both.[44]

But it was not only a matter of citing one part of the Scriptures against another, more so it was an "appeal to origins and reflects a theology and ideology: God's original purpose has priority."[45] If Moses permitted divorce in a particular context, then it was just that—a *permission*. But that was not the intention. "From the beginning it was not so..." The intention, according to Jesus, is that which was revealed at Creation: the original unity of male and female. This unity is what humanity was and is called to. Jesus thus refers not to a mere Mosaic command, but to the will of God at creation: "Have you not read that He who made them..." H. J. Schoeps after scrutinizing rabbinic and other apocalyptic texts declares that the reference to the original will of God is so unique and radical that it must have "stemmed exclusively from His Person. There was no accepted Jewish tradition upon this point."[46] The method of referring to the original will of God was radical, but what was it that Jesus was really saying?

THE ORIGINAL ANDROGYNOUS MAN

And He answered and said to them, (1) "Have you not read that He who made them at the beginning '*made them male and female*', and said, (2)

---

[43] W. D. Davies, *The Setting of the Sermon on the Mount*, 104-105.

[44] Christopher Rowland, *Christian Origins* (London: SPCK, 2002), 155.

[45] William R. G. Loader, *Jesus' Attitude towards the Law: A Study of the Gospels* (Cambridge: Wm. B. Eerdmans, 2002), 89.

[46] Cited from Robert Banks, *Jesus and the Law in the Synoptic Tradition* (Cambridge: Cambridge University Press, 2005), 150.

'For this reason a man shall leave his father and mother and be joined to his wife, and the two shall become *one flesh*'? So then, they are no longer two but one flesh. Therefore what God has joined together, let not man separate."

The *first* statement "made them male and female," by itself at first proves nothing. That men and women were created in no way indicates that they may not divorce. Yet, for Jesus it does. From this statement Jesus deduces in His *second* statement: "For this reason...the two shall become one flesh." The *first* results in the *second*. Why and how? Logically, the first statement— God creating two independent beings—could actually be an argument for divorce. Therefore there must have been something that led Jesus from the first statement to the second. The answer lies in the entire quotation found in Genesis:

> ...in the image of God He created *him*;
> male and female He created *them*.[47]

At this point I should say that what follows is an unusual hypothesis and definitely not in keeping with the understanding of the Church. I only mention it as it is indicative of just how united the original man and woman were called to be (though it no doubt is an extreme and flawed reading).

For some rabbis, and to those familiar with the works of Plato,[48] there was a concept (at times a Judaic doctrine) that the original created being was an ideal *androgynous* man.[49] That is to say, God created the original man as male and female in *one*. They came to this fascinating conclusion from the verse itself, where the singular is used for "created him," and yet somehow "him" is identified with "male and female He created *them*." Perceiving this, as well as the observation that woman came from the rib of man, the ancients and the rabbis with them were left questioning: "What sort of being might it be...of whom one could equally well speak in the singular or plural? Again the answer was that the verse must refer to androgynous man."[50] Put simply, the original creation (as understood by some of the ancient Jews) was a composite being, both male and female.[51] So much so that Rabbi Eleazar

---

[47] Gen 1:27.

[48] Plato, *Symposium* 189d-190d.

[49] *Androgynous:* Both male and female.

[50] David Daube, *The New Testament and Rabbinic Judaism* (London: The Athlone Press, 1956), 72.

[51] Also see *Beresbit Rabba* 8:1; *Babylonian Talmud Erubin* 18a; Philo, *De Opificio Mundi* 24.76.

said: "Any man [*adam*] who has no wife is no proper man [*adam*]; for it is said, male and female He created them and called their name *Adam*."[52] In a *Midrash* on Genesis, the rabbis speak without shadows: "When the Holy One, blessed be He, created Adam, He created him an androgynous."[53] Rabbi Shamuel, son of Nahman, echoes even further: "When the Blessed Holy One created Adam, He created Him with a double face. Then He sawed him apart..."[54]

Though this reading of Genesis may be inexact, it at least reveals just how united the original creation was called to be. If the statement "made them male and female" is understood in the light of this united original creation, then the unity inherent in the original creation is the simple yet irrefutable reason why man may not divorce his wife. Jesus by pointing to the original creation outlaws divorce, for to divorce is to divide the original unity intended by God. Only now may we understand how Jesus moves flawlessly from the statement "made them male and female" to the conclusion "the two shall become one flesh." The inherent unity in creation (though *not* precisely as an androgynous man), whereby man was created as "male *and* female," presses the conclusion that man was and is intended to become one with a woman. Therefore, Jesus teaches emphatically, "what God has joined together, let not man separate."

We should also note that Jesus by referring to Genesis was outlawing polygamy along with divorce on the basis of the original creation. An unknown Church Father remarks: "For it was not two or three ribs that He took from the side of man; and He did not make two or three women. When, therefore, a second or a third wife stands before your face, as then Eve stood before Adam, how could you say to them, 'This is bone from my bones?'"[55] In the words of the eminent Jewish legal scholar, David Daube:

> ... [Jesus' teaching] involves the rejection, not only of divorce, but also of polygamy. It does so because it sees in marriage an *imitation* of the ideal, androgynous state of man. Once marriage is conceived of in this fashion, it becomes just as criminal for a husband to take a second wife while the first lives. The ideal state is disrupted in the former no less than in the latter.[56]

No doubt some will be disconcerted with this somewhat strange concept of the ideal androgynous man; others may claim that the evidence

---

[52] *Babylonian Talmud Yebamot* 63a.
[53] *Midrash Genesis Rabbah* 8:1.
[54] *Babylonian Talmud Berakhot* 61a.
[55] Anonymous, *Incomplete Work on Matthew*, Homily 32, PG 56:800.
[56] David Daube, *The New Testament and Rabbinic Judaism*, 75.

for this concept comes from rabbinic literature post-Jesus. To be clear and to reiterate, I do *not* in any way claim that Adam was a man *and* a woman, nor do I think that the rabbis did for the most part.[57] Yet what stands is that in the description given in Genesis (along with the rabbinic thought that was contemporary with Jesus) there was an understanding that man was created in the image of the *oneness* of God. Therefore man was created in the image of this unity. Furthermore, man was created as "male and female," that is, in some sense the ideal human existence was the union of man and woman. As if to say, men and women were created to become one "human." If such is the case, then man, logically and inherently, may not separate from his wife. But there is, however, one case, when he may.

DIVORCE & THE CHURCH

Matthew in retelling the confrontation on divorce, as well as in the antitheses in the Sermon on the Mount,[58] tells of the singular exception to divorce: *sexual immorality*. Mark is far more radical and gives no exception. And thus it is that we ask: If Jesus points to the original creation of man as the ideal, why then do we find in Matthew: "And I say to you, whoever divorces his wife, *except for sexual immorality*…"[59]

Great debate has centered upon this exceptive clause, *pareketos logou porneias*, perhaps unnecessarily. Many have suggested that if the exception was adultery, then the word used for adultery should have been *moicheia* and not *porneias* in Greek.[60] Others have debated why the clause was in Matthew and not in Mark. Yet in reality it is not important whether Jesus granted the exception or not, for it is the act of adultery itself which separates the marriage, not the divorce. In the words of Cyril of Alexandria: "It is not the letters of divorce that dissolve the marriage in relation to God but the errant behavior."[61] The very act of infidelity destroys that which was made one at the beginning of time. The two existentially cease to be one flesh. It is for a

---

[57] For an illuminating and Orthodox discussion of the original creation see Peter C. Bouteneff, *Beginnings: Ancient Christian Readings of the Biblical Creation Narratives* (Grand Rapids: Baker Academic, 2008), 1-32.

[58] Matt 5:31-32.

[59] Matt 19:9.

[60] Some scholars have even taken this usage of *porneias* to mean "incestuous union."

[61] Cyril of Alexandria, PG 72:380. The Church Fathers were fairly consistent in their view of divorce. For a sample of their views see Chromatius, *Tractate on Matthew* 24.1.1-3, CCL 9a:309; Gregory of Nazianzus, *Orations* 37.8, NPNF 2 7:340; Tertullian, *Against Marcion* 4.34, ANF 3:405; Jerome, *Letter to Amandus* 55.3, NPNF 2 6:109-111.

similar reason that Paul claims that even by lying with a prostitute, the two shall become one flesh.[62] The exceptive clause then simply states what has already been declared:

> According to the Gospel, adultery destroys the very reality, the mystical essence, of marriage… Divorce is but a declaration about the absence, the disappearance, the destruction of love, and therefore it simply declares that a marriage does not exist. It is analogous to the act of excommunication; it is not a punishment, but a post factum determination of a separation that has *already* taken place.[63]

Thus, when the Church "grants" divorce it does not sever a bond that was created by God, but simply "declares" it severed by the desecration of the union by one of the two. Adultery, by either party, amounts to disuniting that which was made in the image of God: "the gift is refused, and marriage does not exist. What occurs then is not only legal 'divorce,' but a tragedy of misused freedom."[64] On the same account, each time the Church in her mercy and with great trepidation "declares" a divorce, she does so by in some sense placing herself *against* the words of her Groom. It is for this reason, that the Church is slow and hesitant in matters of the "economy" of divorce. This, however, is not the place for such a discussion.[65]

What is critical to see is that for Jesus, divorce was neither a function nor privilege of the law. Marriage, the united bond of man and woman, was that which was espoused by the law. Moses may have granted the people permission to divorce because of the "hardness of their hearts." But Jesus called for a renewal of hearts, when humanity shall return to that ideal and original union, in the untainted image of God. For it is in this image that the truth and mystical reality of marriage takes shape.

This mystery is revealed and adequately summated in a most charming Jewish story related by Rabbi Iddi: "It happened once that a woman in Sidon had lived ten years with her husband without bearing him a child. They came to Rabbi Simeon ben Yohai and requested to be parted from one another. He said to them: 'I adjure you, just as you have always shared a festive life together, so do not part save with festivity.' They took his advice and kept holiday and made a great feast and drank very freely. Feeling then in a good

---

[62] 1 Cor 6:15.

[63] Paul Evdokimov, *The Sacrament of Love: The Nuptial Mystery in the Light of the Orthodox Tradition* (New York: SVS Press, 2001), 189.

[64] John Meyendorff, *Marriage: An Orthodox Perspective*, 15.

[65] See Paul Evdokimov, *The Sacrament of Love*, 186-192 and John Meyendorff, *Marriage: An Orthodox Perspective*, 54-58.

humor the husband said to her: 'My wife, pick out any article you want in my house and take it with you to your father's house.' What did she do? When he was asleep she gave an order to her servants and handmaids to lift him up on the bed and take and carry him to her father's house. At midnight he awoke from his sleep, and when the effects of the wine passed from him he said: 'My wife, where am I?' She replied: 'You are in my father's house.' 'And what am I doing in your father's house?' he said. She replied: 'did you not say to me last night, "Take any article you like from my house and go to your father's house?" There is nothing in the world I care for more than you.' They again went to Rabbi Simeon ben Yohai and he went and prayed for them, and they became fertile." The story then continues with a radical conclusion:

> And is not the lesson clear: If a woman on saying to a mere mortal like herself, "There is nothing I care for more in the world than you," was visited [granted a child], does it not stand to reason that Israel who *wait* for the salvation of God every day and say, "We care for nothing in the world but You," will certainly be visited?[66]

Jesus in no way stands against the law of Moses. For indeed, there was no law of divorce but only a specific case of prohibition of remarriage. Rather, Jesus by forbidding divorce refers man once more to the original will and law of God: *Unity.* The union of man and woman, in the image of their Maker, is a symbol of the union of God and His people. Perhaps now we may appreciate why it is that our Creator "hates divorce, for it covers one's garment with violence."[67] Annihilating the union of man and woman pains the Creator, for it does "violence" to His very union with humanity. It is little wonder that the Apostle Paul when writing on marriage concludes: "This is a great mystery, but I speak concerning Christ and the church."[68]

---

[66] *Midrash Canticles Rabbah* 1.4.

[67] Mal 2:16. Also see Tadros Y. Malaty, *The Gospel According to St. Mark* (Alexandria: St. George Church, 2003), 166.

[68] Eph. 5:30-32.

CHAPTER THREE

Jesus & the Law: 'It was said of old'

There are truths which are not for all men, nor for all times.
—VOLTAIRE

THE TORAH WAS, AND IS, FOR JEWS THE MEANS of perfect obedience to God the law-giver. Written by the finger of God on Mount Sinai, the law given to Moses would from then on guide the people unto God. It revealed the will of God to the individual and the community in both public and private existence, in both great and minor concern. In short, Torah defined Israel.[1]

Should a Jew then speak or act against this law (or even question it for that matter), they would not be placing themselves in opposition to social convention or norms; it was opposition to God Himself! It is for this most *crucial* reason—and it cannot be stressed enough—that the words and actions of Jesus that "seem" to be against the law must be examined in this lengthy chapter. How could Jesus, a most perfect Jew, not observe that which

---

[1] N. T. Wright, *Jesus and the Victory of God* (Minneapolis: Fortress Press, 1996), 432. Also see Geza Vermes, *Jesus in His Jewish Context* (Minneapolis: Fortress Press, 2003), 40.

was commanded by the God of Israel? To put the point more dramatically: How could Jesus be disobedient to God His Father?[2]

But first a momentary pause need be made. An important source for contextualizing Jesus' sayings on the law is the rabbinic literature. Rabbinic evidence for what first-century "historical" Pharisees actually thought is to be found in the *Mishnah* specifically. This is a work that was compiled in its final form a few centuries after Jesus. And thus some scholars have claimed that such rabbinic works are irrelevant in that they consist of material that is post-Jesus in thought, type, and purpose. But though perhaps finding "completion" centuries after Jesus, the Mishnah is at least indicative of first-century Judaic thought with much of its material being confirmed by other Judaic sources (for instance Josephus), studies of oral tradition, and archeological evidence. This does not in any way deny the issues of dating and intention, but it does in a very real sense indicate that such material cannot be ignored.[3]

THE SABBATH LAWS

The first law that concerns us (in as far as it concerned Jesus) is that which was commanded in the days of creation:

> And on the seventh day God ended His work which He had done, and He rested on the seventh day... Then God blessed the seventh day and *sanctified* it, because in it He *rested* from all His work which God had created and made.[4]

---

[2] The discussion of how and why the early Church grew apart from the Mosaic law is beyond our scope. Though of interest, our concern limits the discussion to the fundamental attitude of Jesus. But I quite like the words of the Jewish scholar, Joseph Klausner: "Jesus remained steadfast to the old Torah: till His dying day He continued to observe the ceremonial laws like a true Pharisaic Jew... Yet on the other hand, had not Jesus' teaching contained suggestions of such a line of action [the abrogation of some ceremonial laws], the idea would never have occurred to 'Saul the Pharisee,' nor would he have succeeded in making it a rule of Christianity." *Jesus of Nazareth: His Life, Times, and Teaching* (New York: Macmillan Company, 1949), 275-276.

[3] Though I seemingly have not "critically" made obvious which material within the Mishnah goes back to Jesus, this does not mean that I have treated the Mishnah "uncritically." Rather, I have preferred not to present such evidence within this text, since it would somewhat distract in an already lengthy book. For an excellent discussion of the use of such material see John P. Meier, *A Marginal Jew: Rethinking the Historical Jesus* Vol. III (New York: Doubleday, 2001), 305-309.

[4] Gen 2:1-3.

The Sabbath, *shabbath* from the Hebrew verb "to rest," is the sanctified day on which God "rested" from His work of creation. Not resting from exhaustion, as if there were need, He sanctified this day so that man may partake in *His* rest. Theodore of Heraclea notes that it was also to remind man of his Creator: "that they would acknowledge that God is both the One who planned it and that it is He Himself who made the world in six days and on the seventh day rested."[5]

It was a reminder that as God's creation, the people of Israel were to participate in the Holiness of their maker: "The Sabbath trained Israel by degrees to abstain from evil and disposed them to listen to the things of the Spirit."[6] It was the act of offering back to God thanksgiving for the act of Creation. It was not a burden, but a gift.[7] Israel was to hallow the Sabbath, so much so that it was given as one of the Ten Commandments.[8] The Sabbath served to mark out the people of Israel from the surrounding nations. It applied not only to the Israelites, but to any children, servants, foreigners, or even animals in the care of an Israelite. As a mark of the gravity of the Sabbath, it was one of only two positive commandments (requiring action in contrast to a prohibition), and its performance was *visible*. It follows that for a man or woman to perform the Sabbath, as an inherently public action, they were also identifying themselves as an Israelite obedient to the law of God.

The Sabbath, the seventh day or Saturday, was consecrated to God as a day of *rest*. This encompassed all activity from breaking bread to working. The laws prohibited gathering of food, cooking, making a fire, and trading on this sacred day.[9] Food was to be prepared on the day before and was to be eaten on the Sabbath without further preparation. It is, however, generally attested that picking up dishes and placing the food in one's mouth was acceptable. It was also explicitly declared: "in plowing time and in harvest you shall rest."[10] Work therefore was not a justification for non-observance, even if it was of pressing need. A little later the *Mishnah* would stipulate some thirty nine categories of work which were prohibited.[11] The one exception was the obligation of the Sabbath offering—a burnt offering—that entailed work on behalf of the priests, a *necessary work*.[12]

---

[5] Theodore of Heraclea, *Fragment* 84, MKGK 79–80.

[6] John Chrysostom, *The Gospel of Matthew*, Homily 39.3, PG 57:436–37; NPNF 1 10:257.

[7] Alfred Edersheim, *The Temple: Its Ministry and Services as they were at the Time of Jesus Christ* (London: James Clarke & Co, 1959), 174.

[8] Exod 20:8-11, Deut 5:12-15; Also see Exod 34:21, Lev 9:3.

[9] Exod 16, 35:3; Neh 13:15-22.

[10] Exod 34:21.

[11] *Mishnah Shabbat* 7:2.

[12] Num 28:9.

Should one inadvertently transgress the Sabbath by working, the punishment required only a sin offering.[13] However, if it be found that the transgression was deliberate, then the consequences were far more severe: execution and to be "cut off."[14] In another place, stoning to death was named as the punishment for deliberate transgression.[15]

But what if a village was attacked on the Sabbath? Was self-defense a transgression? The book of *Maccabees* relates the tragic tale of many pious Jews dying in the early days of the Maccabean revolt (c. 167 BC), in their insistence on observing the Sabbath. Eventually, though, self-defense was to become an exception. Josephus tells of a similar case. In 63 BC the Roman general Pompey exploited this Jewish observance by constructing battering rams on the Sabbath, yet carefully ensuring no missiles were fired.[16] What is of interest is that the Jews were unable to prevent the construction of these weapons as that would not be direct self-defense, unless they were first attacked.

The next logical question is: If someone is sick may he be given medicine on the Sabbath? The answer lies in the severity of the illness. The general consensus opposed any work that was entailed in a minor healing.[17] Understandably, especially where pain was concerned, a great deal of discussion focused on how to obtain a cure without transgressing the Sabbath. One peculiar case in the *Mishnah* states: "He who is concerned about his teeth may not suck vinegar through them. But he dunks [his bread] in the normal way, and if he is healed, he is healed."[18] That is, vinegar as a cure for a tooth ache may not be used, but if there happened to be vinegar on the bread you ate, well, that would be acceptable. Nevertheless, if we take the Jewish law as a whole, we find it to be softer than one may expect: "The implied definition, 'practicing medicine is work,' and the implied rule, 'no minor cures on the Sabbath,' are tough, but the application is more humane."[19]

The case entirely differed if the illness was severe. If self-defense was permitted on the Sabbath, then likewise was the prevention of serious injury. Generally, the rule for this went as such: If there is doubt whether a life is in danger then the person should be treated. In the words of Rabbi Mattiah b. Harash: "He who has a pain in his throat—they drop medicine into his

---

[13] Lev 4:27-35.

[14] Exod 31:12-17. To be "cut off" was not simply exile, but rather execution, with one's family to also be executed or in other interpretations to no longer be numbered among the people of Israel.

[15] Num 15:32-36.

[16] Josephus, *Jewish Wars*, I:145-147.

[17] *Covenant of Damascus* 11:10; *Mishnah Shabbat* 14:3; *Tosefta Shabbat* 12:8-14.

[18] *Mishnah Shabbat* 14:4.

[19] E. P. Sanders, *Jewish Law from Jesus to the Mishnah* (London: SCM Press, 1990), 13.

mouth on the Sabbath, because it is a matter of doubt as to danger to life. And any matter of doubt as to danger to life overrides the prohibitions of the Sabbath."[20] The ancients were not as versed in modern medicine, yet the principle remained that one could not be sure whether even a minor illness may lead to death, and therefore even a sore throat may be treated. The same principle applies in a multitude of cases found in the Mishnah:

> He upon whom a building fell down –
> [if] it is a matter of doubt whether or not he is there,
> [if] it is a matter of doubt whether [if he is there], he is alive or dead,
> [if] it is a matter of doubt whether [if he is there and alive] he is a Gentile or an Israelite –
> [Therefore] they clear away the ruin from above him.
> [If] they found him alive, they remove the [remaining] ruins from above him. But if they found him dead, they *leave* him be [until after the Sabbath].[21]

Some stricter Jewish groups, such as the *Essenes*, took it upon themselves to strengthen and broaden the Sabbath laws.[22] And, in their usual manner, the School of *Shammai* sought to tighten the law, whilst the School of *Hillel* softened it. For instance, if the School of Shammai said not to spread nets for fish on the Sabbath, then the School of Hillel would permit it.[23] We should not see in such disputes simply a debate of trivialities. In reality and existentially, the Sabbath was one of the divinely ordained commandments, and hence the faithful Jew sought to be obedient to his or her God. To do so, was to ask the question: Is this or that allowed? From this question resulted the great many stipulations of the Sabbath law in a pious attempt to be wholly obedient to that law. Importantly and significantly, we should note, the stricter views of such Schools were held by its constituents, and there is no real evidence that such views were forced upon the common Jew.

The final point that we must take into consideration before examining the controversy surrounding Jesus, is, who exactly delivered the punishment for transgression? More specifically in first-century Palestine, who would and could have reprimanded Jesus if indeed He had transgressed the Sabbath

---

[20] *Mishnah Yoma* 8:6. Perhaps they had rheumatic fever or septicemia in mind.

[21] *Mishnah Yoma* 8:7.

[22] *Covenant of Damscus* 11:13-14.

[23] *Mishnah Shabbat* 1:5-8; This forms one of a list of five disputes between the two schools. Most of the conflicts between these two Schools centered upon what exactly was and was not permitted on a festival day if it happened to fall on the Sabbath. See E. P. Sanders, *Jewish Law from Jesus to the Mishnah*, 8-12, for a fuller discussion.

laws? There are four possibilities. The *Romans* would, to be sure, never have enforced the Sabbath unless of course it was feared to lead to an uprising. Likewise, it is exceedingly unlikely that *Herod Antipas*, Tetrarch of Galilee, would have punished the transgressors—evidently he would have spent most of his time punishing himself! And the most likely chastisers, the *Pharisees*, did not have the authority, and in any event, the death penalty was impossible at the time of Jesus.[24] Finally, the only other real possibility is the *Priesthood*, who more likely than not would have simply persuaded the offender to bring forth a sin offering, for they did not have the authority to enact the punishments of the book of Exodus. Simplistically and briefly, the only real punishment for transgression of the Sabbath (knowingly or unknowingly) in first-century Palestine was moral conviction and the sin offering. And thus we may conclude that within the debates between Jesus and the Pharisees regarding the Sabbath, there is no motive of punishment, but rather an elucidation of the truth. It is to this elucidation that we now turn.

Jesus is accused of opposing the Sabbath laws in two main cases: that of *plucking grain*, and that of *healing*. We begin with the first:

> At that time Jesus went through the grainfields on the Sabbath. And His disciples were hungry, and began to *pluck* heads of grain and to eat. And when the Pharisees saw *it*, they said to Him, "Look, Your disciples are doing what is not lawful to do on the Sabbath!"
> But He said to them, "Have you not read what David did when he was hungry, he and those who were with him: how he entered the house of God and ate the *showbread* which was not lawful for him to eat, nor for those who were with him, but only for the priests? Or have you not read in the law that on the Sabbath the priests in the temple *profane* the Sabbath, and are blameless? Yet I say to you that in this place there is One *greater* than the temple. But if you had known what *this* means, 'I desire mercy and not sacrifice,' you would not have condemned the guiltless. For the Son of Man is Lord even of the Sabbath."[25]

The disciples of Jesus are accused of plucking the heads of grain on the Sabbath. Luke adds "*rubbing* them in their hands."[26] Plucking grain from another's fields is not the actual offense, for there is provision for this within

---

[24] See *Mishnah Sanhedrin*; *Mishnah Shabbat* 7:1. The death penalty is not prescribed in the Pharisaic work of the Mishnah and Talmud, and is not testified to within the Gospels. Hence, the ongoing discussion of who crucified Jesus? A topic, of which is beyond our scope.

[25] Matt 12:1-8; Mark 2:23-28; Luke 6:1-5.

[26] Luke 6:1.

the law.[27] Rather the offense is plucking and rubbing the grain, and therefore *working* on the Sabbath. We should also note that it is fairly unlikely that the Pharisees witnessed the event, for logically and practically speaking why were they away from Jerusalem spying in the grain fields? We must also remember that Jesus was not accused, His disciples were. Therefore it stands to reason that Jesus did not transgress the law. As for His disciples, Jesus claims that a violation of the Sabbath never actually took place. It is from here that He develops His two-fold argument.

Out of hunger, king David "ate the showbread which was not lawful for him." This statement is often misunderstood. Jesus, here, is not purely making a legal argument, and neither is He simply searching for precedence, for this act of David has nothing to do with the Sabbath. Rather, Jesus is claiming that *necessity*—the hunger of David—overshadows the law, and likewise the hunger of His disciples permits them to pluck grain without transgressing the Sabbath.

Secondly, Jesus argues, "the priests in the temple profane the Sabbath, and are blameless." As we have seen previously, the singular exception to work on the Sabbath was the work of the priests in preparing the Sabbath offering.[28] John Chrysostom, the master exegete, further claims that "they were acquitted of charges not by special pleading or indulgence but on reasonable grounds according to the principles of justice."[29] Accordingly, if the priests were blameless in serving the temple on the Sabbath, then likewise were the disciples who served "One *greater* than the temple." To serve Him who is greater than the temple, then becomes not only permissible on the Sabbath, but mandatory, just as the offerings were. Therefore "it is a question of authority rather than legality as such which is at stake."[30]

It is perhaps pertinent at this point to consider Jesus' methodology. Rabbinic interpretation involves a principle known as *qal wahomer*, the "light and the weighty." Though formulated as part of the seven original *Middoth* of Rabbi Hillel (if you like, the rules of Jewish interpretation), this concept was common in rabbinic debate in times contemporary with Jesus. This principle essentially stated that whatever applied in a less important case— the *light*—applies in the more important case—the *weighty*. Fundamentally then, the claim of Jesus rests upon *qal wahomer*:

---

[27] Deut 23:24-25: "When you come into your neighbor's standing grain, you may pluck the heads with your hand, but you shall not use a sickle on your neighbor's standing grain."

[28] Num 28:9.

[29] John Chrysostom, *The Gospel of Matthew*, Homily 39.2, PG 57:435; NPNF 1 10:256.

[30] Robert Banks, *Jesus and the Law*, 117.

Scripture—thus the argument in Matthew runs—ordains that the observance of the Sabbath must *yield* to the temple service... [and thus] it must yield in the present case, where something greater than the temple demands consideration.[31]

If the priests may work on the Sabbath for temple service, so may Jesus' disciples since He is *greater* than the temple. Likewise, if David broke the Sabbath out of hunger, then so may those who serve the *new* King. Intelligibly, the law was not transgressed, and paradoxically by making this case Jesus honors the law: "Appealing to mitigating circumstances (hunger) and precedent (David) shows fundamental respect for the law."[32] Had He not valued the law, there would have been no purpose debating in the first place, for He could have dismissed the matter as altogether trivial.

This brings us to the second accusation: *healing* on the Sabbath. The Evangelists record for us a number of these healings such as the woman with a "spirit of infirmity,"[33] and the man with dropsy.[34] But paramount among the healings is a third, the man with the withered hand:

> And He entered the synagogue again, and a man was there who had a withered hand. So they watched Him closely, whether He would heal him on the *Sabbath*, so that they might accuse Him. And He said to the man who had the withered hand, "Step forward." Then He said to them, "Is it lawful on the Sabbath to do good or to do evil, *to save life or to kill?*" But they kept silent. And when He had looked around at them with anger, being grieved by the hardness of their hearts, He said to the man, "Stretch out your hand." And he stretched *it* out, and his hand was restored as whole as the other.[35]

Of these three healings, a strange thing becomes evident. Jesus only "worked" in healing the woman by laying His hands on her.[36] In the case of the man with a withered hand, He healed by a word, and the account of the man with dropsy only tells us that Jesus "took him and healed him."[37] Yet, in all three cases Jesus is accused of transgressing the Sabbath, irrespective of whether He physically did work or not. And, interestingly it is only in Mark,

[31] David Daube, *The New Testament and Rabbinic Judaism*, 71.

[32] E.P. Sanders, "Jesus and the First Table of the Jewish Law," in *The Historical Jesus in Recent Research*, ed. James D. G. Dunn and Scot McKnight (Indiana: Eisenbrauns, 2005), 221.

[33] Luke 13:10-17

[34] Luke 14:1-6.

[35] Mark 3:1-6; Matt 12:9-14; Luke 6:6.

[36] Luke 13:13.

[37] Luke 14:4.

where Jesus did not work, that His accusers "plotted...how they might destroy Him."[38]

The question thus remains: Did Jesus violate the Sabbath law by healing? It should first be noted that the single case of laying the hand is one of the rare occasions where it is Jesus Himself (and not His disciples) that is accused of transgressing the law. Secondly, the healings of Jesus on the Sabbath are few and the practice was certainly not normative. We must also remember that "talking" is on no account regarded as work, and therefore it is not prohibited on the Sabbath. That said, how then does Jesus respond to the accusation?

In the varying accounts He relates three cases when one would and could legally transgress the Sabbath. First, in the case of the withered hand, Jesus questions: "Is it lawful on the Sabbath to do good or to do evil, *to save life or to kill?*" This is a clear reference to the known allowance within the Judaic teachings that acting to save a life was permitted on the Sabbath. But recall it was only permitted if the illness was severe unto death. Would the healing of a withered hand, likely to have been present for many years, be considered as saving a life? It is doubtful. But then again, in this particular case, Jesus is not recorded as doing any work, for He healed by a word. Athanasius the Great comments:

> Stretch out your hand. I am not touching you so that they may not bring a charge against me. I am speaking with a *speech* so that they may not think that touching is an act of work. God did not say, "Do not speak on the Sabbath." But if speech becomes an act of work, let the one who has spoken be an object of amazement... While the withered hand was restored, the withered minds of the onlookers were not.[39]

What of the other healings, where perhaps He *did* do work? "And behold, there was a woman who had a spirit of infirmity eighteen years, and was bent over and could in no way raise herself up."[40] Once more by healing—in this case by laying His hands—Jesus could not be said to be saving life, for she had lived in such condition for eighteen years. Thus Jesus advances His argument further: "Does not each one of you on the Sabbath loose his ox or donkey from the stall, and lead it away to water it?" Jesus implies: Why then may I not *loosen* this woman "whom Satan has bound"

---

[38] Mark 3:6.

[39] Athanasius of Alexandria, *Homilia de Semente* 28, cf. TLG 2035.069, 28.165.37-44; 165.48-168.1; 168.2-24. cf. PG 28.144-68; cf. E. A. W. Budge, *Coptic Homilies in the Dialect of Upper Egypt* (London: British Museum, 1910).

[40] Luke 13:10-17.

and alleviate her discomfort? If an animal may be *untied* and led to water,[41] then why should a human remain bound? By referring to the urgency in which this woman should be *unbound*, Jesus was reminding Israel of the intention of the Sabbath. Man was called to participate in God's rest:

> Here Jesus is portrayed as taking up and transforming the great theme of Sabbath as *release from work*, bringing into immediate presence and sharp focus the theme of Sabbath as rest after trouble, as redemption after slavery.[42]

To heal on the Sabbath is to grant *rest* to another. Not only is it appropriate to heal on such a day, it is the day on which one *must* heal. For to do so, is to bring humanity once more into the rest of God. Jesus thus, by healing even with the work of placing His hands, is not acting contrary to the Sabbath law, rather He radically enacts it! Similarly, after healing the man with dropsy, Jesus questions: "Which of you, having a donkey or an ox that has fallen into a pit, will not immediately pull him out on the Sabbath day?"[43] A peculiar answer is found in the *Talmud*: "If an animal falls into a dyke, one brings pillows and bedding and places [them] under it, and if it ascends it ascends."[44] Man may "work" in assisting an animal to climb out of a pit. Therefore, if an animal that has fallen into a pit may be saved, why not a man that has "fallen into a pit?" It thus becomes clear that Jesus is claiming *qal wahomer*, the "light and the weighty." If you take animals to water, then may I not alleviate a woman's discomfort of eighteen years? If you run to save an ox, may I not heal a man?

"The Sabbath was made for man, and not man for the Sabbath."[45] Jesus completes His debate on the plucking of grain by reminding Israel that the law was instituted for them, and not they for the law. A rabbinic parallel is found in the words of Rabbi Jonathan b. Joseph: "For it is holy unto you; i.e., it [the Sabbath] is committed to your hands, not you to its hands."[46] Jesus understood the Sabbath as a gift from God to man—to bring man into His rest. Therefore to *deny* healing on the Sabbath is to effectively break the Sabbath. John Chrysostom summates: "Did Christ then attempt to repeal a law so beneficial as the Sabbath law? Far from it. Rather, He greatly magnified the Sabbath."[47]

---

[41] For such an allowance, see *Babylonian Talmud Shabbat* 128b.
[42] N. T. Wright, *Jesus and the Victory of God*, 394.
[43] Luke 14:5.
[44] *Baylonian Talmud Shabbat* 128b.
[45] Mark 2:27-28.
[46] *Babylonian Talmud Yoma* 85b.
[47] John Chrysostom, *The Gospel of Matthew*, Homily 39.3, PG 57:436–37; NPNF 1 10:257.

We may thus conclude that Jesus on no account transgressed the Sabbath: "[He] behaved on the Sabbath in a way which fell *inside* the range of current debate about it, and well inside the range of permitted behavior."[48] In terms of the plucking of grain, Jesus claims that hunger overrides the law, especially when in service of one *greater* than the temple. Even then, He was not accused of the transgression, His disciples were. Jesus justifies His Sabbath stance by responding with the well attested principle of *qal wahomer*: If you are called to bring an animal comfort, why not a human? Likewise, He argues that healing on the Sabbath is justified if it grants "rest" to another, and thus Jesus enacts God's rest on the Sabbath revealing to Israel the very will of God.

THE FOOD LAWS

The Sabbath laws in demanding public observance marked out and identified Israel from among its neighbors. Standing alongside were the food laws. Together they were a fundamental and defining feature of early Judaism.

> Now the LORD spoke to Moses and Aaron, saying to them, "Speak to the children of Israel, saying, 'These are the animals which you *may* eat among all the animals that are on the earth...'"[49]

The food laws placed six main restrictions on the diet of Israel, declaring what food was *clean* and what was *unclean*. Four-footed animals besides sheep, goat, cattle, and some deer, were prohibited, along with shellfish and mollusks. Birds of prey, as well as most insects, were also considered to be unclean. All blood and fat, no matter the source, was unclean and so was Gentile wine (as some of it may have been poured out as a libation before other gods). Essentially then, clean food comprised of sheep, goat, beef, pigeon, dove, and fish that had fins and scales.[50] It need be said that "dietary laws" though considered as part of the "purity laws," differed in one key point: One cannot be purified after eating an unclean food. That is to say, to eat *unclean* food was abominable before God and sinful, whereas to

---

[48] E. P. Sanders, *Jewish Law from Jesus to the Mishnah*, 23.

[49] Lev 11:1-2.

[50] Lev 11; Deut 14. The *Essenes* further deepened these food laws to such an extent that some starved after being expelled from the community, for lack of *pure* food (Josephus, *Jewish Wars*, II:143-144). Also, in their characteristic manner the Schools of Hillel and Shammai loosened and strengthened the laws respectively, *Mishnah Hullin* 8:1; *Mishnah Eduyyot* 5:2.

contract *impurity*, after childbirth for instance, was not. This distinction is paramount in revealing the intention of Jesus' sayings.

Given the food laws were a defining facet of first-century Judaism, we should not be surprised of their presence in the Gospels. The alleged incident is reported both in Matthew and Mark:

> Now when they saw *some* of His disciples eat bread with defiled, that is, with unwashed hands, they found fault... Then the Pharisees and scribes asked Him, "Why do Your *disciples* not walk according to the *tradition* of the elders, but eat bread with unwashed hands?"[51]

Jesus is questioned as to why His disciples are eating with unclean hands. Once more, pertinently, He is not accused, but His disciples are—even then not all of the disciples, but only *some*. The charge being that without the washing of hands, one would be defiled. The real problem arises some verses later in Jesus teaching: "There is nothing that enters a man from *outside* which can defile him; but the things which come out of him, those are the things that defile a man...thus purifying *all* foods."[52] It is this teaching which has caused a great deal of difficulty in understanding Jesus' stance towards the law. If *all* food is declared clean, as E. P. Sanders cautiously notes, then Jesus stands decidedly against the law of God: "this statement, if it really means what it appears to mean, nullifies the food laws and falls completely outside the limits of debate about the law in first-century Judaism."[53] The question must then be: Did Jesus really declare all food clean?

To answer this, we need to follow Jesus' argument from its beginnings. The Pharisees question: "Why do your disciples transgress the *tradition* of the elders?"[54] Jesus, surprisingly, does not answer this directly, but counters:

> Why do you also transgress the commandment of God because of *your* tradition? For God commanded, saying, "Honor your father and your mother"... But you say, "Whoever says to his father or mother, 'Whatever profit you might have received from me is a gift to God'—then he need not honor his father or mother." Thus you have made the commandment of God of no effect by your tradition.[55]

---

[51] Mark 7:2, 5; also see Matt 15:1-20.
[52] Mark 7:15, 19.
[53] E. P. Sanders, *Jewish Law from Jesus to the Mishnah*, 28.
[54] Matt 15:2.
[55] Matt 15:3-6.

In response to why His disciples transgressed tradition, Jesus questions whether tradition allows the transgression of the written law. Instead of obedience to the commandments: "Honor your father...," the Pharisees are accused of citing the *tradition* of *qorban*. Meaning "offering," *qorban* was what was vowed to the temple. Thus, instead of financially supporting one's parents, one could promise such funds to the temple instead. The son, it should be noted, would not derive benefit from the funds as he would lose the funds or property to the temple eventually.[56] The claim here is that the act of saying *qorban* was done out of malice so that no one could derive benefit. In the Mishnah we hear that one could even pronounce food *qorban*: "...he saw people eating figs [belonging to him] and said, 'Lo, they are *qorban* to you!'"[57] Following from this, Jesus declares:

> Hear Me, everyone, and understand: There is nothing that enters a man from *outside* which can defile him; but the things which come out of him, those are the things that defile a man...
> So He said to them, "Are you thus without understanding also? Do you not perceive that whatever enters a man from outside cannot defile him, because it does not enter his heart but his stomach, and is eliminated, thus purifying *all* foods?"[58]

It is the conclusion—"thus purifying all foods"—that is the key to understanding this saying of Jesus. Let us for a moment assume that He did declare *all* food clean. It follows that the Apostles would have adhered to such a clear and unambiguous teaching. But if this is the case, why then did Peter (after Jesus had died), when told in a vision to eat unclean food, respond: "Not so, Lord! For I have *never* eaten anything common or unclean"?[59] Why then was the issue of clean and unclean food so disputed at the council of Jerusalem,[60] as well as in the writings of Paul the Apostle?[61] To confirm the point, there is no recorded instance of Jesus ever eating pork, let alone any

---

[56] Fr. Theodore Stylianopoulos, a Professor of New Testament at Holy Cross Orthodox School of Theology, has brought to my attention that this is in fact not a certainty. It would seem that earlier rabbinic evidence indicates that the son who made the vow could still retain use of the vowed property. On the other hand, some later evidence points to the conclusion that the son who declared his property *qorban* would also be unable to use the property. See S. Zeitlin, "Korban," *Jewish Quarterly Review* 33 (1962): 160-63; J. Duncan M. Derrett, "Korban, ho estin doron," *New Testament Studies* 16 (1970): 364-68; J. Hart, "Corban," *Jewish Quarterly Review* 19 (1907): 615-50.

[57] *Mishnah Nedarim* 3:2.

[58] Mark 7:14-19.

[59] Acts 10:14.

[60] Acts 15.

[61] Gal 2:11-14; Rom 14:1-15:16.

other unclean food. It is thus exceedingly unlikely that the earliest Church would be so uncertain, as well as continuing to eat only clean food, if Jesus had declared all food clean. Indeed, "if Jesus had said, out on the street, that the time has come when God-given taboos, which marked out the Jews from their pagan neighbors, were to be made redundant...He might well have started a riot."[62]

Historically it does not fit that Jesus abolished the food laws, yet this saying "purifying all foods" still plagues us. First, it needs to be placed within context. Jesus is claiming that food does not carry impurity since the stomach purifies all foods. This, then, is *not* a discussion of the stomach purifying *unclean* foods and thus making all food clean. It *is* a discussion of the stomach purifying *clean* foods *from impurity*, for example if an insect made contact with the food or if eating with unwashed hands. To repeat, "food laws" prohibited unclean foods which were an abomination to God, "purity laws" dealt with what led to impurity (as we shall see shortly). In other words, the original incident was concerned with hand washing (therefore impurity) and not unclean food (an abomination and therefore sinfulness). Why then would Jesus take a purity law and transform it into a debate on food laws?[63] The issue at hand was whether the lack of hand-washing led to impurity, not whether certain foods were clean or unclean!

Secondly, the problem lies in the language itself. "Not what goes into the mouth defiles a man; but what comes out of the mouth, this defiles a man."[64] What we have before us is of the formula "not this... but this..."[65] Let us examine this formula elsewhere. Moses tells the people of Israel in Exodus: "Your complaints are *not* against us *but* against the Lord," yet moments earlier the people out of hunger "complained against Moses and Aaron in the wilderness."[66] Thus the statement meant "not *only* against us..., but against the Lord *more so*." A similar example is found in the Gospel of Mark: "...whoever receives Me, receives *not* Me *but* Him who sent Me."[67] To receive Jesus is to receive God, and therefore the statement indicated "whoever receives me, receives not *only* Me but *also* He who sent Me."

---

[62] N. T. Wright, *Jesus and the Victory of God*, 398.

[63] See Phillip Sigal, "Aspects of Mark pointing to Matthean priority," in *New Synoptic Studies: The Cambridge Gospel Conference and Beyond*, ed. William R. Farmer (Macon: Mercer University Press, 1983), 158.

[64] Matt 15:11.

[65] See A. B. Du Toit, "Hyperbolical Contrasts: A Neglected Aspect of Paul's Style," in *A South African Perspective on the New Testament*, ed. J. H. Petzer and P. J. Martin (Leiden: Brill, 1986), 178-186.

[66] Exod 16:2-8.

[67] Mark 9:37.

Again the principle holds in a saying of Jesus we shall examine further in our journey: "I did *not* come to bring peace *but* a sword."[68]

Understood in this manner "not what goes into... but what comes out," becomes "not what goes in *only*... but what comes out *more so*." This corresponds with the language of the Scriptures, as well as seamlessly aligning with the fact that Peter and the early Church seem to have been entirely unaware that Jesus had allegedly declared all food clean.

We should also note that in this present study the intention is not to consider whether or not Jesus "laid the foundation" for the eventual abolition of dietary laws. This is another matter entirely and is beyond our scope. But we may at least say that Jesus did not explicitly dismiss the food laws at this specific point given the confusion of the earliest Church. That Jesus is ever recorded as speaking against or rejecting the food laws is misconceived. What Jesus did reject was "tradition" that transgressed the commandments of God. To promise assets to the temple to avoid the duty to one's parents out of malice was for Jesus the real source of defilement. He cries out to us: that which comes out of man (in this case the verbal vow of *qorban*) defiles far more than unwashed hands. This brings us to the issue of purity.

The Purity Laws

Since Jesus was Jew He must have shared the Jewish concern for purity: "You shall be holy to me; for I the Lord am holy, and I have separated you from the other peoples to be mine."[69] This call to be pure was intimately related to the call to be separated from the rest of the nations. And thus it is of little surprise that the name of those who sought to bring all spheres of life into the purity debate, the Pharisees, was *perushim*, meaning "the separated."[70]

This call of purity, however similar to the food laws, differed in that impurity was not a transgression of the law. Or as James D. G. Dunn puts it: "impurity is not sin; to be impure was not wrong..."[71] Israel was commanded to avoid certain foods which if eaten would lead to sinfulness. Impurity on the other hand was a necessary part of Jewish life. To reproduce or to bury a deceased family member would require one to become impure, and thus

---

[68] Matt 10:34.

[69] Lev 20:24-26.

[70] Jacob Neusner, *From Politics to Piety: The Emergence of Pharisaic Judaism* (New Jersey: Prentice-Hall, 1973).

[71] James D. G. Dunn, "Jesus and Purity: An Ongoing Debate," *New Testament Studies* 48 (2002): 451-452. Also see Jacob Neusner, *The Idea of Purity in Ancient Judaism* (Leiden: Brill, 1973).

impurity was at times an obligation. Impurity *only* became sinful when one
entered the temple in a state of impurity:

> There is no doubt that the temple was the focal point and *reason* for pu-
> rity: if one was to approach the holy God one had to be holy/pure oneself.
> Strictly speaking, purification was only necessary for those who wished
> to attend the temple. That, however, did not mean that impurity could be
> treated lightly when one was distant from the temple.[72]

As impurity could spread from person to person, and perhaps
eventually reach the sanctuary, impurity was to be avoided not only when
wishing to worship at the temple, but also in day to day dealings. That said,
it still remains that failing to remedy this impurity did not necessarily mean
interference in one's everyday life. If it did, few in first-century Palestine
would have been pure for long. So in what manner did one become impure?

Impurity could be contracted by contact with a corpse,[73] following
childbirth,[74] during menstruation or following intercourse with a
menstruating woman,[75] contact with semen[76] or other discharges,[77] contact
with the carcass of an unclean animal or forbidden insect,[78] contact with
a leper,[79] contact with anything impure,[80] or eating anything that died
unnaturally.[81] Once impurity was contracted, the impure would be unclean
for a particular period and may have to bathe and offer a sacrifice depending
on the cause. For example, one was impure until sunset after intercourse and
was required to bathe; whilst touching a corpse would render one impure
for seven days and the sacrifice of a red heifer was required.

We shall focus on a few of the relevant purity laws. The first of which we
have already touched upon: *hand-washing*. The only prescription of hand-
washing in the *Torah* is if a man has genital discharge, in which case he

[72] James D. G. Dunn, "Jesus and Purity: An Ongoing Debate," 452. See Lev 19:8, 20:17,
22:9; Isa 6:7; *1 Enoch* 5:4; *Pss. Sol.* 8:12–13.

[73] Num 19:11-15.

[74] Lev 12.

[75] Lev 15:19-24. In *Mishnah Eduyyot* 1:1, we find a debate on exactly when a woman was
impure, stemming from the fact that a man may *not* touch a menstruating woman. Shammai
says, "For all women it is sufficient [to be regarded as unclean by reason of menstruation] from
the time [of their first having a flow]." Hillel says, "[It is retroactive] from the examination
[at which the blood was found] to the examination [last made, before the blood was found]."

[76] Lev 15:16-18.

[77] Lev 15:2, 25.

[78] Lev 5:2, 11:33-35.

[79] Lev 13:8.

[80] Lev 5:3.

[81] Lev 17:15.

should rinse his hands before touching anything else.[82] The practice may have first become a norm, outside of this commanded case, in the Diaspora among those Jews who were unable to visit Jerusalem. Specifically, many of these Jews would wash their hands before prayer,[83] perhaps in imitation of the priests within the temple.[84] Later, possibly in an attempt to prevent the spread of impurity, many of the Pharisees began to wash their hands before handling food intended for the priesthood, before partaking in a meal on the Sabbath or festival day, and when handling the Scriptures.[85]

The second purity law which intrigues us is *corpse impurity*. Coming into contact with a corpse or even entering a house where a dead body lay would render the Jew impure.[86] Does this mean that a dead Israelite may not be buried? Certainly not. The only transgression against the law was to enter the temple in a state of impurity, thus anyone may be buried as long as the burier was careful to seek purification before approaching the temple. In fact, should a Jew even "overshadow" a corpse by leaning out of a window during a funeral procession in the street or perhaps inadvertently walk over a grave, then he or she would contract impurity. It was such a pressing concern, Josephus relates, that Herod Antipas was unable to convince the Jews to inhabit the city of Tiberias for it was built (in part) over a large graveyard.[87] The single exception was for the priesthood, who were commanded to avoid corpse impurity at all costs apart from their closest relatives.[88]

Having briefly examined the purity laws, we may now ask: Did Jesus dispute these commandments? The major debate surrounds *hand-washing*. The disciples (not Jesus) are accused of not subscribing to the practice of washing their hands from defilement before eating, whilst we are told: "the Pharisees and all the Jews do not eat unless they wash their hands in a special way."[89] Needless to say "all the Jews" places the disciples at odds with the rest of their kinsman. Yet biblically the single prescription for hand-washing is after intercourse, and the only other indication that laymen had adopted

---

[82] Lev 15:11.

[83] *Aristes* 305-306; *Sibylline Oracles* 3:591-593.

[84] E. P. Sanders, *Jewish Law from Jesus to the Mishnah*, 30. For a discussion on hand-washing see also R. P. Booth, *Jesus and the Laws of Purity: Tradition History and Legal History in Mark 7* (Sheffield: JSOT, 1986) 194–202, and T. Kazen, *Jesus and Purity Halakhah: Was Jesus Indifferent to Impurity?* (Stockholm: Almqvist & Wiksell, 2002), 62–72, 81–5.

[85] *Mishnah Bikkurim* 2:1; *Mishnah Berakhot* 8:2; *Mishnah Yadayim* 3:5.

[86] Num 19:11-22.

[87] Josephus, *Antiquities of the Jews*, XVIII:36-38.

[88] Lev 21:1-3. In the *Mishnah*, there is further loosening of these laws for the priesthood—R. Eliezer said: "Let a priest contract corpse uncleanness, for he does not have to bring an offering on account of his uncleanness." (*Nazir* 7:1)

[89] Mark 7:3.

the practice in other circumstances was in the Diaspora, not in Galilee. To this we must add that the Pharisees themselves, in their own writings, are generally not claimed to have washed their hands before ordinary meals. Even then should it be shown that hand-washing was the norm; the matter at hand is *impurity* not *sin*. They were not accused of eating unclean food, but rather of eating clean food that may have contracted impurity through their unwashed hands. Once again, one is sinful, the other is not.

The same principle is applied in the matter of Jesus' occasional *corpse impurity*. The primary incident is that of the dead son of the widow of Nain, where "He came and *touched* the *open* coffin."[90] If one as much as overshadowed a coffin impurity was contracted, yet Jesus here has direct contact. In itself, as described previously, this is not transgressing the law. Jesus would simply have been ceremonially unclean for seven days and was required to offer a red heifer. Similarly when entering the house of Jairus, the ruler of the synagogue, to heal his daughter, Jesus would have been rendered impure by simply entering the house, let alone that He "took her by the hand."[91] Once more the matter was impurity not transgression: "the action could scarcely be termed a breaking of the law, for it would simply have necessitated His fulfillment of the regulations associated with the removal of such defilement, which are provided *in* the law itself."[92]

These findings allow us to hear the parable of the *Good Samaritan* through first-century Jewish ears.[93] It was not intended to be merely a moral tale, but also perhaps a criticism of the priesthood. To perceive this we need to remember the nature of corpse impurity. "The priests, the sons of Aaron," are commanded to avoid corpse impurity except in the case of close relatives, else it was a transgression and thus *sin*.[94] In the parable, the Levite and the priest did not tend to the "half dead" man, lest they contracted impurity.[95] The issue is that they were unsure whether he was actually dead or not. Jesus' criticism is that they should have rescued the man, and thus *risked* impurity (and perhaps transgression of the law for the priest as the man was not a relative), if there was even the slightest chance of life.[96] Corpse impurity is thus a key to an often overlooked aspect of the parable.

In touching a corpse, or for that matter eating with unclean hands, the stance of Jesus towards the law rests in the crucial distinction between

---

90 Luke 7:14.
91 Luke 8:54.
92 Robert Banks, *Jesus and the Law*, 105.
93 Luke 10:30-37.
94 Lev 21:1.
95 Luke 10:30.
96 *Mishnah Nazir* 7:1.

impurity and sin. Jesus at no time spoke against the purity laws. The only possible exception being hand-washing (of which He was not guilty), and even then it was a *tradition* and not a commandment, and an inconsistent one at that. If we also take into account that Jesus was in perfect agreement with the other purity laws such as those on leprosy—"*show* yourself to the priest and *offer* the sacrifices that Moses commanded for your cleansing"[97]— the only feasible summation is that He did not oppose, but rather stood firmly within the law.

LET THE DEAD BURY THEIR DEAD...

> Then He said to another, "Follow Me." But he said, "Lord, let me first go and bury my father." Jesus said to him, "Let the dead bury their own dead, but you go and preach the kingdom of God."[98]

It is quite easy to gloss over this saying seeing in it nothing more than a dramatic example of the pressing nature of discipleship. Is that how it would have resounded in a first-century crowd? Or would they have heard a violation of *filial duty*, that familiar cringe we experienced on reading this passage for the very first time? To the more discerning, no doubt, it may have been received as a *direct* violation of the fifth commandment: "Honor your father..."[99]

In Matthew it stands as the second of two calls to discipleship, in Luke it is the second of three.[100] What first greets us is that the would-be disciple seems not to be seeking permission, but more so stating his obvious and necessary plans, as if permission were a *given*. The second initial observation is that the saying is remarkably unique in that it is original relative to what came before (early Judaism) and what came after (Christianity). To appreciate this let us succinctly survey the practice of burying one's dead.

"Abraham stood up from before his dead," and sought a burial place for his beloved Sarah.[101] More than a sentimental expectation, God in a certain sense commanded such burial as law: "Honor your father and your mother..." Burying one's dead, in rabbinic works, displaced even religious observance: "One whose dead is lying before him [awaiting burial] is *exempt*

---

[97] Mark 1:44. This is an exact fulfillment of the purity laws of leprosy. "Show the priest" (Lev 13:49), "examination" (Lev 14:1-2), and "sacrifice" (Lev 14:3-32).

[98] Luke 9:59-60.

[99] Exod 20:12.

[100] See Luke 9:59-60; Matt 8:21-22.

[101] Gen 23:3.

from the recitation of the Shema,[102] and from [wearing] phylacteries."[103] Later the teaching went so far as to *permit* a high-priest or Nazirite to contract corpse impurity for the sake of his immediate family.[104] Tobias in the book of Tobit, on the eve of marrying, feared meeting the fate of his fiancé's late seven husbands not out of mortal concern but lest he violate filial duty: "for they have no other son to *bury* them."[105] To avoid this most sacred duty then is not only to defy human nature, but to essentially dishonor the law. In the words of E. P. Sanders: "Disobedience of the requirement to care for one's dead parents is actually disobedience to God."[106] Is Jesus thus calling the disciple to disobey God?

Before answering this grave question we need to remember that there was in fact *no* law stipulating the burial of one's parents, but only an interpretation of the fifth commandment. Secondly, from a purely logical line of thought, if we have seen that burial of father or mother displaced the obligation of the recitation of certain prayers in Judaic law, why then is it strange that the "kingdom of God" displaces the obligation of burial? What stands is priority before God. Thirdly, and oddly, this may be one of the only times where Jesus actually called for a transgression of the law (if it indeed was a law), and yet out of all of Jesus' debates on the law it yielded the *least* consequence. Not a single one of His disciples, or for that matter early or late Christian, ever followed in this supposed "transgression" and prohibited the burial of one's dead on account of this saying.

Joachim Jeremias further muses that in first-century Palestine to wait for the burial would simply have not been feasible: "burial took place on the day of death, but it was followed by *six days* of mourning on which the bereaved family received expressions of sympathy. Jesus cannot allow so long a delay."[107] Others have sought to claim that the father was not actually dead, introducing an indefinite delay to discipleship. Kenneth E. Bailey, intimately acquainted with Middle Eastern peasant culture, suggests: "the phrase 'to bury one's father' is a traditional idiom that refers specifically to the duty of the son to remain at home and care for his parents until they are laid to rest respectfully."[108] This would then entirely alter the importance and meaning of the saying. The would-be disciple would have been placing a familial

---

[102] *Shema*: A central Jewish prayer, "Hear, O Israel! The LORD is our God! ...," that was to be recited twice daily.

[103] *Mishnah Berakhot* 3:1.

[104] *Mishnah Nazir* 7:1.

[105] *Tobit* 6:13-15.

[106] E. P. Sanders, *Jesus and Judaism*, 253.

[107] Joachim Jeremias, *The Proclamation of Jesus* (London: SCM Press, 1971), 132.

[108] K. E. Bailey, *Through Peasant Eyes* (Grand Rapids: Wm. B. Eerdmans, 1980), 26-27.

attachment above the kingdom, and not the burial of his dead. Though a possibility, this approach misses the primary purpose of the saying.[109]

The father was, we can confidently assume, really dead. The kingdom was placed sovereign to duty. The *urgency* of preaching the kingdom of God overshadowed all else. Ezekiel the prophet was forbidden by God to mourn and weep for his wife who had died in the evening, as a symbolic message to the people of Israel.[110] And Jeremiah is told: "Do not enter the house of mourning... they shall not be buried,"[111] in order to proclaim the coming judgment. God thus commanded His prophets to break with convention in order to radicalize an impending need or message. Jesus does the same:

> If Jesus demanded even more incisively of His prospective follower that he should override the fifth commandment and the "works of love," He was demanding this, basically, in a way in which in the Old Testament *only* God Himself enjoined obedience on individual prophets in regard to the proclamation of His approaching judgment.[112]

The call of Jesus, of the same gravity as the judgment of the prophets, was to seek those fit to usher in the kingdom. Not for the mere purpose of discipleship to a Teacher, but to "preach the kingdom of God." Loyalty to the kingdom thus displaced filial duty. This was, to be sure, not a point of legal dispute, but a radical declaration of what was at hand. It was "a one-time-only requirement,"[113] calling those "fit" for the kingdom. Cyril of Alexandria echoes: "Whoever wishes to serve God must not let any ties of kinship become an excuse, on grounds of preoccupation, for not following Christ."[114] This was not a teaching that all who followed Christ should shun away from burying their parents. It was and is a call to the more vital and urgent prerogative. In this Origen rightly judges:

> It seems inhumane. But Jesus does not in fact forbid people from burying the dead, but rather He puts before this the preaching of the kingdom of heaven, which makes people *alive*. As for burying the body, there were many people who could have done this.[115]

---

[109] Vesilin Kesich, *The Gospel Image of Christ* (New York: SVS Press, 1991), 170.

[110] Ezek 24:15-24.

[111] Jer 16:5.

[112] Martin Hengel, *The Charismatic Leader and His Followers* (Edinburgh: T. & T. Clark, 1981), 12.

[113] E. P. Sanders, *Jewish Law from Jesus to the Mishnah*, 4.

[114] Cyril of Alexandria, *Fragment* 98, MKGK 183–84.

[115] Origen, *Fragment* 161, GCS 41.1:80.

CHAPTER FOUR

Jesus & the Law: 'But I say to you'

The force of necessity is irresistible.
—AESCHYLUS

THERE ARE A FEW FACTS IN LIFE. THEY DO NOT CHANGE. We may, but they do not. Law in Israel was one such fact. No matter what one said or did it persisted. Weathered by time, trial, or blood, it endured decade after decade, century after century. It was the one *unalterable* fact in the life of the Jew.

Surpassing man-made laws, Torah did not concern itself with justice or humanitarian cause. It knew no motive, cause, or precedent. Torah was no mere summation of the finer and more practiced feelings currently preoccupying humanity. It knew no time, convention, or consensus. Torah, law, was *fact*. The laws of humanity changed as humanity changed. Torah, on the contrary, knew but one Legislator "the most ancient of them all."

Consequently, Josephus, an ancient Jewish historian, professes it absolute and unchanging:

> ...for amongst most other nations it is a studied art how men may transgress their laws; but no such thing is permitted amongst us; for though we be deprived of our wealth, of our cities, or of other advantages we have, our law *continues* immortal...[1]

A second fact: Jesus was a Jew. Law, then, was an unalterable fact in the life of Jesus. But if Jesus really was the Messiah, the chosen of God, how could He be anything but observant of the law? How could the Son disobey the immutable law of the Father? To answer these most fundamental of queries we have seen the stance of Jesus relative to specific *points* in the law, such as divorce and the Sabbath. But (in modern terms) it is one thing to agree or disagree with a particular law such as the legal speed of a vehicle; it is quite another to affirm or dispute the entire constitution, the law proper. Similarly, now let us advance one step further. In what manner did Jesus approach the law as a *whole*? The answer comes in what was to be His most celebrated and yet most tragically misunderstood sermon.

THE SERMON ON THE MOUNT

"Nowhere in literature is there anything to match the Sermon on the Mount: If there is, let men bring it forward."[2] This fated sermon is recorded in its longer form in Matthew where it is preached on the mount.[3] Luke's account is shorter and we are told that Jesus descended and "stood on a level place" before delivering the sermon.[4] Both begin with the beatitudes and both end with the parable of the house in the storm. Likewise both of the Gospels reveal ambiguity as to who the sermon was actually preached to. The sermon begins with: "when He was seated His *disciples* came to Him. Then He opened His mouth and taught them,"[5] and concludes with: "the *people* were astonished at His teaching."[6] From this many scholars have moved to claim that the core teaching was given only to the disciples, as though it

---

[1] Josephus, *Against Apion*, II:276-279.
[2] Gerard Manley Hopkins, *The Major Works* (Oxford: Oxford University Press, 2002), 278.
[3] Matt 5:1-7:29.
[4] Luke 6:20-49.
[5] Matt 5:1-2; also see Luke 6:20.
[6] Matt 7:28-29; also see Luke 7:1.

was only for the "more pious." This is entirely unfounded and rests more upon a medieval understanding than reality. In any case, what was delivered to the disciples was intended for the multitudes, and, in the words of John Chrysostom: "do not think of Him as discoursing with His disciples only, but rather with all *through* them."[7] The early Church knew no Gnostic elitism, all were called to perfection.

In Matthew and Luke, we see Jesus in the light of Moses. As Moses and the elders climbed Mount Sinai, Jesus and His disciples ascend the mountain. As Moses then ascended alone into the cloud, Jesus spent the night alone in prayer on the mountain. As the Israelites waited expectantly at the foot of Mount Sinai to receive the commandments, Jesus descends to a "level place" to deliver His teaching. We cannot but see the parallel. The Mosaic law and the teaching of Jesus stand in the same place. Is one then at opposition to the other? Does Jesus come to bring a *new* law and dispel the *old*? Knowing the now perturbed thoughts of first-century Palestine (and ours with them) Jesus is quick to alleviate the unrest:

> Do *not* think that I came to destroy the Law or the Prophets. I did not come to destroy but to fulfill. For assuredly [*Amen*], I say to you, till heaven and earth pass away, one jot or one tittle will by no means pass from the law till all is fulfilled. Whoever therefore breaks one of the least of these commandments, and teaches men so, shall be called least in the kingdom of heaven... For I say to you, that unless your righteousness *exceeds* the righteousness of the scribes and Pharisees, you will by no means enter the kingdom of heaven.[8]

These verses stand as the prologue to the so-called *antitheses* (which we shall consider promptly) and set the scenery for Jesus' defining stance relative to the law: "Do not think that I came to destroy the law... I did not come to destroy but to *fulfill.*" The word "fulfill" in Greek is given as *plerosai*, meaning to "complete," or "make perfect." Before even uttering a single word of teaching Jesus makes His purpose extremely clear: I do not stand against the law; I have come to complete it. So much so that even "one jot or one tittle will by no means pass from the law."

"Jot," in Greek *iota*, in Hebrew *yod*, is the smallest letter in its respective alphabet. "Tittle" is an artistic embellishment or distinguishing mark such as a dot placed over a letter. The meaning is simple. Jesus is dreadfully clear. Take away even a letter, no, even a dot above a letter of the law and

---

[7] John Chrysostom, *The Gospel of Matthew*, Homily 15.1, NPNF 1 10:91.
[8] Matt 5:17-20.

you risk the kingdom: "Even small things point to the great future of the kingdom of heaven."[9] Jesus asserts the permanence of the law even in its minute details. "Till heaven and earth pass away," nothing shall pass from the law. Rabbi Alexander reiterates: "If all men in the world were gathered together to destroy the 'yod,' which is the smallest letter in the law, they would not succeed."[10] The smallest detail, the least of the commandments, is of the greatest consequence. "Be heedful," Rabbi Judah the Prince warns, "of a light commandment as of a grave one."[11] An *iota* is immutable, unalterable, and with it, the entire law which rests upon it. Unlike the laws of humanity, these precepts are "not in any way relative to any time or place: they are absolute because they are from God."[12] And when we place such words in the context of another saying of Jesus, "Heaven and earth will pass away, but *My words* will by no means pass away,"[13] the consequence becomes drastically apparent. If Jesus claims that His words are just as permanent as even the smallest detail in the law, then the only possible conclusion is that the two must exist *timelessly* in harmony. One does not oppose the other.

But, Jesus continues, even living out the law in its smallest letter is not enough. "Unless your righteousness *exceeds* the righteousness of the scribes and Pharisees, you will by no means enter the kingdom of heaven." Chrysostom keenly notes: "If they were not acting in a commendable fashion, He would not have spoken of them as righteous."[14] The scribes and Pharisees were obedient to the smallest detail of the law, and yet it was not enough. Jesus was calling Israel to go beyond the letter of the law, to perceive its true meaning. The Pharisees were righteous, but the kingdom required more. It was "a challenge to Israel to *be* Israel."[15] This was not the realization or germination of a new law, rather it was a challenge to move towards what the law really was and is. How then could one exceed the righteousness of the Pharisees? Moreover how may one reach the kingdom? A reply is to be found in the *antitheses* that follow this brief yet crucial prologue to the sermon.

---

[9] Chromatius, *Tractate on Matthew* 20.2.1-3, CCL 9a:292.

[10] *Canticles Rabbah* 5:2.

[11] *Mishnah Abot* 2:1. Also see Origen, *Fragment* 99, GCS 41.1:56.

[12] Bishop Dmitri Royster, *The Kingdom of God: The Sermon on the Mount* (New York: SVS Press, 1992), 44.

[13] Matt 24:35.

[14] John Chrysostom, *The Gospel of Matthew*, Homily 16.4, PG 57:244; NPNF 1 10:107.

[15] N. T. Wright, *Jesus and the Victory of God*, 288.

You have heard... But I say to you

Imagine that we sat down on that Galilean mount and heard the words:

> *You have heard that it was said* to those of old, "You shall not murder, and whoever murders will be in danger of the judgment." *But I say to you* that whoever is angry with his brother without a cause shall be in danger of the judgment.[16]

What would be our initial reaction? I suggest that first we would understand Jesus to be saying something *new*: "You have heard" a thing of old, but now I am saying something else, something different. It is quite easy to come away from this with the conclusion that the old is over, and the new has begun. Should, however, we take our imaginings more holistically and contextually, our conclusion would radically differ. If we truly sat on those Galilean slopes then we would have also heard the statements that immediately preceded these. The statements in question are: "I did not come to destroy but to fulfill..." which we have seen previously. Now our imaginings take us elsewhere. Anything we have just heard must be taken as a follow on of "I did not come to destroy." That is, the saying "you have heard... but I say..." cannot possibly "destroy," but necessarily must "fulfill" the law. We may not and cannot take this text apart from its introduction. Each word must be appreciated in its context.

I am, of course, referring to the supposed six *antitheses*. So-called because these are six statements uttered by Jesus that set a *thesis*: "You have heard that it was said..." *against* something else: "But I say to you..." All six are found in the Sermon on the Mount in which they are introduced by the statements of Jesus on fulfilling the law, and are concluded by a call to perfection: "you shall be perfect, just as your Father in heaven is perfect."[17] They deal with the laws against murder, adultery, divorce, oaths, justice, and the love of the neighbor.[18] Whilst scholars ordinarily assert that there are six antitheses, closer examination reveals only five, with divorce really being a sub-teaching on adultery.

To begin, we should note that Jesus did not say in any of the six cases "*Moses* said," but rather, "you have *heard* that it was said." Thus Jesus' words are not being placed in opposition to what Moses commanded in the law, but rather what was "heard." At hand, therefore, is a discussion of the

[16] Matt 5:21-22.
[17] Matt 5:48.
[18] Matt 5:21-47.

interpretation of the law—what was "heard"—not the law itself. Secondly, the Greek conjunction *de* may either mean "and" or "but," therefore giving the *antitheses* the character of "you heard," "and I say." The point is further strengthened when we consider the rabbinic literature. Whenever an interpretation of Scripture is made amongst the rabbis it begins: "Rabbi so and so, said…" E. P. Sanders summates: "The verb 'to say' in [rabbinic] legal debate means 'to interpret.'"[19] The usage of "but I say to you" by Jesus then fits in neatly with rabbinic terminology as an introduction into His *interpretation* of the law. In the same vein, we question why Jesus preferred "you have *heard* it was *said*" and not "you have *read* that it was *written*"? If it was a matter of the law itself, then the argument should have proceeded upon what was written and not that which was said.

David Daube, a rabbinic scholar, offers another explanation. By examining the phrase as well as similar usages within the Jewish works of the *Mishnah* and *Midrash*, he concludes: "there is good reason, then for translating the first part of the Matthean form by: 'You have literally understood.'"[20] This would introduce a debate of understanding, rather than law. In other words, the antitheses to the ears of first-century Palestine would have taken the form of "you have understood the law to mean… but what it really signifies is…" A rabbinic example is very telling. Rabbi Judah the Prince comments on the passage, "Then the Lord came down upon Mount Sinai…,"[21] that is found in the book of Exodus:

> I might *hear* this as it is *heard* [i.e. literally]. *But you must say* [i.e. its true meaning]: If the sun, one of the many servants of God, may remain in its place and nevertheless be effective beyond it, how much more He by whose word the world came into being.[22]

Understanding the statements of Jesus in this manner helps us solve a problem that most of us never even knew existed. In the first and sixth antitheses the laws that Jesus quotes do *not* actually exist in that form. Once more I remind you that He preferred "heard…said" instead of "read… written," a point most pertinent. Jesus in the first antithesis quotes: "You shall not murder, *and whoever murders will be in danger of the judgment*,"[23] and in the sixth: "You shall love your neighbor and *hate your enemy*."[24]

[19] E. P. Sanders, *Jewish Law from Jesus to the Mishnah*, 93.
[20] David Daube, *The New Testament and Rabbinic Judaism*, 56.
[21] Exod 19:20.
[22] *Mekhilta on Exodus* 19:20.
[23] Matt 5:21.
[24] Matt 5:43.

The problem is that the extra clauses ("whoever murders will…" and "hate your enemy") simply do not exist in the Scriptures. If Jesus was debating the law itself then we would have a real issue. If it were, on the contrary, a matter of debating interpretation of the law, then Jesus would be free to quote an interpretation (what was "heard") and not only the actual verse of the law.

And thus the antitheses of Jesus become far clearer if taken in the context of the prologue to the Sermon on the Mount, as well as the contemporary rabbinic debate. His words may have been received on the Galilean slopes as such: "I did not come to destroy but to fulfill the law. But to belong to the kingdom you need to exceed the righteousness of the Pharisees. The Pharisees have 'heard' and interpreted the law as thus. But you need to go further and do what the law really signifies. If you do this, you will be perfect, as your Father is perfect." Understood in this manner these statements *cease* being antithetical to the law and instead become an illustration of their introduction: "I did not come to destroy but to fulfill the law."[25]

Paradoxically, the mistakenly-termed "antitheses" are in fact *point by point* demonstrations of the fulfillment of the law.[26] "He from this point," Chrysostom discerns, "begins to legislate, not simply, but by way of comparison with the ancient ordinances…*not as contending* with the former, but rather *in great harmony* with them."[27] This is not a dispute between that of old, and that of the new. Jesus does not dismiss fasting, prayer, tithing or any other of the laws, but points to their proper and inner observance *as well*. It was a seeking out of the real significance of the precept, "pressing behind some specific law to the more fundamental issue within or behind the law."[28] But that said, we should be careful not to swing in another unfortunate direction, that of outer versus inner observance:

> The antitheses do not, then, focus on the contrast between "outward" and "inward" keepings of the law. They are not retrojections into the first century of a nineteenth-century Romantic ideal of religion in which outward things are bad and inward things good.[29]

Now let us question what precisely Jesus was claiming in His interpretation of the law. The "antitheses" may be paraphrased as such:

---

[25] Matt 5:17-20.

[26] See W. D. Davies, *The Setting of the Sermon on the Mount*, 107.

[27] John Chrysostom, *The Gospel of Matthew*, Homily 16.7, NPNF 1 10:107. Also see David Daube, *The New Testament and Rabbinic Judaism*, 60.

[28] James D. G. Dunn, *Jesus Remembered* (Wm. B. Eerdmans, 2003), 579.

[29] N. T. Wright, *Jesus and the Victory of God*, 290.

If it was said not to murder, I say do not become angry;
If it was said not to commit adultery, I say do not lust;
If it was said not to swear falsely, I say do not swear at all;
If it was said an eye for an eye, I say turn the cheek;
If it was said to love your neighbor, I say love your enemy.[30]

A simple observation is that if one followed Jesus' interpretation alone, then transgression of the law would be impossible: "In no case would the following of Jesus' precepts have placed a person actually outside the law."[31] Far from opposing the law, Dorotheos of Gaza discerns within the "antitheses" instructions on avoiding transgressing the law from the beginning: "I repeat that the aim of Christ, our Master, is precisely to teach us *how* we come to commit all our sins; how we fall into all our evils."[32] To forbid lust, was to cast away adultery. To forbid anger, is to make murder impossible: "whoever fulfills the commandments of Christ implicitly fulfills the commandments of the law. For one who does not get angry is much less capable of killing."[33] Augustine similarly teaches: "He who teaches that we should not be angry, does not break the law not to kill, but rather fulfils it."[34] Jesus reveals to Israel the significance of the law. It is not a boundary, where one is safe till crossing to the other side of transgression. It is a declaration of the separation of humanity from God. He thus cries out to Israel: Uproot the beginning of sin lest it lead to separation.[35]

Finally, before concluding our discussion of the sermon we must consider a single word: *Amen*. There is nothing strange or unique in the word itself. What captivates our interest is the place it has in the words of Jesus: "*Amen*, I say to you [*Amen lego hymin*], till heaven and earth pass away..."[36] Jesus here *begins* His sentence with amen which is often translated

---

[30] Matt 5:21-48.

[31] A. E. Harvey, *Jesus and the Constraints of History* (London: Duckworth, 1982), 55-56.

[32] Dorotheos of Gaza, *Discourses and Sayings*, tr. Eric P. Wheeler (Michigan: Cistercian Publications, 1977), 80.

[33] Anonymous, *Incomplete Work on Matthew*, Homily 11, PG 56:689-90.

[34] Augustine, *Our Lord's Sermon on the Mount*, Book 1.21, NPNF 1 6:11.

[35] These commands have been subject to the inquiry whether the modern Christian should take them as timeless truths or as a past teaching specific to the first-century context. Sadly, both miss the point. To turn the sayings into timeless truths is to neglect their *historical context*. To relegate them to the past is to render Jesus' teaching inapplicable and *inconsequential* to our times. A single example will suffice. To turn the cheek is a timeless and absolute message of forgiveness, a crucial introducer into the kingdom (Matt 5:38-42). But to be slapped on the *right* cheek, historically, implies that one was struck with the back of the right hand, literally the greatest insult in the orient (then and now). In short, then, the words of the Jesus apply in our day, for they are timeless as well as historic, just as He is.

[36] Matt 5:18.

as "assuredly." Yet in all other literature, biblical and extra-biblical, "amen" normally *follows* a statement to confirm another's belief, for it means "so be it" or "truly." The usage by Jesus is, according to the eminent scholar Gustaf Dalman, "unfamiliar to the entire range of Jewish literature."[37] It is one thing to say "amen" to conclude a statement, it is altogether another to begin a statement with it. And it comes not as a single coincidence or error, but "seventy-five times throughout the four Gospels...exclusively in the sayings of Jesus."[38]

The point being that Jesus has no *need* for anyone to confirm His words: "'Amen, I say to you' emphasized that He knew and taught God's will with absolute certitude."[39] The antitheses, along with His entire teaching, bear this authority. His words were marked not as *an* interpretation, as though He were just one of the rabbis, but as *the* interpretation of the law. In the words of Vesilin Kesich:

> "Thus saith the Lord" was an introductory formula used by a prophet to indicate that his prophecy was *not* the product of his own insight or wisdom, but a message received from God. When Jesus introduced a saying with "Amen, I say to you," He spoke on the *basis* of His own authority and knowledge, which were rooted in His union with the Father, in His experience of the certainty of God's presence, and in the intimacy of His relationship with God.[40]

It is quite clear, then, that Jesus in His Sermon on the Mount was not giving "antitheses" to the law of Moses, but rather was instructing as to the proper interpretation and hence fulfillment of the law. But would this have been enough to calm his hearers? To a first-century Jew, obedience to the law meant to observe *both of its tables*.

THE TWO TABLES OF THE LAW

A lawyer came before Jesus and questioned Him: "Teacher, which is the great commandment in the law?" The response was the *two tables* of the law:

---

[37] Gustaf Dalman, *The Words of Jesus* (Edinburgh: T & T Clark, 1909), 226.

[38] Jaroslav Pelikan, *Jesus Through the Centuries: His Place in the History of Culture* (New Haven: Yale University Press, 1985), 15.

[39] John P. Meier, "Reflections on Jesus-of-History Research Today," in *Jesus' Jewishness: Exploring the Place of Jesus in Early Judaism*, ed. James H. Charlesworth (New York: Crossroad Publishing Company, 1996), 95.

[40] Vesilin Kesich, *The Gospel Image of Christ*, 147.

"You shall love the Lord your God with all your heart, with all your soul, and with all your mind." This is the *first* and great commandment. And the *second* is like it: "You shall love your neighbor as yourself." On these two commandments hang all the Law and the Prophets.[41]

In a few words the entire law could be summarized as the love of *God* and the love of *man*. Jewish law from its inception had been perceived as two tables of law: that of the commandments relating to God—*mitzvot ben adam le-Maqom*—and that of the commandments relating to man—*mitzvot ben adam le-adam*.[42] Each of the tables is evident in the Ten Commandments.[43] On the question of whether Jesus opposed the law of Moses and thus the religion of the Jews (which we should remember was also His), we must therefore question whether He spoke against either or both of the tables of the law. E. P. Sanders preempts: "I cannot find evidence that He attacked either table. His debates and arguments with His contemporaries fall within the parameters of disagreement in His place and time."[44]

It would be a severe mistake and singularly unintelligent to claim that Jesus was against the second table of the law (love of man). His entire life, word as well as deed, was for the sake of His neighbor, along with His enemy. To make the point, if it need be made, almost every controversial debate concerning the first table (love of God) results from Jesus' insistence on abiding by the second table. To cite two examples: He defends His disciples' apparent transgression of the Sabbath by plucking grain because they were *hungry*, and He heals on the Sabbath to alleviate *discomfort*. Thus we are left with whether Jesus opposed the first table of the law, the laws concerning the relation of God to man.

This is a question we have discussed at length bar the impending controversy in the temple to be examined shortly. We have shown that Jesus did not in any way place Himself in opposition to the law of Moses. He stood firmly within the laws of Sabbath, diet, and impurity. As for divorce, Jesus forbade it, returning marriage to its original and inherent unity (we should also remember that to strengthen a law is not to oppose it). He did, however, at times reveal a negative attitude to developments of the law or *tradition*:

[41] Matt 20:34-40. For a rabbinic parallel to this as well as Matt 7:12, see *Babylonian Talmud Shabbat* 31a: A Gentile once asked Hillel to teach him the Torah quickly, Hillel responded "Do nothing to your fellow that you would hate to be done to you! This is the entire Torah; all the rest is merely interpretation."

[42] See *Sifre Ahare Mot pereq* 8.1 and Philo, *Special Laws* 2.63, for evidence that this division was well known.

[43] Exod 20:1-17.

[44] E. P. Sanders, "Jesus and the First Table of the Jewish Law," 236.

"[He is shown as] interpreting Torah, even though He frequently comes to very different conclusions from those which were commonly held."[45] Jesus reminds Israel that the law was made for her, and not her for the law. Far from destroying or abrogating, His words reveal that He seeks to radically fulfill the law. He fulfills it by revealing the true significance and meaning of the law, not as a mere boundary of human behavior, but as a means and guide into the kingdom. Moreover Jesus came not only to fulfill the law, but mystically to have it fulfilled in Him:

> The Son of God, who is the *author* of the law and the prophets, did not come to abolish the law or the prophets. He gave the people the law that was to be handed down through Moses, and He imbued the prophets with the Holy Spirit for the preaching of the things to come... He fulfilled the law and the prophets in this way: He *brought to pass* those things that had been written about *Him* in the law and the prophets.[46]

That said, Jesus fits no known mould, neither before nor after Him: "He appears as 'the man who fits no formula,' whether Jewish or modern."[47] He speaks on His own authority, revealing that His is not *an* interpretation, but *the* interpretation of the law. Understood as such, His words need no confirmation. He provides His own *Amen.*

---

[45] Christopher Rowland, *Christian Origins*, 156.
[46] Chromatius, *Tractate on Matthew* 20.1.1-2, CCL 9a:291.
[47] Robert Banks, *Jesus and the Law*, 263.

CHAPTER FIVE

The Temple: 'I desire mercy and not sacrifice'

A religion without its mysteries
Is a temple without a God.
—ROBERT HALL

THERE IS ONE INCIDENT SINGLED OUT FROM AMONG MANY that stands at the centre of the life and death of Jesus: The "cleansing" of the temple. Alongside this often misunderstood action sit a number of sayings related to the destruction of the temple. Strictly speaking, however, one may ask whether this has anything to do with the law at all. Surely crying out against one or two merchants and overturning a few tables is not a point of contention with the law? Yet all takes a drastic turn when it dawns that the temple sacrificial system was a fundamental command from the God *of* sacrifice. Temple, in fact, has everything to do with the law. The two "formed an unbreakable whole."[1]

[1] N. T. Wright, *The New Testament and the People of God* (Minneapolis: Fortress Press, 1992), 228.

THE ACTION IN THE TEMPLE

It has been called "the greatest public deed which He performed during His lifetime."[2] Let us then consider three questions: What did Jesus do? What did He say? And significantly: What does it mean? We begin with the first:

> Then Jesus went into the temple and began to *drive* out those who bought and sold in the temple, and *overturned* the tables of the money changers and the seats of those who sold doves. And He would not allow anyone to carry wares through the temple. Then He taught, saying to them, "Is it not written, 'My house shall be called a house of prayer for all nations'? But *you have made it* a 'den of thieves.'" And the scribes and chief priests heard it and sought how they might *destroy* Him…[3]

On initial glance the matter is really quite simple. Jesus entered the temple and was witness to something that forced Him to react.[4] There are thus two things we must consider: the "something" and the "reaction." Should we examine the entirety of the life of Jesus in the Gospels we would find Him a rather composed and tranquil Man. Accordingly for Him to *react* by "driving" out merchants and "overturning" tables, some have inferred that He saw *something* that He had never seen previously. From this, many scholars have concluded that Jesus was reacting to something which He perceived to be a defilement of the temple. It was once a "house of prayer," but now *they* have "defiled" it and made it a "den of thieves." It was *once* one thing, now it has become another. What then was the original state of the temple? And what "defiled" the temple?

Before considering the possible answers to these queries a pivotal note must be made. Many biblical scholars, of all persuasions, have seen in this "cleansing" of the temple a conflict that in fact never existed. The alleged claim is that Jesus sought to return the "outward" show of the temple to "pure" religion. Unfortunately this has more foundation in nineteenth-century Romantic Protestantism than in first-century Judaism. The debate of *outward* "works" versus *inward* "religion" was not in any way known by

---

[2] Joseph Klausner, *Jesus of Nazareth*, 312.

[3] Mark 11:15-18; Also see Matt 21:12-17; Luke 19:45-48; John 2:13-22.

[4] Some of the Church Fathers on examining the different accounts of the incident found John to be unique in order and detail. They then concluded that there were in fact two "cleansings," that is, two incidents in which Jesus demonstrated within the temple. There is little evidence to prove or disprove such findings. For example see John Chrysostom, *The Gospel of Matthew*, Homily 67.1, PG 58:631-33; NPNF 1 10:409; and Augustine, *Harmony of the Gospels* 2.67.129, NPNF 1 6:160.

first-century Jews. For them, the external was simply the reflection and manifestation of the internal. And thus to "return" the temple to a "pure" purpose would necessarily mean a cessation of sacrifice:

> Those who write about Jesus' desire to return the temple to its "original," "true" purpose, the pure worship of God, seem to forget the principal function of any temple is to serve as a place to sacrifice, and that sacrifices *require* the supply of suitable animals.[5]

Being the single point of sacrifice for all Jews, in Palestine and beyond, the Jerusalem temple would have required a constant supply of animals. To then claim that the day to day trading involved in such sacrifice was a "terrible desecration,"[6] seems to me to miss the mark widely. If we return to our initial question of the original state of the temple before its "defilement," the matter becomes clearer. Essentially there never was a time when the temple was "*undefiled*." Selecting and sacrificing unblemished animals would have from the beginning "defiled" the temple. So then, what was Jesus returning the temple to? Claiming that Jesus sought to purify the temple to return it to its original purpose begs the question: what purpose *other* than sacrifice? Put simply: Jesus, being a Jew (and not a nineteenth-century Protestant), would have known that the sacrificial act, central to any Jew's life, would have required the supply, purchase, and selection of unblemished animals. How then could He envision sacrifice without its necessary means? It is similar to storming into the Liturgy of the Eucharist and forbidding the purchase of candles or the supply of bread and wine. To the early Jew (and thankfully, some Christians) the concept of outward versus inward basically did not exist. The external was necessary for the internal and vice versa—they were one and the same. In short, the temple without sacrifice is *not* a temple:

> And what did they sell there? Things which people needed in the sacrifices of that time... It was not a great sin, then, if they sold in the temple that which was bought for the purpose of offering in the temple: and yet He *cast* them out thence.[7]

The great Augustine concludes that to buy and sell was not to err, and "yet He cast them out thence." Something else was at play. Having thus brushed

[5] E. P. Sanders, *Jesus and Judaism*, 63.

[6] Alfred Edersheim, *The Life and Times of Jesus the Messiah* (Grand Rapids: Wm. B. Eerdmans, 1953), 370.

[7] Augustine, *Tractates on John* 10.4, NPNF 1 7:70.

away these invalid retrojections, we are left with *three* general possibilities.[8] The first is that Jesus purposely reacted against the *sacrificial system* itself. We have already touched upon the fact that sacrifice was absolutely necessary in that it was commanded by God. It was out of this very need for sacrifice, Josephus points out, that the temple became a political asset:

> ...those that could get [the temple] into their hands had the whole nation under their power, for without the command of them it was not possible to offer their sacrifices; and to think of leaving off those sacrifices, is to every Jew plainly *impossible*, who are still more ready to lose their lives than to leave off that divine worship which they have been wont to pay unto God.[9]

But if Jesus reacted against the system, then we must also consider the *moneychangers* whose tables were overturned. These were those entrusted with the conversion of various coinages from the entire Diaspora into acceptable coinage (likely Tyrian[10] coinage) for paying the temple tax[11] as well as the purchasing of animals for sacrifice.[12] The *buyers* and *sellers* were likewise absolutely vital to the temple's operation. To see this, imagine that you were a Jew on pilgrimage from Alexandria who happened to also own a turtledove. You would hardly bring a turtledove with you from Alexandria and risk the dove dying en-route, or perhaps being rejected for a particular blemish. Not to mention the added burden of carrying an animal with you on the harsh journey. Instead, you would likely sell the dove before you left, and use the resulting funds to purchase another dove "certified" by the temple. In other words, if sacrifices were commanded by God, then moneychangers and their like were required to facilitate this commandment: "The business arrangements around the temple were *necessary* if the commandments were to be obeyed."[13]

---

[8] There are others, all with far less credibility. One is that Jesus sought to reform and *purify* the temple by moving trade altogether outside of the temple precincts. It is generally attested that the trade was conducted in the Court of the Gentiles (so-called because Gentiles could not advance beyond it), an area still strictly within the temple. There is little support for this possibility—biblically and extra-biblically—though it does fit in some ways with the saying "a house of prayer for all nations." Gentiles, the nations, were only allowed in this single part of the temple which now was witness to trade. Some have suggested that perhaps Jesus was seeking out a place for the Gentiles within the temple?

[9] Josephus, *Antiquities of the Jews*, XV:248.

[10] *Mishnah Bekhorot* 8:7.

[11] The temple taxes, of a half-shekel, were used to pay for the daily offerings offered on behalf of all Jews.

[12] *Mishnah Sheqalim* 1:3.

[13] E. P. Sanders, *Jesus and Judaism*, 65.

Perhaps then Jesus reacts not so much against the system, but against the corruption of its constituents. This superficially becomes more likely when we consider what Jesus actually said during the act: "You have made it a 'den of *thieves*.'" But the Greek word for thieves, *lestes*, and the Hebrew, *parisim*, found in the original quotation from Jeremiah,[14] do not mean "swindler" but rather "raider" or "one who robs with violence."[15] Therefore the accusation does not fit with a charge of corruption. Even if it did, some degree of corruption would always be associated with a sacrificial system which necessitated the supply of sacrifice on such a grand level. And if admitted that the buyers, sellers, and moneychangers, were all corrupt, the same could not be said of the system itself.

We thus return once more to the "something" and the "reaction." Why *now* would Jesus choose to react to the corruption of individuals, when His past reactions to the likes of Zacchaeus the tax collector were altogether amicable?[16] It is more plausible that if Jesus were to react against corruption, that it would be against the priesthood.

This brings us to our second possibility: that Jesus reacted against the *priesthood*, the caretakers of the sacrificial acts. It is reasonable to ask whether He would have been the first to attempt to "cleanse" the defilement of the priesthood. In the book of Malachi the priests are accused of offering cursed sacrifices by "putting away" their wives and exploiting the poor.[17] The *Psalms of Solomon* deride the priesthood for committing adultery and "robbing the sanctuary," along with the charge of offering sacrifice after coming into contact with menstrual blood.[18] Likewise are they charged in the *Covenant of Damascus*: "they *convey* uncleanness to the sanctuary, inasmuch as they do not keep separate according to the law, but lie with her that sees 'the blood of her flux.'"[19]

But if Jesus wished to follow suit why does He not lay a charge of impurity, dishonesty, or exploitation, against the priesthood? Furthermore had He intended to cleanse the temple from the impurity of the priesthood, Jesus no doubt would have made His way to the actual place where the sacrifices were being prepared *by* the priests: "we must recall that Jesus' symbolic action occurs in the outer court, far from priests and sacrifices and the temple building [proper]."[20] The buyers, sellers, and moneychangers, could

---

[14] Jer 7:3-15.
[15] A. E. Harvey, *Jesus and the Constraints of History*, 132.
[16] Luke 19:1-9.
[17] Mal 2-3.
[18] *Psalms of Solomon* 8:9-14.
[19] *Covenant of Damascus* 5:6-8.
[20] Lloyd Gaston, *No Stone On Another: Studies in the Significance of the Fall of Jerusalem*

have *only* undertaken their business within the outer court of the temple, an area known as the Court of the Gentiles.[21] The point being that the act of "cleansing" must therefore have also taken place in this outer court, and thus *away* from where the priesthood in fact performed its function. This outer court was then inherently unsuitable for an attack against the priesthood. Once more another possibility becomes unsustainable.

SYMBOL OF DESTRUCTION

Now let us advance to the final possibility. Once more imagine that you are a first-century Jew standing in a queue to purchase a turtledove for a purification offering. As you stand in the Court of the Gentiles a Man suddenly enters through the gate, strolls past the temple guards, and then proceeds to overturn tables, and making a "whip of cords," drives out merchants. Looking around another thing strikes you: the Court is incredibly *large*. Modern estimates place the area at around four hundred square meters. If this be of surprise, consider that the whole temple occupied almost a quarter of the city of Jerusalem.[22]

In overturning tables and driving out merchants, Jesus, therefore, would not have in any way brought the buying and selling to an *end*. Practically, it would have required a mob, perhaps an army, in any event more than a few disciples, to attempt any real disturbance to trade in such a large area. Those present would have known that by interfering with a small and probably public *part* of the Court, Jesus was not intending a mass "cleansing" of the temple but rather was making a point. Consistently throughout His ministry, Jesus showed Himself to be keenly intelligent and ever practical. Why then would He not be aware that as one Man it was impossible to "cleanse" the temple there and then? Indeed, if He had intended to drive out all that "defiled" the temple in that moment, why were the blind and lame permitted to come to Him for healing *in* the temple immediately afterwards?[23] Or for that matter why was Jesus

---

in the Synoptic Gospels (Leiden: Brill, 1970), 88.

[21] See Joseph Klausner, *Jesus of Nazareth*, 314, for a study against the generally accepted thesis that the trade was conducted in the outer Court of the Gentiles. *Mishnah Berakot* 9:5: "One should not enter the Temple mount with his walking stick, his overshoes, his *money* bag, or with dust on his feet." This needs to be qualified with the dating of the Mishnah, which found its final form centuries after the destruction of the temple in 70 AD.

[22] N. T. Wright, *The New Testament and the People of God*, 225.

[23] Matt 21:14.

permitted to continue "teaching daily in the temple?"[24] Martin Hengel identifies a further consequence:

> ...it was not a matter of driving out all who sold, and the money-changers—for such an action would not have been possible *without* a large contingent of troops and a corresponding general riot, and would inevitably have led to intervention on the part of the temple guards and the Romans.[25]

Jesus, if we may dare to speak of His intention, sought not in that moment to remove every last portion of "defilement" from the temple. Instead *He enacted a symbol*. In the words of E. P. Sanders: "Those who saw it, and those who heard about it, would have known that it was a gesture intended to make a point rather than have a concrete result; that is, they would have seen the action as *symbolic*."[26] At various points in His ministry "Jesus acted as, and saw Himself as, a prophet, standing within Israel's long prophetic tradition."[27] And prophets, at least in Israel's history, often acted symbolically. Jesus was not alone. Ezekiel took a clay tablet and portrayed upon it the destruction of Jerusalem.[28] Isaiah went barefoot and naked as a symbol of "the Egyptians as prisoners and the Ethiopians as captives, young and old, naked and barefoot, with their buttocks uncovered."[29] Closer to home, Jeremiah smashed a potter's flask in the presence of the people to symbolize that God "will break this people and this city, as one breaks a potter's vessel."[30] This leads us to an obvious question: What did Jesus *intend* to symbolize?

A first insight is to be found in the original passage of Jeremiah that is quoted by Jesus:

> Will you steal, murder, commit adultery, swear falsely, burn incense to Baal, and walk after other gods whom you do not know, and then come and stand before Me... Has this house, which is called by My name, become a *den of thieves* in your eyes?... Behold, My anger and My fury will be *poured* out on this place...[31]

---

[24] Luke 19:47.
[25] Martin Hengel, *Was Jesus a Revolutionist?*, tr. William Klassen (Philadelphia: Fortress Press, 1971), 17-18.
[26] E. P. Sanders, *Jesus and Judaism*, 70. Also see Augustine, *Explanation of the Psalm* 130.2-3, CCL 40:1899-1900.
[27] N. T. Wright, *Jesus and the Victory of God*, 415.
[28] Ezek 4:1-17.
[29] Isa 20:2-4.
[30] Jer 19:1, 10-11.
[31] Jer 9-11.

In the action of Jesus the crucial word is *overturning*. A word that is laced with sentiments of *destruction*, and one which pans well with the sense given in the original passage in Jeremiah. To physically take hold of a table upon which sat hundreds of coins, as well as the odd animal cage, and then to overturn it, is to enact a symbol of destruction. We should note once more that Jesus being a religious Jew knew that God had commanded sacrifices. Therefore to disrupt (even symbolically) the sacrificial system was to place Himself, at the very least in the eyes of a significant few, as one who publicly confronted the God of the sacrifices.

But that said, what exactly is to be destroyed? The sacrificial system? The priesthood? Or perhaps, the temple itself? Two of these have already been ruled out. If Jesus had intended to reveal the destruction (symbolically) of the priesthood or the system of sacrifices surely He would have said something to that effect. In contrast, when it came to the temple He *did* say something:

(1) Do you see these great buildings? Not *one* stone shall be left upon another that shall not be thrown down.[32]
(2) Jesus answered and said to them, "Destroy this temple, and in three days I will raise it up."[33]
(3) *We* heard Him say, "I will destroy this temple made with hands, and within three days I will build another made without hands."[34]

When we look at what Jesus had to say about the temple, the theme is destruction. Two of the sayings come directly from His mouth; the third is a hearsay accusation. Of interest, in (2) Jesus says: "[*If you*] destroy this temple...," whilst in (3) His accusers charge Him with saying: "*I will* destroy." Immediately following (1) Jesus delivers the *apocalypse*, a collection of prophecies of an undisclosed time in the future. Also, the saying in (1) only entails destruction without any mention of a rebuilding. It is the second saying, no doubt upon which (3) is based, that introduces the concept of *restoration*. Destruction in this case is not absolute, but is a preparation for the rebuilding of the temple "made without hands." John the theologian immediately follows (2) with: "But He was speaking of the temple of His body."[35] Origen further clarifies that the false witnesses accuse Jesus of saying that He would "build": "He did not say that He would build the temple but raise it up. The verb *build* does not designate a sudden action, but '*raise* it up' does."[36]

---

[32] Mark 13:2; Luke 21:5; Matt 24:2.
[33] John 2:18-19.
[34] Mark 14:58; 15:29; Matt 26:61, 27:39; Acts 6:14.
[35] John 2:21.
[36] Origen, *Commentary on Matthew* 132, GCS 38.2:268–69.

We thus remain unsure as to whether Jesus actually threatened the temple as the phrase, "I will destroy," is hearsay at the mouth of "false witnesses."[37] But we can conclude that He did indeed predict a destruction of the temple as well as the destruction of His body which would be rebuilt in three days. In the sayings there are therefore four different aspects: the destruction of the temple, the prediction of His death, the restoration of His life, and the restoration of the temple. If we place the act of "cleansing" the temple within this context then "the action and the saying form a unity."[38] The act of *overturning* corresponds with His vision of destruction. Driving out the merchants and *restoring* a "house of prayer" aligns with the restoration and rebuilding of a new temple. If we consider "destroy this temple made with hands, and within three days I will build another made without hands,"[39] as actual words of Jesus and not hearsay, then the deed entirely corresponds with the saying.

Jesus was symbolizing the destruction and restoration of the temple. But *why* is it to be destroyed? Some have claimed that it was not so much a matter of whether the old temple was impure, but rather that the old was to be destroyed to make way for the new and perfect temple.[40] Others agree that this destruction was an inevitable step in the restoration of the temple, but perceive within it *judgment* as well. If we take into account the cursing of the fig tree which is found immediately before and after the cleansing of the temple, the message is clear. "By intercalating the temple incident with the cursing of the fig tree Mark had Jesus declare God's judgment on the temple."[41] Add to this the tearful scene where Jesus on approaching Jerusalem cries out: "they will not leave in you one *stone* upon another, because you did not know the time of your visitation," [42] and the conclusion becomes irresistible. Jesus judged in deed and action the temple: "He symbolically and prophetically enacted judgment upon it—a judgment which, both before and after, He announced verbally as well as in action."[43] The Fathers of the Church are in this vein unanimous. The destruction of Jerusalem and the temple, though to eventually be restored in the coming age, is a consequence of neglecting their "visitation":

---

[37] Matt 26:60.
[38] E. P. Sanders, *Jesus and Judaism*, 75.
[39] Mark 14:58; 15:29; Matt 26:61, 27:39; Acts 6:14.
[40] E. P. Sanders, *Jesus and Judaism*, 75.
[41] William R. G. Loader, *Jesus' Attitude towards the Law*, 116.
[42] Luke 19:41-44.
[43] N. T. Wright, *Jesus and the Victory of God*, 417.

Because [Jerusalem] had not accepted the law, He cursed [the fig tree], so that there might no longer be fruit on it, according to its law... He sought fruit from the fig tree at an inopportune time [when it was not its season], that it might be a symbol of one who had deceitfully withheld the fruits of the law at the opportune time. For, if He had sought fruit from it at the opportune time, no one would have known that there was a figurative meaning embedded here. Instead of the fig tree, therefore, He showed that it was Jerusalem that He was reproaching, for He had sought love in her, but she had despised the fruit of repentance...[44]

As with all prophecies, it was a reaction to a historical event as well as an indication of a loftier truth. It found roots in *history* (a reaction to trade), grew as *revelation* (destruction of the old temple), and flowered in *prophecy* (restoration of the new temple). But let us press further.

THE NEW TEMPLE

Is there any evidence that early Judaic thought ever envisioned that the sacred temple would be destroyed or rebuilt? Lloyd Gaston, in his great study on the temple, denies any concept of a new temple within the early literature, discerning instead a new Jerusalem:

We find no background in Jewish apocalyptic before 70 AD for the statement "I will destroy this temple and in three days I will build it." The future salvation was couched in terms of the new *Jerusalem*, even if the temple should occasionally be presupposed as part of this... Although it might be natural, it is never explicitly said that the old temple must first be removed before the new one comes."[45]

Others by equating "Zion" with the temple as well as Jerusalem have seen otherwise: "The descriptions of the New Zion *presuppose* a new temple, for no good Israelite could think of one without the other."[46] Should we examine the literature itself we would find a similar claim. Isaiah calls for a new temple: "Saying to Jerusalem, 'You shall be built,' And to the temple,

---

[44] Ephrem the Syrian, *Commentary on Tatian's Diatesseron*, 164, 168, 170; JSSS 2:243–46. See also Augustine, *Sermons On New Testament Lessons* 48.3, Cetedoc 0284, 98.38.592.39; NPNF 1 6:413-14; and Gregory the Great, *Letter 39 to Eulogius*, Cetedoc 1714, 140A.10.21.32; NPNF 2 13:48.

[45] Lloyd Gaston, *No Stone On Another*, 119.

[46] R. J. McKelvey, *The New Temple: The Church in the New Testament* (Oxford: Oxford University Press, 1969), ii, n. 2.

'Your foundation shall be laid.'[47] Ezekiel advances further, providing detailed instructions on the building of this new temple.[48] In the book of Tobit we hear a prophecy in which "they shall *build* a temple, but *not* like to the first, until the time of that age be fulfilled... as the prophets have spoken thereof."[49] Entailed within this hope for the new temple is therefore the end of the old:

> And I stood up to see till they folded up that *old* house...till the Lord of the sheep brought a *new* house greater and loftier than the first, and set it in the place of the first...and all the sheep were within it.[50]

Our inevitable conclusion is that the Jewish expectation, at least for some, consisted in a restoration of Israel in which there would be a new Jerusalem closely associated with a new temple.[51] And to build anew necessitates the destruction of the old. If such concepts were familiar to Jewish thinkers, in different parts of space and time, then it stands to reason that such expectations may have been held by, or at least were known by, some of Jesus' hearers. Similarly, if Jesus mentioned destruction (either at His hands according to the false witnesses, or by others) and rebuilding, surely some must have been privy to the connotations of the end of the age. This expectation needs to be coupled to another of equal, if not more, significance and consequence:

> When your days are fulfilled and you rest with your fathers, I will set up your seed after you, who will come from your body, and I will establish his kingdom. He shall build a *house* for My name, and I will establish the throne of his kingdom *forever*. I will be his Father, and he shall be My *son*.[52]

Through Nathan, God reveals to David the mystery of the *temple-builder*. He, who would come from the seed of David, would be established in an eternal kingdom, and would build a new temple. He shall be called the Son. This clearly was a messianic expectation, and thus "any claim to rebuild the temple could all too readily be read as a claim to royal messiahship,

---

[47] Isa 44:28.
[48] Ezek 40-43.
[49] *Tobit* 14:4-5.
[50] *1 Enoch* 90:28. Also see *1 Enoch* 91:13.
[51] At this point we are not discussing the restoration or return of the *Gentiles*. But we should point out that the new temple comes in the context of, in a surprisingly great number of texts, the Gentiles returning to true religion. See Isa 56:1-8, 60:3-7, 66:18-24; *Tobit* 14:6; *1 Enoch* 90:30; *Jubilees* 1:15-17; *Sibylline Oracles* 3:702-720, 772-774.
[52] 2 Sam 7:12-14.

and divine sonship."[53] That the Messiah would rebuild the temple is testified to in multiple places, importantly at the mouths of Rabbi Yohanan Ben Zakkai, Rabbi Judah Ben Ilai, and Rabbi Akiba.[54] It is then not surprising that, on hearing the accusation that Jesus would destroy and rebuild the temple, the high-priest erupts immediately: "Are You the Messiah, the Son of the Blessed?"[55]

In Judaic thought the temple was wrapped in garments of messianic expectation and divine sonship. To claim to rebuild was to evoke anticipation of the messianic temple-builder. If we place these words side by side with the action then no doubt "among the reverberations set off by Jesus' action in the temple would be the question, 'Could this be the expected Davidic Messiah?'"[56]

Whether understood as an attack on the commercialism of the temple, the priesthood, the sacrificial system, or the temple itself, the action would be far reaching. The temple was central to the life of the Jew: "To evoke, even conditionally, the destruction of 'this temple' was to touch not just stone and gold and not only the general well-being but history and hope, national identity, self-understanding, and pride."[57] A public demonstration against *anything* associated with the temple would have been perceived as dangerous at the least. The Gospel writers thus immediately state bluntly: "the scribes and chief priests heard it and sought how they might *destroy* Him."[58] It is no shock that at the trial of Jesus the accusers never claim that He had claimed to be the Messiah. Instead the charge focuses upon the saying of destroying the temple. The temple, and therefore Jesus' action and saying, stand at the very centre of His death and for the Church, His resurrection.

With this in mind, we may now consider the true meaning of the action within the temple. Our summations fall within a number of themes. First, Jesus in both word and deed *symbolized the overturning* of the old temple. By doing so He reveals to Israel that He intends to draw the present age to an *end* in ushering in a *new* kingdom. The temple will, however, once more be restored and will be made *anew*, a true "house of prayer." In claiming to

---

[53] James D. G. Dunn, *The Parting of the Ways: Between Christianity and Judaism and their Significance for the Character of Christianity* (London: SCM Press & Philadelphia: Trinity Press International, 1991), 167.

[54] For numerous references as well as a commentary on the temple-builder expectation see Joseph Klausner, *The Messianic Idea in Israel: From Its Beginning to the Completion of the Mishnah* (New York: The Macmillan Company, 1955), 513-514.

[55] Mark 14:61.

[56] James D. G. Dunn, *Jesus Remembered*, 640. Also see Irving M. Zeitlin, *Jesus and the Judaism of His Time* (Cambridge: Polity Press, 1988), 151.

[57] Ben F. Meyer, *The Aims of Jesus* (London: SCM Press, 1979), 183.

[58] Mark 11:18.

rebuild the temple, Jesus subtly beckons the first-century mind to recognize in Him the foretold *temple-builder*, the Son, a ruler of an everlasting kingdom. Mysteriously and majestically, this very temple, which is to be made anew in the kingdom, is His body. The saying thus unfolds the deed: "The old temple would be replaced by the resurrected Christ, the new locus of God's revelation and forgiveness."[59]

If the meaning of the action is such, we must finally ask: What then does the composite unit of word and deed reveal about Jesus' attitude to the law? Jesus did not in any way seek to destroy the sacrificial system or the temple. His action symbolized the end of the old, and the ushering in of the new. The saying and deed must be understood within this context. Put simply, Jesus did not violate the law in reference to the temple, though perhaps on that fated day He created quite a scene. Even after the action, Jesus continued to teach and heal in the temple.[60] Should we look further into the future after His death, we would find that the disciples continued to worship in the temple.[61] If Jesus Himself, along with His disciples, did not sense an immediate break with the temple, surely our only possible conclusion must be that this action was not intended to undermine the sanctity nor *current* necessity of the temple. We must also remember that He paid the prescribed temple tax,[62] commanded a healed leper to offer the required sacrifice,[63] and called for purity of heart *before* sacrificing.[64] In short, Jesus in no way showed Himself to be at odds with the temple of Israel, in principle or deed. He did, however, prophetically enact its imminent destruction on two levels, as a building, and as His body. That it was destroyed is an event of history. But that it was rebuilt, mystically, is a truth of glory.

All this may be summarized in a single incident. At the *Feast of Tabernacles* on each of the first seven days of the festival a water libation ceremony was performed.[65] Especially on the "great day of the feast," water (to encourage rain and blessing) was carried in a joyous musical procession from the spring of Gihon to the temple. Entering by the water gate, the priest carrying the water would then pour it out on the *foundation stone* of the altar and the temple. By pouring water on this central stone of the temple, the faithful would be confident that, in return, water would flow in rivers to Israel. Long ago, Ezekiel had prophesized that living water would one day

[59] Vesilin Kesich, *The Gospel Image of Christ*, 172.
[60] Luke 19:47.
[61] Acts 3:1, 21:23-26.
[62] Matt 17:24.
[63] Mark 1:40-44.
[64] Matt 5:23.
[65] The ceremony is described in *Mishnah Sukkah* 4:9-5:5.

flow from the new temple.[66] As they performed this ceremony some two millennia ago, One stood up:

> Now the Jews' *Feast of Tabernacles* was at hand... On the last day, that great day of the feast, Jesus stood and cried out, saying, "If anyone thirsts, let him come to Me and *drink*. He who believes in Me, as the Scripture has said, out of his heart will flow rivers of living *water*."[67]

Jesus stands and declares to all who will hear Him: I am the living water. I am the foundation stone of the temple from whom all life flows. I am the *temple*.

---

[66] Ezek 47:1-12.
[67] John 7:2, 37-39.

PART TWO:

The People of the Kingdom

CHAPTER SIX

The Unforgivable Sin: 'Blasphemy against the Spirit'

Perhaps there is not in all Holy Scripture found
A more important or more difficult question.
—SAINT AUGUSTINE

AT THE TURN OF THE FOURTH CENTURY in an ancient city of Algeria, a middle aged man quietly approached the pulpit. As all eyes turned and focused intently upon him, he looked towards the ground. In a barely audible voice he humbly confessed: "I have always in my discourses to the people avoided the difficulty and embarrassment of this question…" It took painful moments of silence for the people to even imagine such a thing. Silently, some murmuring, each man and woman, young and old, inquired: O' father, what is this question that plagues you, and how is it that you, a master of the Gospel, are unable to answer it? Knowing their thoughts, the unpretentious father replied: "I tell you, my beloved; perhaps there is not in all Holy Scripture found a more important or more difficult question."[1]

---

[1] Augustine, *Sermons on New Testament Lessons* 21.8, NPNF 1 6:320-321.

This confession was not made by an illiterate or perhaps unlearned priest. Here before us is the embarrassment of the great Church Father and master rhetorician, Augustine. But he was not alone. His embarrassment has been shared throughout the centuries. What then is this source of confusion, this question of questions?

Immediately after exorcising a demon possessed man, Jesus with unyielding eyes warns:

> Anyone who speaks a word against the Son of Man, it *will* be forgiven him; but whoever speaks against the Holy Spirit, it will *not* be forgiven him, either in this age or in the age to come.[2]

Augustine, and with him centuries of Christian thought, thus pondered: What is this blasphemy, and why will it never be forgiven? Is God not merciful and capable to forgive any sin for which repentance is given? And how is it that blasphemy against the Son of Man *will* be forgiven, whilst that against the Holy Spirit will *not*? Is the Son of Man *less* than the Spirit? Now, perhaps, we may appreciate with Augustine the gravity of this declaration of Jesus. First we shall turn to exorcism in general, before examining the specific case of exorcism that led to this warning against blasphemy.

A First Century View of Exorcism

In the previous chapters, Jesus interpreted and transformed the law of Moses *into* the law of the kingdom. Yet as He made to usher it in, an enemy arose. Against Jesus stood not Rome, nor an oppressing army, but the real adversary. Evil was no longer an enemy without; in first-century Palestine it was *within*. Not beyond Israel's border among pagans, but "within the chosen people."[3] Evil, with *Satan*[4] as its forerunner, had Israel in its grip. And thus any motion

---

[2] Matt 12:32.

[3] N. T. Wright, *Jesus and the Victory of God*, 446.

[4] Whilst I will refer to him as "Satan," a more accurate representation is "the Satan." *Satan* comes from the Hebrew root *stn* meaning "to obstruct" or "to oppose." He was thus "the obstructer," and in Greek was translated as *ho diabolos—the devil* in English—meaning "the adversary." In both cases we find "the" before Satan indicating that this name described a function: "to obstruct." For a discussion see Elaine Pagels, "The Social History of Satan, the 'Intimate Enemy': A Preliminary Sketch," *The Harvard Theological Review* 84, 2 (1991), 106. Also see her other work, *The Origin of Satan* (New York: Random House, 1995); H. Van Der Loos, *The Miracles of Jesus* (Leiden: Brill, 1968), 350. On demonology in general see James D. G. Dunn, "Demon Possession and Exorcism in the New Testament," in *The Christ and the Spirit* Vol. II (Grand Rapids: Wm. B. Eerdmans, 1998), 178. Also see Henry Ansgar Kelly, *Satan:*

to establish the kingdom would first necessitate dealing with the enemy, and with him the grip of evil.[5]

This brings us to the practice of exorcism, the binding and casting out of demons. Jesus was neither the first nor the last to cast out demons. Demonic *obsession* (whereby a person was afflicted externally) and demonic *possession* (the invasion of the person internally) were ideas that were prevalent in ancient culture.[6] Sumerian and Akkadian religion had formal rites of exorcism, indicating that it was common enough to be formalized. Likewise do we find the practice in the ancient Babylonian, Assyrian, and Egyptian religions. Pre-exilic Judaism (before 587 BC), however, has little to offer by way of possession or exorcism, the single exception being king Saul who was afflicted by a "distressing spirit."[7] Post-exilic Judaism on the other hand is another matter entirely.

In the book of Tobit we find a characteristic example of demonic obsession. Seven husbands of Tobias' wife-to-be are killed by a demon named Asmodeus who is said to "love her."[8] Later Josephus, the great Jewish historian, tells of the reputation of king Solomon as an exorcist. He also relates an exorcism he witnessed by a Jew called Eleazar, who cast out a demon in the presence of the Roman Emperor Vespasian (69-79 AD), by using a special ring and invoking the name of Solomon.[9] And in the *Prayer of Nabonidus*, the Babylonian king Nabonidus tells of a Jewish exorcist from among the exiled Jews of Judah.[10] A fascinating though no doubt fictional work known as the *Genesis Apocryphon* narrates that even Abraham once exorcised Pharaoh.

If Jesus is thus seen on this scenery of first-century Judaism, and if He was perceived by His hearers to be a miracle worker or prophet in any way, then it follows that He would have in some way or form been confronted with at least a few cases of demonic possession. Indeed, as John P. Meier notes, it "would be surprising *not* to find any trace of exorcism" in His thought and practice.[11]

A Biography (Cambridge: Cambridge University Press, 2006); *The Devil, Demonology, and Witchcraft* (Oregon: Wipf & Stock, 2004).

[5] Jeffrey Burton Russell, *The Devil: Perceptions of Evil from Antiquity to Primitive Christianity* (Ithaca: Cornell University Press, 1977), 222. For a discussion of Satan in the thought of the early Church Fathers see Jeffrey Burton Russell, *Satan: The Early Christian Tradition* (Ithaca: Cornell University Press, 1982).

[6] John P. Meier, *A Marginal Jew*, Vol. II, 405.

[7] 1 Sam 16:14-23.

[8] *Tobit* 6-8.

[9] Josephus, *Antiquities of the Jews*, VIII:45-49. The *Testament of Solomon*, dated c. 100-300 AD gives a fuller exposition on Solomon as an exorcist.

[10] 4 QprNab.

[11] John P. Meier, *A Marginal Jew*, Vol. II, 406.

The Gospels would obviously agree. Six specific exorcisms are mentioned,[12] forming the largest group of the healing miracles, as well as numerous summaries of unmentioned exorcisms where He "cast[s] out many demons."[13] Even beyond the New Testament, the Jewish work of the Talmud remembered Jesus as one who "practiced sorcery."[14] Of interest is also the *manner* in which He cast out demons which finds no real parallel, either before or after Him. Jesus did not use a heart or liver like Tobit, nor the "smell of a root" like Eleazar, and neither did He pray before exorcising as the Jewish holy man Hanina ben Dosa.[15] Without resorting to ritual, the authoritative word alone was sufficient for Jesus, and thus He "commands" demons to "be silent," and to "come out."[16]

But before moving onto the fated incident itself, we do well to address the concerns of modernity. The western mind has a particular revulsion to the entire concept of exorcism for at least three reasons. Chief among these is that advances in medicine explain away the majority of possessions as schizophrenia, paranoia, or epilepsy. More significantly, to admit exorcism admits not only the existence of the supernatural, but more-so the existence of the supernatural *among* the natural. The third and last reason concerns media portrayals, which transform evil into a horror caricature, thereby designating it "unintelligent" to the "informed."

The last of these reasons will not be considered for media by nature is generally untrue to life, and the second is beyond our scope for I take it as a simple Christian truth.[17] As to the first we should remember that the ancients (though perhaps medically primitive) were not by any means naïve. They did not attribute *all* illnesses to possession, and thus we find a distinction between the "demon-possessed, epileptics, and paralytics"[18] that Jesus healed. That said, though a particular illness was a medical entity (and not possession), this does not mean that it could not be attributed to Satan. Job was not possessed, and yet was afflicted with "medical" boils that were attributed to Satan.[19] A disease may have a spiritual dimension and thus

---

[12] Mark 1:23-28, 3:22-27, 5:1-20, 7:24-30, 9:14-29; Matt 12:22-23; Luke 11:14-23.

[13] As well as the summary references in Mark 1:39; 3:11; Luke 7:21, 13:32.

[14] *Babylonian Talmud Sanhedrin* 43a. For further references see H. Van Der Loos, *The Miracles of Jesus*, 156-167.

[15] See *Babylonian Talmud Berakhot* 34b. For a discussion on this fascinating holy man contemporary with Jesus, see Geza Vermes, *Jesus the Jew: A Historian's Reading of the Gospels* (London: SCM Press, 1983), 72-78.

[16] Matt 12:43; Mark 1:25; and Mark 9:25 respectively.

[17] Even if the reader does not hold this as a fact, it does not affect the argument in play.

[18] Matt 4:24.

[19] Job 2:7.

some influence from Satan, or for that matter, from God. Therefore, there is no need to "demythologize" these cases of possession or illness in general:

> We recognize, after all, that mental disorders can have physical symptoms—that is, that many physical ailments are rooted in a person's mind. As soon, then, as we recognize that a person is *also* spirit as well as body and mind, it becomes equally obvious that physical or mental illness can have spiritual causes. The label "demon possession" never was particularly specific, and if on one side it needs to be more carefully delimited to take account of our fuller knowledge... on the other side it needs to be given more scope to take fuller account of the evil active in the spiritual dimension...[20]

THE BEELZEBUB CONTROVERSY

In casting out demons Jesus was not simply freeing a few individuals from the grip of evil. He was freeing the entire chosen community. By rupturing Satan's control over personal and historical life, Jesus was in fact "making possible the renewal of the people of Israel."[21] For Hilary of Poitiers, the entire race was represented in the "dramatic definitive form of a single person."[22] And if "the whole world was offered to Him in one man,"[23] then exorcising a single demon, could wrestle the entire world from the grip of Satan into the kingdom of God:

> Then *one* was brought to Him who was demon-possessed, blind and mute; and He healed him, so that the blind and mute man both spoke and saw. And all the multitudes were amazed and said, "Could this be the Son of David?" Now when the Pharisees heard it they said, "This fellow does not cast out demons except *by* Beelzebub, the ruler of the demons."[24]

---

[20] James D. G. Dunn, "Demon Possession and Exorcism in the New Testament," 185. Also, for a fuller discussion, specifically on mental illness and spirituality, see Jean Claude-Larchet, *Mental Disorders & Spiritual Healing: Teachings from the Early Christian East* (San Rafael: Sophia Perennis, 2005).

[21] Richard A. Horsley, *Jesus and the Spiral of Violence: Popular Jewish Resistance in Roman Palestine* (Minneapolis: Fortress Press, 1993), 160.

[22] Hilary of Poitiers, *On Matthew* 12.11, SC 254:276–78.

[23] Anonymous, *Incomplete Work on Matthew*, Homily 29, PG 56:781. Also see Gerd Theissen, *The Miracle Stories of the Early Christian Tradition* (Edinburgh: T & T Clark, 1983), 280.

[24] Matt 12:22-24.

This passage is known as the Beelzebub controversy that immediately precedes the *blasphemy* saying.[25] The first thing we note is that the one who was possessed was "mute." Cyril of Alexandria, from experience perhaps, teaches us that, "mute devils are difficult for any one of the saints to rebuke. They are more obstinate than any other kind and excessively bold."[26] The man is then healed without any mention of ritual. All who were witnesses then cried out in amazement: "Could this be the Son of David?" To which the Pharisees respond that Jesus casts out demons by "Beelzebub, the ruler of the demons."

The meaning of "Beelzebub" is not entirely clear, but it likely refers to *ba'al zebub* which in Hebrew could mean "Lord of the heavens" or "Lord of the flies." But whatever its meaning, Jesus responds by taking Beelzebub to mean Satan.[27] Two possibilities are then evident, either Jesus casts out demons by Satan or He does so by God. And if we should think about the matter, these were the *only* two possible options: "No third option was available. Within the world of first-century Judaism, someone who did such things must be either from the true God or from the enemy."[28] He was either more powerful than the demon and thus with God, or was more evil than the demon. Jesus is quick to react by dispelling the possibility of the latter:

> But Jesus knew their thoughts, and said to them: "Every kingdom *divided* against itself is brought to desolation, and every city or house divided against itself will not stand. If Satan casts out Satan, he is divided against himself. How then will his kingdom stand? And if I cast out demons by Beelzebub, by whom do your sons cast them out? Therefore they shall be your judges. But if I cast out demons by the Spirit *of* God, surely the kingdom of God *has* come upon you. Or how can one enter a strong man's house and plunder his goods, unless he first binds the strong man? And then he will plunder his house. He who is not with Me is against Me, and he who does not gather with Me scatters abroad."[29]

The key to the argument of Jesus is that division *precipitates* the collapse of a house or kingdom. This principle is echoed among the Jewish works:

---

[25] For a discussion on the original context of these sayings, besides other references, see Burton Scott Easton, "The Beelzebul Sections," *Journal of Biblical Literature* 32, 1 (1913): 57-73.

[26] Cyril of Alexandria, *Commentary on Luke*, Homily 80, CGSL 327.

[27] H. Van Der Loos, *The Miracles of Jesus*, 409: "The name Beelzebub does not occur in Jewish literature as a name for Satan. The Pharisees mean by Beelzebub the prince of the devils, whilst Jesus associates him with Satan..."

[28] N. T. Wright, *Jesus and the Victory of God*, 452.

[29] Matt 12:25-30.

"A house in which there is division in the end will be laid waste,"[30] as well as among the Church Fathers: "Every power is pulled down by division, and the strength of a kingdom separated from itself is destroyed."[31] Dissent, therefore, in any system, house or kingdom, leads to desolation. From this Jesus concludes that He obviously does not cast out Satan by Satan. Yet, how did Jesus arrive at such a conclusion?

Jesus claims (1) that to cast out demons by Satan, the kingdom must be divided, for He would be going against Satan for Satan's sake. Therefore (2), if the kingdom is divided it will not stand. He then affirms (3) that He casts out demons by the "Spirit of God." It then becomes clear that a step of logic is missing between (2) and (3). Simply, (2) must *not* be true, to prove (3). In other words, if the kingdom of Satan is divided and therefore is laid to waste, then Jesus has no grounds to claim (3) that He does not cast out demons by Satan. But if the kingdom of Satan is not laid to waste, and therefore not divided, then Jesus consequently cannot be in league with Satan. For if He was with Satan then Satan's kingdom would have already fallen, as it would be divided. Therefore this missing step between (2) and (3) is something like: Satan's kingdom still stands and is not laid to waste, hence it is not divided.

The logic then runs as such: "If I was with Satan, then his kingdom would be divided and thus it would fall. Quite obviously it has not fallen yet, as some are still being possessed. The fact that it has not yet fallen proves that it is not divided, and therefore I have not cast out Satan by Satan." Clearly the observation is that "Satan remains strong, and this fact exposes the fallacy of [the] charge" that Jesus is in allegiance with Satan.[32]

But if the kingdom of Satan is not divided and thus is still strong, then how is it that Jesus has authority over demons? In the Gospel of Luke, Jesus answers: "When a *strong man*, fully armed, guards his own palace, his goods are in peace. But when a *stronger* than he comes upon him and overcomes him, he takes from him all his armor in which he trusted, and divides his

---

[30] *Derekh Erez Rabba* 5.

[31] Hilary of Poitiers, *On Matthew* 12.13-14, SC 254:278-280.

[32] W. L. Lane, *The Gospel of Mark* (Grand Rapids: Wm. B. Eerdmans, 1974), 142-143. To the discerning reader an apparent contradiction emerges in that Jesus implies here that the kingdom of Satan still stands. Yet some verses later, we hear that the "stronger" (Jesus) has bound the "strong man" (Satan), thus weakening his kingdom. Whether or not there is an actual conflict is in question. The fact that it still stands is a hypothetical position, whereas that fact that Jesus has bound Satan in some manner is not. Even then the former has to do with division within, the latter entails division without. In any case the bearings of such a conflict do not change the results in the present study, and are therefore beyond our scope. For an analysis of the possibilities see Joel Marcus, "The Beelzebul Controversy and the Eschatologies of Jesus," in *Authenticating the Activities of Jesus*, ed. Bruce Chilton and Craig A. Evans (Leiden: Brill, 2002).

spoils."[33] Jesus claims that He is the "stronger" who has bound Satan, the "strong man," by the Spirit of God and thus captures the "spoils"—souls—in his possession. In saying so Jesus was declaring that He had already begun to bind Satan,[34] else how could He cast out demons and free the possessed? In this battle "he who is not with Me is against Me, and he who does not gather with Me scatters abroad."[35] Either one stands with the "one constructive *unifying* redemptive power in a distracted world,"[36] or else one is against this kingdom. He who is lukewarm will be vomited out.[37] Far from being a "sign of allegiance," the acts of exorcism were ultimately the signs of the battle *against* Satan.[38]

The real significance, however, does not lie in the exorcism, but in the kingdom: "But if I cast out demons with the *finger of God*, surely the kingdom of God has come upon you."[39] It should be noted that here Luke gives it as "finger" instead of Matthew's "Spirit." This phrase "finger of God," *en daktylo theou*, occurs nowhere else in the New Testament. And in its various usages in the Old Testament as the Hebrew *esba* or Greek *daktylos*, it never indicates the manifestation of God's miraculous power.[40] That is, with the intriguing exception found in the book of Exodus.

> For Aaron stretched out his hand with his rod and struck the dust of the earth, and it became lice on man and beast. All the dust of the land became lice throughout all the land of Egypt. Now the magicians so worked with their enchantments to bring forth lice, but they could *not*. So there were lice on man and beast. Then the magicians said to Pharaoh, "This is the *finger of God*."[41]

In this third plague of lice, the power of God is manifested in an action of Moses and Aaron. The magicians were unable to replicate the miracle

---

[33] Luke 11:21-23. Matthew (12:29) and Mark (3:27) do not indicate that the one who binds the "strong man" is "stronger," but the fact that he overcomes the "strong man" is indicative enough.

[34] See Luke 10:18.

[35] Matt 12:30.

[36] T. W. Manson, *The Sayings of Jesus* (London: SCM Press, 1954), 87.

[37] Rev 3:16.

[38] Anonymous, *Incomplete Work on Matthew*, Homily 29, PG 56:786.

[39] Luke 11:20. Matthew (12:28) has it as "Spirit of God." The original is likely to have been "finger" given the unique usage, and the possible allusion to Exodus. In any case, both serve to designate the power of God. See, Heinrich Schlier, "daktylos," *TDNT* 2 (1964): 20-21: "'finger of God' denotes God's direct and concrete intervention…"

[40] Psa 8:4; Exod 31:18; Deut 9:10; and Dan 5:5. A similar usage is likewise not found in the Pseudepigrapha or other similar works.

[41] Exod 8:17-19.

and thus conclude, "This is the finger of God." And hence by referring to the *finger of God*, Jesus is likely indicating that He alongside Moses and Aaron, is empowered to perform miracles that liberate Israel from her captivity.[42] But there is far more to this reference. If we turn to the Jewish *Midrash Rabbah* on Exodus,[43] our eyes begin to open: "When the magicians saw that they could not produce the lice, they recognized immediately that the happenings [the plagues] were the work of God and *not* the work of demons."[44]

How radical! In the first two plagues, by implication, the magicians were doing the work of something other than God. And to their knowledge *so* was Moses. But now that they were *incapable* of replicating the third plague, they exclaim that Moses was doing the work of God. This squares perfectly with the logic of Jesus. The magicians of Pharaoh summate that if this work is not of Satan (for they were working with Satan, and yet they could not replicate the third plague) then this work must be of God. Likewise in the time of Jesus: "If then demons are out of the question, His opponents will be constrained to say as the Egyptian magicians said: It is the finger of God."[45] It was one or the other. It is then quite probable that Jesus had this commentary on Exodus in mind, and thus purposely referred to the "finger of God." Else, it would seem rather strange that He spoke of this "finger" only once in His entire ministry, especially in such a coincidental manner.

In sum, then, the argument of Jesus thus far may be followed in this manner:

A. You accuse Me of casting out demons by Satan.
   B. If this be true then Satan has a divided kingdom,
      C. And thus his kingdom should have fallen.
      C'. But we both know it has not yet fallen, for souls are still captive in Satan's possession.
   B'. Since it has not fallen, quite obviously it is not divided.
A'. If it is not divided, then I cannot be in league with Satan.
D. But if I am not in league with Satan, who then am I in alliance with except God?
E. If I work by the power of God; then the finger of God displaces the kingdom of Satan.
F. If Satan's kingdom is displaced; then the kingdom of God has surely come upon you.

---

[42] John P. Meier, *A Marginal Jew*, Vol. II, 411.

[43] Though the Midrash may have found its final compilation after Jesus, it "does not preclude the possibility that the tradition goes back to the first century." Norman Perrin, *Rediscovering the Teaching of Jesus* (New York: Harper & Row Publishers, 1976), 67.

[44] *Midrash Rabbah on Exodus* 10:7.

[45] T. W. Manson, *The Teaching of Jesus: Studies of Its Form and Content* (Cambridge: Cambridge University Press, 1945), 83.

THE UNFORGIVABLE SIN

Immediately following this Beelzebub controversy, Jesus sternly warns:

> Therefore I say to you, every sin and blasphemy will be forgiven men, but
> the blasphemy *against* the Spirit will not be forgiven men. Anyone who
> speaks a word against the Son of Man, it *will* be forgiven him; but whoever
> speaks against the Holy Spirit, it will not be forgiven him, either in this age
> or in the age to come.[46]

This fated teaching cannot be answered in any other way, except by
the lengthy path we have taken. It is not an isolated text, but rather forms
the conclusion of the Beelzebub controversy. We must then consider four
questions within this question that at least one Church Father claimed as
"the most important" of Scripture. The first is seemingly obvious: Why
did Jesus talk about blasphemy against the Spirit in the first place, who
blasphemed and why is Jesus talking about it now? This brings us to the
second: What is this sin which is unforgivable? The third is closely related:
Why is it unforgivable? And the final question is a fearful one: Why is sin
against the Son of Man to be forgiven, if that which is against the Holy Spirit
is not? Are they not equal?

The answer to the first (for once) is especially simple but evades us if
we neglect to take the text as a whole. Jesus had cast out the demon from
the blind and mute man. He was then accused of casting out demons by
the power of "Beelzebub." He then replies that He exorcises by the power
of the "Spirit of God." In other words, *the Pharisees had equated the Spirit
of God with Satan.* A point made succinctly by Mark who concludes the
blasphemy saying by explaining that Jesus' reaction resulted "because they
said, 'He has an unclean spirit.'"[47] There is no harsher word that may be
spoken about the Holy Spirit, than to slander Him as Satan. It is to this that
Jesus reacts forcefully.

To answer the second question we must return to the great Augustine
as he stood in front of the pulpit confessing his embarrassment over this
difficult saying. Before he had even approached the pulpit, he had been
listening intently to the reading of the Liturgy, this very Gospel we are now
considering. He relates the following: "As I listened to today's lesson, upon
which it was my duty to discourse to you, as the Gospel was being read, there
was such a beating at my heart, that I believed that it was God's will that

[46] Matt 12:31-32.
[47] Mark 3:30.

you should hear something on the subject by my ministry."[48] Something had happened. His heart began to beat. An answer had come.

Augustine begins by asking: "Who is not convicted of having spoken a word against the Holy Ghost [Spirit], before he became a Christian?"[49] What about the pagans or the Jews, who may still blaspheme Him till this day? What of the heretics? Are they never to be forgiven, even upon leaving behind their past and becoming Christian? Augustine concludes that possibly the only ones without this unforgivable sin are those literally born in the Church. He for one was not, and thus now we appreciate his discomfort in approaching this saying.

Perhaps, Augustine continues, blaspheming means to commit a "deadly" sin after Baptism with the Holy Spirit?[50] But did Jesus not warn *everyone*, even those who were not baptized? "The Lord did not say, 'the *baptized* Catholic who shall speak a word against the Holy Ghost;' but 'he who,' that is whoever speaks, be he who he may..."[51] Therefore, baptized or not, the unforgivable sin may be committed. Having dispelled that possibility, Augustine slowly draws his fourth-century Church to the answer. Augustine first posits that Jesus did not say "whoever speaks *any* word against...," but rather "whoever speaks *a* word." Therefore it is not "every" blasphemy or word against the Holy Spirit that is not to be forgiven, but rather a "specific" blasphemy:

> ...there is no necessity for anyone to think, that *every* blasphemy or every word which is spoken against the Holy Spirit has no remission; but necessary it plainly is, that there should be *some* certain blasphemy, and some word which if it be spoken against the Holy Spirit can never attain to pardon and forgiveness. For if we take it to mean "every word," who then can be saved?[52]

What then is this specific word or blasphemy? In a lengthy discourse, Augustine argues that Jesus forgives sins *only* through the power of the Holy Spirit. Secondly, by the admission of Jesus, He also casts out demons through the very same Power. When granting authority to His Apostles to forgive sins, it is likewise by the authority and indwelling of the grace of the

---

[48] Augustine, *Sermons on New Testament Lessons* 21.8, NPNF 1 6:320-321.

[49] Augustine, *Sermons on New Testament Lessons* 21.5, NPNF 1 6:319.

[50] Augustine, *Sermons on New Testament Lessons* 21.7, NPNF 1 6:320.

[51] Augustine, *Sermons on New Testament Lessons* 21.7, NPNF 1 6:320.

[52] Augustine, *Sermons on New Testament Lessons* 21.10, NPNF 1 6:321. Note this distinction is found in the first clause against the Son of Man, and Augustine extends it to the second. He acknowledges this, and even defends this position.

Holy Spirit.[53] It is here that Augustine reveals his brilliance.

To then speak against the Holy Spirit, is to speak against the gift of forgiveness: "Against this gratuitous *gift*, against this grace of God, does the impenitent heart speak. This impenitence then *is* 'the blasphemy of the Spirit.'"[54] To speak against the Spirit who casts out demons and forgives sins, necessarily makes the sin unforgivable. For how can He forgive, if He is denied? The specific word or blasphemy is then "understood to be *not* every kind of blasphemy, but a *particular* sort, and that as I have said or discovered, or even as I think clearly shown to be the case, the persevering hardness of an impenitent heart."[55] For Augustine it is this "persevering hardness" of heart that is blasphemy, for it rejects the Holy Spirit who solely is able to grant forgiveness of sins. This is why blasphemy even against the Son of Man will be forgiven, but not that against the Holy Spirit:

> Therefore not only every word spoken against the Son of Man, but, in fact, every sin and blasphemy shall be forgiven unto men; because where there is *not* this sin of an impenitent heart against the Holy Ghost, *by* whom sins are remitted in the Church, all other sins are forgiven. But how shall that sin be forgiven, which *hinders* the forgiveness of other sins also?[56]

If one has "stopped the source of forgiveness against himself"[57] by persevering with an impenitent heart, then who will forgive him? One may understand the thought of Augustine in the following manner. A child runs to his father crying that he is unable to reach a toy at the top of the shelf. Just as the father makes to lift up the child so that he is within reach of the toy, the child menacingly looks at his father and says: "You do not have the strength to lift me up so high, and even then I do not trust that you will do it, thus I do not want you to lift me." The father, the only means to reaching the toy, has been denied, necessarily making the child's goal unattainable. No matter what is said or done, the child will not get his toy. And all the while, his father will weep for him.

We now are able to appreciate what the sin is and *why* it is not forgivable, but what of our other questions? John Chrysostom, the Golden Mouth, likewise finds this saying troubling. Chrysostom calls us to remember that this was not the first time the Pharisees had blasphemed against Jesus and

---

[53] Augustine, *Sermons on New Testament Lessons* 21.19, NPNF 1 6:324.
[54] Augustine, *Sermons on New Testament Lessons* 21.20, NPNF 1 6:325.
[55] Augustine, *Sermons on New Testament Lessons* 21.21, NPNF 1 6:325.
[56] Augustine, *Sermons on New Testament Lessons* 21.23, NPNF 1 6:326.
[57] Augustine, *Sermons on New Testament Lessons* 21.34, NPNF 1 6:330.

the Spirit.[58] So why does Jesus react now, and not then? Chrysostom teaches that Jesus wished to show the people further divine miracles so that they would be without excuse.[59] This great Church Father then begins to unveil the mystery of why blasphemy against Jesus will be forgiven. In humility Jesus has become the Son of Man, and thus to the uninitiated He is seen as a mere man:

> ...they might have been *ignorant* of Jesus and who He might be, but of the Spirit they could not be ignorant due to their own *previous* experience. For the prophets had spoken by the Spirit. The Old Testament as a whole had an exalted understanding of the Holy Spirit. What he says, then, is this: "So be it—you may be offended at me, *because of the humanity I have assumed.* But you cannot say the same of the Holy Spirit. You cannot claim not to know the Spirit. Therefore your blasphemy has no excuse..."[60]

Sin against Jesus is sin against One who has become truly human, thus it is forgivable in as far as ignorance of Jesus' true nature goes. But to sin against the Spirit of God is to explicitly blaspheme the divinity of God, He who is able to liberate. How then may it be forgiven? N. T. Wright has cautiously commented: "To say such a thing was to paint oneself into a corner from which there is no escape. *Once* define the battle for your liberation as the work of your enemy, and you will never be free."[61] Even to the extent of the crucifixion,[62] men will be forgiven: "Father, forgive them, for they do not know what they do."[63]

Some scholars, however, have sought to take a different path round by focusing on the words "son of man," which may be taken in two different ways. That is to say, was Jesus referring to blasphemy against Himself (the "Son of Man") or simply to a mere "son of man" (in other words a mere human)? Cyril of Alexandria,[64] as always, pre-empts modern scholars and early on had already perceived the Son of Man debate.[65] If, Cyril

---

[58] Matt 9:34.

[59] John Chrysostom, *The Gospel of Matthew*, Homily 41.1, NPNF 1 10:264.

[60] John Chrysostom, *The Gospel of Matthew*, Homily 41.5, PG 57:449; NPNF 1 10:266-67.

[61] N. T. Wright, *Jesus and the Victory of God*, 454.

[62] John Chrysostom, *The Gospel of Matthew*, Homily 41.5, NPNF 1 10:266.

[63] Luke 23:34.

[64] For his argument see, Cyril of Alexandria, *Commentary on Luke*, Homily 88, CGSL 357-358.

[65] See Daniel Fanous, "Son of Man," in *The Person of the Christ*, 165-183. For an interpretation as "a mere man," see F. F. Bruce, *The Hard Sayings of Jesus* (Illinois: Intervarsity Press, 1983), 92. Owen Evans rightly concludes that in either case "the important thing to realize is that the contrast drawn by Jesus was one between blasphemy against the *human* and blasphemy against the *divine*." Owen E. Evans, "Expository Problems: The Unforgivable Sin," *The Expository Times* 68 (1957): 240-244.

hypothesizes, Jesus meant Son of Man to mean "a mere man," then there is no difficulty. For it has never been contested that blaspheming a fellow man may be forgiven. If, however, "the declaration has *reference to Christ, the Savior of all,*"[66] then we have a real problem on our hands. How can one blaspheme Jesus, who is God-enfleshed, and still be forgiven? Cyril assures us that the answer is to be found in the Incarnate Nature of Jesus. He is the Word of God enfleshed, and therefore in humility took upon Himself our limitations. And thus blasphemy against the Son of Man may well be forgiven as "being spoken inconsiderably *from ignorance.*"[67] In the flesh Jesus was a perfect man, and thus He willingly took to Himself the consequences of His flesh. To sin against the Word-enfleshed is therefore forgivable "on the excuse of their *ignorance of the mystery,* His self-abasement and humility shown as a man."[68]

On the other hand, he "who criticizes God in action,"[69] may never be forgiven. Cyril of Alexandria is adamant that to blaspheme the Holy Spirit is to effectively sin against the Godhead itself. If in the Old Testament to blaspheme against the Name of God was to warrant stoning without possibility of forgiveness, what of the blasphemy against the Godhead *itself*?

> On another hand, condemnation and the eternal punishment both in this world and in that which is to come is inevitable for those who have blasphemed the Godhead *itself.* By "the Spirit," He means not only the Holy Spirit but also the whole nature of the Godhead, as understood [to consist] in the Father, the Son and the Holy Spirit... Blasphemy against the Spirit is against the whole supreme substance.[70]

Of this Severus of Antioch warns: "They could not use ignorance as a pretext for their defense."[71] Sergius Bulgakov aptly concludes that blasphemy against Jesus "in whom the divinity is *hidden,* is not the sin of direct rebellion against God, but the blasphemy against the Holy Spirit *is* the sin of direct rebellion."[72]

---

[66] Cyril of Alexandria, *Commentary on Luke,* Homily 88, *CGSL* 357.

[67] Cyril of Alexandria, *Commentary on Luke,* Homily 88, *CGSL* 357.

[68] Severus of Antioch, *Cathedral Sermons,* Homily 98, PO 25:154–55.

[69] P. M. Casey, *From Jewish Prophet to Gentile God: The Origins and Development of New Testament Christology* (Louisville: Westminster John Knox, 1991), 50.

[70] Cyril of Alexandria, *Commentary on Luke,* Homily 88, *CGSL* 358. Cyril is not claiming that the Person of the Holy Spirit is to be identified as the essence of God (as if the *hypostasis* was identical with the *ousia*). Rather he is claiming that what is spoken against the Spirit is also spoken against the Godhead, since the Spirit is a Person of the Godhead.

[71] Severus of Antioch, *Cathedral Sermons,* Homily 98, PO 25:154–55.

[72] Sergius Bulgakov, *The Lamb of God* (Grand Rapids: Wm. B. Eerdmans, 2008), 307.

It was this "direct rebellion" against God which prompted so forceful a reaction from Jesus. Blasphemy against Jesus may be forgiven even to the pain of the crucifixion, for it is a sin in "ignorance of the mystery" of the God-enfleshed. On the other hand, in identifying the exorcisms of Jesus with the "ruler of demons," the Pharisees blasphemed the Holy Spirit whom they had known of old. Cyril perceives that within this blasphemy, one actually blasphemes the Godhead *itself*, of which there can be no turning back. It is this which inherently makes the sin unforgivable. To deny the Holy Spirit is to deny the *sole* source of forgiveness. How can He who is denied forgive? To identify the life-giver as the enemy, to see truth as false, to trade good for evil, to reduce one's life to death, is to deny the very hope of humanity. It is to see one's liberator as one's captor. There can be no freedom, there can be no salvation. It is a betrayal of humanity, a life *of* lifelessness.

CHAPTER SEVEN

'Throw not the children's bread to the dogs'

In a place where there are no humans, one must strive to be human.
—RABBI HILLEL

MBARRASSED. THAT IS ONE WAY TO PUT THE FEELING that many Christians have known. A Gentile woman weeps in desperation for her possessed daughter. Jesus *ignores* her. Looking away with disinterest, He declares: "I have come *only* for the Jews." She bows down before Him. Eyes down, heart broken, she manages a few words: "Lord, help me." Still not looking at her, Jesus, far from acknowledging her pain, states bluntly, "I cannot take the food of the children, and give it to the little *dogs*." No longer embarrassed, we begin to cringe.

Is this really the same Jesus we have known? The One who had compassion upon harlots and tax collectors? The very same Jesus who bore the suffering of all He encountered? We then become excruciatingly uncomfortable as another detail begins to dawn upon us. This is not only the rejection of a desperate Syrophoenician woman seeking aid for her daughter. It is not only the seemingly distasteful insult of a woman in need.

This *is* an apparent rejection of the Gentiles. We should remember that the divide was not between Jew and Christian, for the first Christians were Jews; rather it was between Jew and the non-Jewish Gentile. But I for one, as far as I am certain of my ancestry, am not a Jew. Am I, along with the greater part of Christianity, to be rejected? Are we then "dogs" as well? Was it by some mistake or oversight that the message of Jesus *accidentally* found its way to our Gentilic ancestors?

In the first part of this book, we saw that the Jesus was making known His authoritative interpretation of the law as an essential introducer into the kingdom. The question now becomes: Who will be called into this kingdom and who will be rejected? In the previous chapter Satan was subjugated to Jesus as an enemy. Now, were Gentiles enemies as well? Where did they stand, inside or outside the kingdom? This will be our primary concern in two chapters. This first awkward incident of the Syrophoenician woman from *Tyre* will introduce us into the second. In view of this let us look to the border between Jew and Gentile.

THE BORDER BETWEEN TYRE AND GALILEE

Tyre was a rural territory north of Galilee.[1] We never actually hear in the Gospels that Jesus visited the *city* of Tyre, but only the surrounding "region."[2] Similarly, the crowd that comes to Jesus may be presumed to come in part not from Tyre, but rather its surroundings. Josephus also reveals that there were Jewish villages in the "country" of Tyre.[3] Historically, then, in the rural hinterland of Tyre, as well as in the territory of Decapolis, Jews would have been living side by side with Syrians and Phoenicians. From this we may now make sense of Jesus' journeys, in that He would have only traveled to those Gentile territories *where* Jews lived: "It would have been to these outposts of Israelite population and Jewish religion that the mind of Jesus first turned when He extended His activity so far to the north."[4] This does not in itself, to be sure, deny that He cared for the Gentiles. Only that His journeys would have been among Jews and any other meetings with Gentiles were incidental. In the specific case of the Syrophoenician woman this becomes evident:

[1] Josephus, *Wars of the Jews*, III:38.

[2] Matt 15:21.

[3] Josephus, *Wars of the Jews*, II:478, 588.

[4] Albrecht Alt, cited in Joachim Jeremias, *Jesus' Promise to the Nations* (London: SCM Press, 1958), 36.

> From there He arose and went to the region of Tyre and Sidon. And He en-
> tered a house and wanted no one to know *it*, but He could not be hidden…
> The woman was a *Greek*, a *Syro-Phoenician* by birth, and she kept asking
> Him to cast the demon out of her daughter.[5]

It is exceedingly unlikely that this was a missionary journey to the
Gentiles. For one, Jesus would have no doubt been among the Jews in the
rural hinterland of Tyre, especially given that He "entered a house" there.
Secondly, Jesus did not choose to go to Tyre, but was *compelled* to "depart"
after conflict with the leaders of the Jews.[6] Furthermore, once there, Jesus
did not seek to preach or heal but "entered a house and wanted no one to
know it." In short, in *this* instance "Jesus was not going there to preach,"[7] nor
heal, nor in any way manifest the kingdom to the Gentiles. Had Jesus placed
the journey as a missionary concern, He would have willingly went, or at the
very least once there, not wished to be concealed.

This brings us to the woman herself. She is called a "Canaanite" woman
in the Gospel of Matthew, which simply designates a non-Jew.[8] Mark
is more specific in revealing that she was a Greek who was born in the
Syrophoenician city of Tyre. The Evangelists are both careful to note that
she met Jesus after He had departed into the regions of Tyre and Sidon,
thus dispelling the possibility that she may have been an "émigré resident"
in Galilee.[9] Many of these Tyrians were known to be bilingual in Greek and
Phoenician. This, in part, may explain her familiarity with Aramaic, and
hence her ability to converse with Jesus. For Phoenician and Aramaic are
closely related, so much so, that Josephus once identified the language of the
Phoenicians with the language of the Jews.[10]

That she was a Greek is also indicative of her social status. A Hellenized
woman in Phoenicia was likely to be a member of the upper class. She was
not alone. Tyre itself was a wealthy city that produced metal works, and
given its geography on the coast would have been crucial in trade with
the whole Mediterranean. In fact its currency was one of the most stable

---

[5] Mark 7:24, 26.

[6] Matt 15:21: "Jesus went out from there and *departed* to the region of Tyre." In the Gospel
"departed" always stands to mean "the departing from danger." Also see "withdrew" in Mark
3:7.

[7] John Chrysostom, *The Gospel of Matthew*, Homily 52.1, PG 58:517–19; NPNF 1 10:321.

[8] See *Mekhilta on Exodus* 21:26. There were not actually any Canaanites at the time,
though the area was previously of Canaanite origin, so much so that the name of the city Sidon
comes from Zidon the son of Canaan.

[9] T. A. Burkill, "The Syrophoenician Woman: The Congruence of Mark 7:24-31," *ZNW*
57 (1966): 35.

[10] Josephus, *Against Apion*, I:173.

of its time. It is of little wonder that the temple moneychangers traded in Tyrian coinage. But its geography was also a problem. Tyre, given that it was on the coast, had only a narrow strip of farmable land and therefore was dependant on agricultural imports from the Mediterranean as well as the Galilean territories:

> The Galilean hinterland and the rural territory belonging to the city (partly settled by Jews) were the "breadbasket" of the metropolis of Tyre... [Thus] the farmers in the territory inhabited by the Jews would often, and justly, have had the *feeling* of having to produce for the rich city-dwellers while they themselves lived in want.[11]

The rich Tyrians, then, in some sense were living off the poor Galileans. It is not hard to imagine that the "let the children be fed first" of Jesus—in effect, let the poor Jew eat first—may have been received (at least by some) with feelings of social injustice.

To deepen this context of the somewhat harsh words of Jesus we should also remember the open hostility between Galilee and Tyre. Even in the times of the Old Testament, Tyre was a threat to the Israelites.[12] Josephus, a Jew, names the Phoenicians as the "bitterest of our enemies."[13] At the beginning of the Jewish War, the Tyrians are said to have executed and imprisoned many of the Jewish minority in the region.[14] And during the reign of the "Tyrant of Tyre," Marion (c. 41 BC), Jewish property in Tyre was seized and the Jewish people in the region enslaved.[15] It may then be possible to see within the words of Jesus, at least as understood by His hearers, an expressed "bitterness that had built up within the relationships between Jews and Gentiles in the border regions between Tyre and Galilee."[16] This does not necessarily mean that Jesus had intended the words as such, but to the hearers in such a context the thoughts were inevitable.

It is from this context that the Syrophoenician woman approaches Jesus. She was one of the *affluent* seeking the aid of her *needy* neighbor (and at times enemy). All the more is this indicative of Jesus' fated words. To be ignored, and then to be called a dog by a superior is one thing. To receive such insult from One perceived to be inferior, a mere Galilean, is another.

---

[11] Gerd Theissen, *The Gospels in Context: Social and Political History in the Synoptic Tradition*, tr. Linda A. Maloney (Minneapolis: Fortress Press, 1991), 74.

[12] Isa 23; Jer 47:4; Ezek 27, 28; Joel 3:4-8.

[13] Josephus, *Against Apion*, I:70.

[14] Josephus, *Wars of the Jews*, II:478.

[15] Josephus, *Antiquities of the Jews*, XVI:321.

[16] Gerd Theissen, *The Gospels in Context*, 65.

T. A. Burkill aptly surmises: "We may safely assume that any intelligent *Hellenistic* woman, addressed in such terms by a *barbarian* [as Jesus would have been perceived by Greeks], would have immediately reacted…"[17] That her reaction was not disgust but altogether humility, is a testament to her glory to this day.

THE CHILDREN AND THE LITTLE DOGS

Despite being an exorcism, the real value of this incident is found in the dialogue between a Jew and a Gentile. It should be noted that the exorcism of the daughter of this Gentile woman is perhaps the singular instance where someone healed by Jesus is definitely known to be a Gentile pagan.[18] We should also be careful to avoid softening the uncomfortable harshness of the words of Jesus, either by applying His traditional gentleness or by our long familiarity with the text which may "obscure the shocking intolerance of the saying."[19]

> And behold, a woman of Canaan came from that region and cried out to Him, saying, "Have mercy on me, O Lord, Son of David! My daughter is severely demon-possessed." But He answered her *not* a word. And His disciples came and urged Him, saying, "*Send her away,* for she cries out after us." But He answered and said, "I was *not* sent except to the lost sheep of the house of Israel." Then she came and worshiped Him, saying, "Lord, help me!" But He answered and said, "It is not good to take the children's bread and throw it to the little *dogs*."[20]

She begs Jesus for the healing of her "severely" possessed daughter.[21] Jesus stands silently answering "her not a word." The disciples unable to contain themselves urge Him: "Send her away, for she cries out after us." Jerome, a fourth century saint, understands this statement to mean one of

---

[17] T. A. Burkill, "The Historical Development of the Story of the Syrophoenician Woman (Mark VII: 24-31)," *Novum Testamentum* 9, 3 (1967): 172-173.

[18] The Centurion's servant may have been of faith (and for that matter so may have been the Centurion himself) (Matt 8:5-13). Likewise we have no details concerning the Gerasene Demoniac. We know that he lived in the outskirts of the Syrian countryside though we remain ignorant of his race and faith (Mark 5:20).

[19] S. G. F. Brandon, *Jesus and the Zealots* (Manchester: Scribners, 1967), 172.

[20] Matt 15:22-26. Also see Mark 7:24-30.

[21] She does not beg for herself, but as the esteemed Hilary of Poitiers notes, she is begging "for her daughter—that is, the Gentile people in the *grips* of unclean spirits." Hilary of Poitiers, *On Matthew* 15.3, SC 258:36–38. See also Epiphanius the Latin, *Interpretation of the Gospels* 58, PL Supp 3:953.

two things. Either the disciples, sensing the reluctance of Jesus, sought to beseech Him on behalf of the woman, or on the other hand, they sought to be "rid of this importuning woman."[22] The truth may be close to both. We should remember that this was a patriarchal society:

> She is a woman, and Jesus is a man. Even today in the Middle East, in conservative areas, men and women do not talk to strangers across the gender barrier. In public rabbis did not talk to female members of their own families. Furthermore, the woman in this story is a Gentile seeking a favor from a Jew.[23]

For a *woman* who was a *non-Jew* (and of the hostile *Tyrians* at that) to throw herself in *desperation* at Jesus' feet, she would consciously be making a significant scene. To the disciples she could easily be perceived as a nuisance, especially since she "cries out after" them. By calling Jesus to "send her away," they may have been suggesting: "Just quickly heal her daughter, so that she can leave us alone." If this were the case then the response of Jesus seems logical: "I was not sent *except* to the lost sheep of the house of Israel." The disciples may have been beseeching Jesus to do away with their nuisance, not by sending her away, but by healing her daughter so that she may go away. But Jesus is clear: I cannot heal her Gentile daughter, as I have come for Israel alone.

"The silence of our Lord elicited an even *deeper* cry."[24] Undeterred, the Syrophoenician woman throws herself at Jesus' feet exclaiming: "Lord, help me!" He had kept silent and ignored her the first time she had begged Him, so why does she ask again? Is this *just* desperation?[25] Jesus not only ignored her, but pointedly also dismissed the request of the disciples to send her away (with healing or without). Perhaps within this she found hope that He had not dismissed her altogether, and thus she presses Him once more. This time, however, Jesus' silence would be easier to bear than His words: "It is not good to take the children's bread and throw it to the little dogs." In Mark

---

[22] Jerome, *Commentary on Matthew* 2.15.23, CCL 77:132–33. Also see Hilary of Poitiers, *On Matthew* 15.4, SC 258:38: "the pitying disciples join in a plea."

[23] Kenneth E. Bailey, *Jesus Through Middle Eastern Eyes: Cultural Studies in the Gospels* (Illinois: Intervarsity Press, 2008), 220.

[24] Ephrem the Syrian, *Commentary on Tatian's Diatessaron*, JSSS 2:196–97.

[25] Ibn al-Tayyib, a physician and theologian of the eleventh century, notes that the woman said: "Have mercy on me," not: "Have mercy on my daughter," for her own distress was severe. Accordingly, Jesus does not say: "Your daughter is healed," but rather: "Let it be as you desire." This old sage, thus discerns that the mother is in need of healing as well. Ibn al-Tayyib, cited from Kenneth E. Bailey, *Jesus Through Middle Eastern Eyes*, 220.

it is given as: "Let the children be filled *first*…"[26] The significance of the latter will be seen in the next chapter. But for now, why does Jesus call her a dog? In what manner is she to be identified with an animal? Is she not in need for the sake of another? Why then is she deserving of such words?

Biblically, in a few words, the word "dog" was a derogatory term. Goliath shouts out at the young David: "Am I a dog, that you come at me with sticks?"[27] At other times, a dog stands for something of disgust: "As a dog returns to its vomit, so a fool repeats his folly."[28] In the New Testament Jesus employs the image of a "dog" to convey the misery of the beggar Lazarus,[29] as well as the warning: "Do not give what is holy to the dogs."[30] In like manner the Apostles compared heretics and adversaries to dogs.[31] To *some* of the rabbis, Gentiles were like dogs for they were uncircumcised: "Anyone who eats with an idolater is like someone who eats with a dog; as the dog is uncircumcised, so is the idolater."[32] And we do well to remember that to the Jew a dog was an unclean animal that could not be eaten. Likewise is the Gentile unclean, and thus the identification is fairly easy to make: "[The Gentiles] are like to dogs on account of their using various meats and practices."[33] The association of Gentiles with dogs, then, was well known and attested to as a derogatory insult of the worst kind. To be sure, "metaphor or not, proverb or not, Jesus in fact compares her and her people to dogs…"[34]

But is being associated with a dog, necessarily an insult? Though an animal, a dog may also be a close friend if domesticated. This becomes a possibility when we recall that Jesus was careful to call her a "*little* dog." The "little dog," or puppy, may be close to the heart,[35] and in the book of Tobit accompanies the parents as they see off their son.[36] Further, the word

---

[26] Mark 7:27.

[27] 1 Sam 17:43. Also see Isa 56:10-11.

[28] Prov 26:11; Also see 2 Kngs 8:13; Ecc 9:4; 1 Sam 24:14; Deut 23:18; Exod 22:31.

[29] Luke 16:21.

[30] Matt 7:6.

[31] 2 Pet 2:22; Phil 3:2; Rev 22:15.

[32] *Pirqe Rabbi Eliezer* 29. It is often disputed that in the rabbinic texts it is more a comparison than a metaphor. But should we consider that the insult is found on the mouths of many different people in first-century Palestine, Jew and Christian alike, for another group that is viewed negatively, then the matter becomes clear.

[33] *Pseudo-Clementine Homilies*, Homily 2.19, ANF 8:232. These writings were attributed to Clement of Rome, but in fact are likely to have been of Ebonite origin. It is by no means canonical, but given its dating in the second or at the latest third century, it is reflective of Jewish-Christian thinking that may have been contemporary with Jesus.

[34] Hisako Kinukawa, *Women and Jesus in Mark: A Japanese Feminist Perspective* (New York: Orbis Books, 1994), 59.

[35] *Epictetus Dissertationes* 4.1.111.

[36] *Tobit* 5:16.

in Greek for little dog is *kynarion*, a diminutive noun, literally meaning "puppy." Had Jesus meant "dog of the street," He could have used *kyon*, but instead He chose "puppy." In other words Jesus chose a specific word that denoted something smaller than the noun, similar to choosing "duckling" over "duck." But whilst this neatly softens the harsh words of Jesus it must be admitted that such an approach is simply *untrue*.

Untrue for it is speculation with no basis. It is exceedingly difficult to show that this distinction between dog and puppy was known in first-century Palestine. It is in fact impossible. The Aramaic which Jesus spoke, unlike the Greek, has no corresponding form of this diminutive noun and therefore there was no distinction between dog and puppy in Aramaic. Even if the Evangelists were aware of the distinction, and chose "puppy" with intent, the limitations of the original Aramaic would have prevented Jesus from following suit. In any case, the Jews rarely, if ever, domesticated dogs as in the upper classes of the Greeks. They in general were not pet-lovers: "To them dogs were the dirty, unpleasant and savage animals which roamed the streets in packs, scavenging for food."[37]

Even if it be accepted that Jesus meant "puppy" and not "dog," it still stands that a puppy when placed in relation to a man is an irrational animal. Softening dog *to* puppy "does not make the image any nicer."[38] Nor does it obliterate the "difference in ontological status between the children and the dogs."[39] A dog was not a member of the household; it was a secondary adopted creature. By "throwing" the bread to the dogs, Jesus implied that the dogs are in fact *outside* the house, or at best *under* the table, and in any event not *at* the table. The children, on the contrary, are primary members of the household and are seated at the table. The children eat what is set *for* them; the dogs receive what haphazardly and unintentionally *falls* to them. At worst (puppy or not), this insult is inhumane; at best, it is deprecating and scandalous.

Similarly ridiculous is the claim of some scholars that Jesus' words were intended in jest with "a twinkle in His eye," or a half-playful "smile," or a comical "tone of voice."[40] This is unfounded speculation. Had Jesus invited

---

[37] Francis Dufton, "The Syrophoenician Woman and Her Dogs," *Expository Times* 100 (1989): 417.

[38] Gerd Theissen, *The Gospels in Context*, 62.

[39] T. A. Burkill, "The Historical Development of the Story of the Syrophoenician Woman," 172.

[40] J. Ireland Hasler, "The Incident of the Syrophoenician Woman," *Expository Times* 45 (1934): 460; Also see Caird and Hurst, *New Testament Theology* (Oxford: Oxford University Press, 1995), 395: "Jesus' words, which in cold print seem so austere, were almost certainly spoken with a *smile* and a *tone* of voice which invited the woman's witty reply."

the "woman's witty reply" by disarming His words with a smile, why then did He exclaim: "O woman, great is your faith!"[41] Had the words not been severe and had she perceived this jest, in what manner did she show great faith? Jesus called her and her people dogs. He spoke the words harshly, after ignoring her previously. This is the uncomfortable reality. Yet though this may be the case here, Jesus is never recorded as addressing a Gentile so harshly in any other place. The question then is, why did He say such a thing, and why *now*?

THE TABLE OF THE MASTER

Jesus throughout the Gospels does not give Himself out as a mere magician, dispensing remedies whenever requested. He had come to unbind Israel from the grip of the enemy to restore Israel into the true kingdom. Why then should He loosen the bonds of one who did not even worship His God? He had come for the house of Israel alone. Faith and communion were thus the *precursors* of His miraculous acts. The Syrophoenician woman was neither in communion nor held the faith of the Jews. Thus how could He enact a miracle, if the very basis for a miracle was missing?

But does she not call Him "Lord, Son of David"? Surely she believed in Jesus by knowing such titles? Realistically it is quite improbable that she knew the Jewish Scriptures and it is even more impossible that she had a developed conception of the Davidic Messiah. Rather, previously her townspeople had been witness to Jesus' teaching and miracles, and then no doubt would have spread word about One called the "Son of David."[42] And now that this desperate woman was in need, she addressed Jesus with that which was significant to her, the "Son of David" of whom she had *heard*, a famed exorcist. The problem is that the power of Jesus was closely connected to the faith of those who sought His aid.[43] How then could she reveal her faith, if she did not even know who He really was?

> But He answered and said, "It is not good to take the children's bread and throw *it* to the little dogs." And she said, "Yes, Lord, yet even the little dogs eat the crumbs which fall from their masters' table."[44]

[41] Matt 15:28.
[42] Mark 3:7-8.
[43] T. W. Manson, *Only to the House of Israel? Jesus and the Non-Jews* (Philadelphia: Fortress Press, 1964), 22-23.
[44] Matt 15:26-27.

The only possible way to reveal her faith, or rather bring her to faith, was to place the woman in a compromising situation. Rabbi Hillel once said: "In a place where there are no humans, one must strive to be human."[45] It is not that one should strive to be a human in a world devoid of the humane. It is that one can only truly become human in such a world. Without the difficulty of suffering and pain, humanity cannot shine as humanity. Only when one is pressed, does one grow. In this anguish, the tears of the eyes strengthen the heart, and children become men. If the woman has not proven her faith by being a Jew nor shares His beliefs, then Jesus positions her in "a place where there are no humans." She is undeserving of insult, yet He shames her. She is in need, He neglects her. She is a Hellenized woman, He is a poor Jew. She sits at His feet begging, and He brands her a dog. Whatever hope she held for her "severely" distressed daughter, Jesus shuns away. And for all this, with tears in complete and utter humility, all she returns is: "Yes, *Lord*, yet even the little dogs eat the *crumbs* which fall from their masters' table."

She still calls Him Lord! Jesus called her a dog, and now she willingly takes this insult upon herself. And, as Epiphanius perceives, she feels no shame in placing herself in the position of a dog: "I know, Lord, that the Gentile people are dogs in worshiping idols and barking at God."[46] But do not even the little dogs eat the crumbs that fall off the table? She confesses her humility. She is *only* worthy to sit at the feet of the master, worthy to eat crumbs. She seeks nothing more. To be at His feet is enough. Instead of defense, or attack, she simply accepts that the crumbs once fallen from the table are after all left for the dogs. The Syrophoenician woman was careful enough not to dishonor the Master, and clever enough to sit at His feet. Her perfection is that "she honored His rejection and still found a *place* for her request."[47]

Jesus does not act without purpose, nor does He speak without intention. He seeks not to hurt a woman in need, but to bring her to glory. He places her in abandonment, and watches in amazement as the mustard seed within her becomes a majestic forest. As He insults her, His heart weeps. As she grows, His heart rejoices. The compassionate One seeks not pain for man, but that man may become *truly* man. In her humility the woman attained what multitudes of "faithful" could not. When the Gentile Centurion declared in humility: "Lord, I am not worthy that You should come under my roof,"[48] Jesus proclaimed that authentic faith was found: "I have not found such

---

[45] *Mishnah Abot* 2:5.

[46] Epiphanius the Latin, *Interpretation of the Gospels* 58, PL Supp 3:954.

[47] David Rhoads, "Jesus and the Syrophoenician Woman in Mark: A Narrative-Critical Study," *Journal of the American Academy of Religion* 62, 2 (1994): 359.

[48] Matt 8:8.

great faith, not even in Israel!"[49] And *then* the healing occurred. When the Syrophoenician woman declared: "even the little dogs eat crumbs," Jesus once more pronounced faith: "O woman, great *is* your faith!"[50] Finally her humility-produced-faith is confirmed:

> Then Jesus answered and said to her, "O woman, great *is* your faith! Let it be to you as you desire." And her daughter was healed from that very hour.[51]

Without realizing, the woman was begging to be seated under the table *of* the kingdom. The Gentiles may have been in the throngs of evil, "but He is their Master still, and they under *His* table."[52] If one was within the kingdom of God, even as a dog, then one was necessarily *not* in the kingdom of Satan. The crumbs she sought were crumbs of life. This woman found a place within the kingdom through her humility "having changed what she was."[53]

And thus we sit at the feet of our Master's table with the Syrophoenician woman and her daughter. With them we beg to be freed from the bonds of evil so that we might live within the kingdom by partaking in those fated morsels that fall from His table. Yet as we sit in amazement of this grace, in full satiety, it is not nearly enough for Him. Yearning for us, He takes us by the hand, and lifting our hearts, minds, and bodies, He seats us at the table besides the children. We take our places at the table of Abraham, Isaac, and Jacob, the table of the kingdom. Though we were content to sit even at His feet and receive those glorious remnants, it was not enough for Him. We sit as sons, as the children of the Master, all the while in wonder, for were we not satisfied even with a single glorious crumb?

---

[49] Matt 8:11.

[50] Matt 15:28. See Augustine, *Sermon* 77.11-12, PL 38:487–88; NPNF 1 6:345–46 [Sermon 27].

[51] Matt 15:28.

[52] Alfred Edersheim, *The Life and Times of Jesus the Messiah*, ii.37. Also see J. Duncan M. Derrett, "Law in the New Testament: The Syro-Phoenician Woman and the Centurion of Capernaum," *Novum Testamentum* 15, 3 (1973): 172.

[53] *Pseudo-Clementine Homilies*, Homily 2.19, ANF 8:232.

CHAPTER EIGHT

'I was not sent except to the House of Israel'

In those days ten men from every language of the nations
Shall grasp the sleeve of a Jewish man, saying,
"Let us go with you, for we have heard that God is with you."
—ZECHARIAH 8:23

I F YOU ASKED TEN SMALL CHILDREN WHO JESUS THE CHRIST had come to save, nine of them would innocently state: All of us. Should we ask them again, whether He had *especially* come for the Jews, eight of the nine remaining would confidently reply: No.

The strange thing is that I think the very same results would be reproducible had we asked a series of adults. Their answers inevitably would be slightly more intelligent, but still inherently the same. The even stranger thing is that should one actually read the Gospels, one would find the situation to be in the shocking *reverse*. At a glance, Jesus was seemingly focused on the people of Israel. It was only decades after His death that this focus began to shine brightly on the Gentiles. The question then is: If Jesus had been so keen to focus on the Jews, why did His disciples turn to the

Gentiles? In fact if we look a little deeper, Jesus not only came for the Jews but in some regards He appears to have come for them *alone*. The simplicity of our imaginary children then becomes apparent. But who among the Christians is a Jew? Who is a Gentile? Surely the numbers must show or prove something? Why would Jesus reject the majority of the *now* Christians and not expect His disciples to follow suit? And, for that matter, why did His disciples follow a different model? Should not they have been obedient to His mission?

We have seen that through humility the Syrophoenician woman (a Gentile) was able to place herself at the table of the kingdom, even if it be at the feet of the table. But who of us has shown such humility or faith? Why then are we at the table? Hesitantly we dare to ask, are we actually at the table?

GENTILES IN EARLY JUDAIC THOUGHT

To grant some context to the words of Jesus, we need to first appreciate two things. The first is the way in which His fellow first-century Jews would have viewed the Gentiles. The second is whether these same Jews had envisioned the salvation of the pagan Gentiles, and if so, did they view this as part of their mission? (It should also be mentioned that the word Gentiles in Hebrew is *goyim*, literally meaning the "nations." Therefore in the biblical texts the word "nations" is always identified with the Gentiles.)

Early Jewish views of the Gentiles were not uniform and varied from writer to writer.[1] This was a result of the vast period of time in which such views took shape. To this we must also add the influence of political circumstance. For instance, one would hardly envision an oppressing Gentilic ruler entering the kingdom of God; a kind ruler on the other hand, perhaps. Furthermore, different groups had differing ideologies, complicating matters endlessly. Even the individual writers themselves were not uniform. Micah tells us that many nations, *goyim*, will come and say of the Lord: "He will teach us His ways, and we shall walk in His paths."[2] But only a few chapters later these nations "shall lick the dust like a serpent."[3] Zephaniah declares the word of the Lord: "My determination is to gather the *nations*...to pour on them My indignation."[4] Yet the very next verse tells us of the salvation of these very same nations: "For then I will restore to the

---

[1] John P. Meier, *A Marginal Jew*, Vol. II, 314.
[2] Mic 4:2.
[3] Mic 7:17.
[4] Zeph 3:8.

peoples a pure language, that they all may call on the name of the Lord."[5] It thus is increasingly difficult to find consensus:

> A full study of Jewish attitudes towards Gentiles from the inside would have to take account of the shifting political fortunes of Judaism in a predominantly Gentile world and also of differences among different groups at different times.[6]

We may, however, briefly discern a number of themes (as variable as they may be). A prevalent feature was that the nations would one day *bow down to Israel*: "They shall bow down to you with their faces to the earth, and lick up the dust of your feet."[7] Other texts pointed to the utter *destruction of the Gentiles*: "I will destroy your cities and I will execute vengeance."[8] This subjugation at times was closely tied to the *salvation of the Gentiles*: "Also the sons of the foreigner... Their burnt offerings and their sacrifices will be accepted on My altar."[9] Here we find that the Gentiles have even found a place in the temple. Finally, the consummation of this salvation is the *eschatological banquet* at the end of times: "The Lord of hosts will make for all people a feast ...And He will destroy on this mountain...the veil that is spread over all nations."[10] But notice that this is no mere "salvation-of-all" theology; the Gentiles are to be saved only *through the Jews*: "I will also give You as a light to the Gentiles, that You should be My salvation to the ends of the earth."[11]

In all of these texts, biblical and extra-biblical, it becomes clear that Israel is the focus. It is the relationship between her and her God that is paramount. The nations are subjugated not for her sake, but for *her God's*. The Gentile kings bow down before her not as a testament to her, but to *her God*. Bonded to God, Israel then becomes a light for all nations. She attracts all nations to come worship the *true* God. But we should be careful to note that this movement is *centripetal* rather than *centrifugal*. Israel does not reach out to convert the nations, but the nations run to her to worship her God.[12] In a way—and this is by no means uniform—Israel's election as the

---

[5] Zeph 3:9.

[6] E. P. Sanders, *Jesus and Judaism*, 213.

[7] Isa 49:23; Also see Isa 45:14, 23; Mic 7:17; *1 Enoch* 90:30.

[8] Mic 5:14-15. Also see Zeph 2:10; *Ben Sira* 36:7, 9; *1 Enoch* 91:9.

[9] Isa 54:1-7. Also see Zech 2:11; Isa 45:22; *1 Enoch* 90:30-33; *Tobit* 14:6-7.

[10] Isa 25:6-8. Also see *1 Enoch* 62:14; 1Qsa 2:11-22 even gives instructions to the Qumran community on etiquette when eating with the Messiah.

[11] Isa 49:6. Also see Isa 51:4; 2:1-4; Micah 4:1-4.

[12] S. G. Wilson, *The Gentiles and the Gentile Mission in Luke-Acts* (Cambridge: Cambridge University Press, 1973), 2.

people of God is not compromised "but is in a sense fulfilled when Gentiles come to join the people of God."[13]

Paramount to this survey is the *timing* of these happenings. Most of the passages which we have seen are concerned only with the end of times and are thus *eschatological*. In part this may be explained by historical circumstance. In later Judaism we find an increasing number of images portraying the destruction of the Gentiles that parallels the increasing oppression of the Jews. The Gentiles, represented by the non-Jewish empires, "continued to hold Israel in subjugation, [and] were continuously visible as the enemies of God's people."[14] How could one envision the salvation of another who was an enemy? It is difficult to imagine such a thing, let alone to expect it. This oppression at the hands of hostile Gentiles, at least in part, was to leave an indelible mark on the later Jewish texts. But rather then dismissing the salvation of the Gentiles altogether, it relegated it to the end times:

> A Jew need not have been an admirer of Gentiles in the *present* in order to think that at the *end*, when Israel would be restored and victorious, Gentiles would repent and turn to God.[15]

The same sentiments are to be found among the rabbis. They, like the Scriptures, were not uniform in portraying the Gentiles. As to whether the Gentiles would find a place in the kingdom there was "continuing uncertainty, not to say disquiet."[16] And in like manner the matter was not whether a Gentile may be righteous *now*, but whether they would be saved *at* the end of days. Even then, if one such as Rabbi Eleazar thought that the Gentiles would not have a "portion in the world to come," another such as Rabbi Joshua would disagree by teaching that the "righteous among the nations" would also be saved.[17] And if we recall that Paul the Apostle was no less than a Pharisee, then it becomes an even stronger possibility that at least a few of the Pharisees envisioned the salvation of the Gentiles in the last days.[18]

That said, given the inherent variability which we have seen, it is difficult to discern the prevailing thought at the time of Jesus. Indeed the thoughts of whom? The Pharisees? The Saduccees? What about the common people

---

[13] N. T. Wright, *The New Testament and the People of God*, 267.

[14] E. P. Sanders, *Jesus and Judaism*, 215. Also see Joachim Jeremias, *Jesus' Promise to the Nations*, 40.

[15] E. P. Sanders, *Jesus and Judaism*, 216.

[16] N. T. Wright, *The New Testament and the People of God*, 268.

[17] *Tosefta Sanhedrin* 13.2.

[18] 1 Thes 1:9-10.

who may have had day to day dealings with Gentiles? Given the evidence, it is difficult to judge. But at the very least a significant portion of the Jews (if the texts are indicative) envisioned the Gentiles in some manner turning to the God of Israel at the end of days.

JESUS & THE GENTILES: FOR OR AGAINST?

"The evidence is at first sight puzzling."[19] If early Judaic thought was uncertain as to the fate of the Gentiles, we could expect the same of the individual thoughts of a first-century Jew. Should we look at the sayings and deeds of Jesus, we would find two fairly distinct themes: one negative, the other positive.

Jesus at times elevates the place of the Gentile: "Many will come from east and west, and *sit* down with Abraham, Isaac, and Jacob in the kingdom of heaven;" "The gospel must first be preached to all the *nations;*" "Go therefore and make disciples of all the *nations*, baptizing them;" "The queen of the South will rise up in the judgment with this generation and condemn it;" "My house shall be called a house of prayer for all *nations.*"[20] These passages point to the inclusion of the Gentiles in the kingdom and even a mission to them.[21]

On the other hand there are also a number of decidedly negative sayings: "Do *not* go into the way of the Gentiles, and do not enter a city of the Samaritans. But go rather to the lost sheep of the house of Israel;" "I was not sent except to the lost sheep of the house of Israel;" "It is not good to take the children's bread and throw it to the little dogs;" "Do not give what is holy to the dogs."[22] In contrast to Israel, in the words of Jesus, the Gentiles are materialistic, their rulers are tyrants, and their prayers are vain repetitions.[23] To this we add the reluctance of Jesus to preach or even go among the Gentiles,[24] and importantly the reluctance of the early Church for the same.[25]

Before we begin to consider the *negative* sayings we should bear in mind that Jesus was a Jew living among Jews. Consequently, "His understanding

---

[19] N. T. Wright, *Jesus and the Victory of God*, 309.

[20] Matt 8:10-13; Mark 10:10; Matt 28:19-20; Matt 12:41-42; Mark 11:17, respectively.

[21] To this list we will not add the marriage banquet parable (Matt 22:1-14), as it is not specifically mentioned that it refers to the Gentiles (though it may well have) and in any case it does not add to the argument.

[22] Matt 10:5-6; Matt 15:24; Matt 15:26; Matt 7:6, respectively.

[23] Mark 6:32; Mark 10:42; Matt 6:7, respectively.

[24] Mark 7:24.

[25] For example Acts 10:28.

of His mission was naturally in terms of His own people."[26] His was not the modern era where one may travel from country to country in hours. Jesus, thus, would have lived and reacted to His *local* context. The question of the Gentiles was not at the foreground. The question of the lost sheep of Israel was, and thus Jesus begins in the place of "*direct* contact with the need of God's people."[27] This did not mean that Jesus did not care for the Gentiles, but rather explains the difficulty in eliciting His attitude towards them. Similarly in the case of the Syrophoenician woman when Jesus claims that He has come only for the "house of Israel," we may now understand His hesitancy. Hilary of Poitiers saw this truth earlier than we:

> Not that salvation was not to be imparted also to the Gentiles, but the Lord had come to His own and among His own, awaiting the *first* fruits of faith from those people He took His *roots* from.[28]

With this qualification we may proceed to the *negative* sayings. "Do not go into the *way* of the Gentiles..." These were the words that Jesus used to define the first mission of the Apostles before He sent them out. The mission was to the "lost sheep of Israel." By closing off the *way* of the Gentiles, Jesus was effectively closing off the North, East, and West. By adding "do not enter a city of the Samaritans," He did away with the South. He was thus succinctly defining His mission (and that of His disciples) among the Jews and them *alone*. If we then wish to show the continuity between Jesus and the later missions of the early Church to the Gentiles, the signs are not encouraging.[29] However we should be careful to note that this did not *necessarily* exclude the Gentiles from the kingdom at the end of days. This was exclusion in the here and now. But how deep did this exclusion really run?

Jesus never sought to heal the two or possibly three Gentiles (the Centurion, the Syrophoenician woman, and the Gerasene demoniac) that we hear of in the Gospels. His only healings of non-Jews came out of the initiative of the sick not the Physician. And even when He performed healings or exorcisms in the neighboring areas "it was clearly the exception, and never included teaching."[30] So much so, that when "compelled" into the Gentilic areas Jesus would seek to remain concealed: "He entered a house

---

[26] Morna D. Hooker, "The Prohibition of Foreign Missions," *The Expository Times* 82 (1971): 364.

[27] T. W. Manson, *Only to the House of Israel*, 20.

[28] Hilary of Poitiers, *On Matthew* 15.4, SC 258:38.

[29] James D. G. Dunn, *Jesus Remembered*, 537.

[30] Geza Vermes, *The Authentic Gospel of Jesus* (London: Penguin Books, 2004), 377.

and wanted no one to know it."[31] Had Jesus envisioned His mission to be among the Gentiles, we would assume that He would have "sought" to go among them or at the least whilst there not wish to remain unseen:

> [When] it is recognized in all three cases the initiative is not taken by Jesus, it becomes abundantly clear that these stories afford no ground for assuming that Jesus extended His mission to the Gentiles, but, on the contrary, that they confirm the fact that He limited His activity to Israel.[32]

This reluctance to go among the Gentiles is mirrored in the history of the early Church. Paul in the epistle to the Galatians shows that only after significant debate did the Jerusalem Church accept the mission to the Gentiles. In the book of Acts we are told that Peter required a vision to convince him that it was no longer unlawful "for a Jewish man to keep company with or go to one of another nation."[33] God, Himself, it would seem, had to persuade him not to "call any man common or unclean."[34] We also note that this entire confused debate took place after they had been told by the risen Jesus: "You shall be witnesses to Me in Jerusalem, and in all Judea and Samaria, and to the end of the earth."[35] To this we add that there was a significant "time-lapse" between the resurrection and the early Church's mission to the Gentiles, once more indicating uncertainty as to the fate of the Gentiles.

This confusion and reluctance of the early Church indicates that Jesus did not expressly command mission among the Gentiles. But neither did He entirely deny it. Else, why would the early Church eventually move beyond the borders of Judaism? It is likely, then, that the confusion stemmed from the simple fact that the mission to the "lost sheep of Israel," and that alone, was at the foreground. Jesus had come to save *His* people.

This brings us to the *positive* sayings. We have seen the reluctance of the early Church to begin its mission among the Gentiles. But the very observation that they did *eventually* begin the mission says something of tremendous importance. It argues that the first Apostles did *not* understand Jesus (not just a few of His sayings, but His entire life) to have rejected the Gentiles. If Jesus had wholly rejected the Gentiles, His disciples would not and could not have welcomed them into the kingdom: "As far as we see from Galatians…no Christian group objected to the Gentile mission; they

---

[31] Mark 7:24.
[32] Joachim Jeremias, *Jesus' Promise to the Nations*, 31.
[33] Acts 10:28.
[34] Acts 10:28.
[35] Acts 1:8.

disagreed only as to its terms and conditions."[36] But their hesitancy also reveals that they were not expressly commanded to welcome them either. The only possibility is that they were unsure. They knew not whether to reject or to accept. What remains of great import is that the *possibility* of mission among the Gentiles, for the early Church, was to be found in the teachings of Jesus. In what manner, then, did they find this potential of mission if Jesus had so clearly commanded: "Go not into the way of the Gentiles"?

In rare exceptions Jesus' compassion extended to the Gentiles in the form of healing and exorcism.[37] The act of healing was for Jesus "always the sign and pledge of the breaking in of the messianic age, an anticipatory participation in its blessings."[38] Jesus was loosening the bonds of the kingdom of Satan, and was ushering in the kingdom of God. Therefore in healing a Gentile (as rare as it was), He was inviting them to participate in the "kingdom of God which was, in a partial and hidden manner, in the process of realization."[39] One could discern a hidden participation in the kingdom, a "future offer of salvation."[40] Thus we find the Syrophoenician woman seated in the kingdom, irrespective of whether it was at or under the table. The kingdom follows closely behind each and every healing. The same, therefore, is to be said of the healing of the Centurion's servant. The Gentile beseeches Jesus: "Lord, I am not worthy that You should come under my roof. But only speak a word..." Jesus marvels:

> Assuredly, I say to you, I have not found such great faith, *not* even in Israel! And I say to you that *many* will come from east and west, and *sit* down with Abraham, Isaac, and Jacob in the kingdom of heaven. But the sons of the kingdom will be cast out into outer darkness. There will be weeping and gnashing of teeth.[41]

This was a double-sided parable. It included a promise of salvation for the "many" from east and west, and a threatening exclusion of the "sons of the kingdom." Some scholars have debated whether the "many" actually refers to

---

[36] E. P. Sanders, *Jesus and Judaism*, 220.

[37] The same may be said of Jesus' attitude towards the Samaritans. Though not strictly Gentiles, they were not Jews, and thus were to inherit the same fate as the Gentiles. Whether it is in healing a Samaritan leper, having compassion on a Samaritan woman, or teaching the parable of the Good Samaritan, we find that again and again Jesus had compassion on the Samaritans. For a further discussion see Daniel Fanous, "The Samaritans," in *The Person of the Christ*, 25-31.

[38] Joachim Jeremias, *Jesus' Promise to the Nations*, 28.

[39] S. G. Wilson, *The Gentiles and the Gentile Mission in Luke-Acts*, 18.

[40] John P. Meier, *A Marginal Jew*, Vol. II, 660.

[41] Matt 8:10-12; Also see Luke 13:25-30.

the Gentiles. In our previous survey, we found a recurrent image of the end of times in which the Gentiles would worship the God of Israel. Since Jesus shared this hope for the restoration in the kingdom, it is fairly likely that He refers to the Gentiles by the phrase "many." To this end, who else are the sons of the kingdom other than the Jews? And if the "sons" are Jews, then those who are not "sons" must be the Gentiles. Further, this saying of Jesus follows immediately after the declaration of faith of the Centurion—a Gentile.

As for the "sons of the kingdom," does it refer to *all* of the Jews? Is the *entire* nation of Israel to be cast out into the "outer darkness"? Hardly. Abraham, Isaac, and Jacob are seated in the kingdom, and if we look to Luke, so are "all the prophets."[42] Seated next to them are the Jewish disciples. And at the head of the table sits Jesus Himself, a Jew and a Son of the kingdom! Therefore, as John P. Meier notes, "there are no grounds for speaking of the 'rejection of *all* Israel.'"[43] This is not so much a matter of Gentiles accepted and Jews rejected, rather, in the words of Gregory the Great: "There were at that time *some* from among the Jews who were to be called, and *some* from among the Gentiles who were not to be called."[44] The entire nation of Israel was not to be rejected, but those *among* the Jews who were disobedient:

> The difference of status between Israel and the Gentiles can be put quite simply in this way, that when the perfect kingdom is being considered the question with regard to the Israelites is: Who, if *any*, will be excluded? While with regard to the Gentiles it is: Who, if *any*, will be admitted?[45]

And thus, Jesus could hardly have rejected the Gentiles if He seated them in the kingdom next to the great Patriarchs of Israel. Yet there is more to be found here. Within this saying of Jesus lies the key to our present dilemma: The eschatological or "end-times" messianic banquet is *placed* in the kingdom. "The saying moves in the world of the regular Jewish symbolism of the messianic banquet."[46] It had been prophesized that at the end of days, the Messiah will bring all nations to Himself and destroy the "veil that is spread over all nations" by inviting them to a divine banquet.[47] By referring to this banquet situated in the kingdom, Jesus subtly was looking "forward to a time when the Gentiles would share in the glory of the age to come."[48]

---

[42] Luke 13:28.
[43] John P. Meier, *A Marginal Jew*, Vol. II, 316.
[44] Gregory the Great, *Forty Gospel Homilies* 4.1, PL 76:1089.
[45] T. W. Manson, *The Teaching of Jesus*, 257.
[46] Norman Perrin, *Rediscovering the Teaching of Jesus*, 162.
[47] Isa 25:6-8.
[48] Christopher Rowland, *Christian Origins*, 147.

Were the Gentiles, then, to be rejected till the end of days when the table would be set? But what if, as Jesus pronounced, the "kingdom of God has come upon you,"[49] did this imply that the moment of salvation for the Gentiles had *already* arrived?[50]

THE MESSIANIC BANQUET AS KEY

Jesus at times rejects the Gentiles as "dogs" not worthy of the "bread" of the Jews who were the "children" of the kingdom. Elsewhere, however, He seats the Gentiles at the table of the kingdom side by side with the greatest of the Jews. How may these two conflicting attitudes be reconciled? And if, as we have seen, Jesus thought that the Gentiles would be welcomed to the banquet at the end of days, why did the Church begin a historical mission *before* the end of days?

One suggested solution to this problem is to differentiate between the present and the end of days. The majority of the *positive* sayings of Jesus regarding the Gentiles point to their salvation at the *end* of time as part of the apocalypse. Consequently there is no real conflict since the disciples were called to preach to the Jews in the present, and the Gentiles were not of concern till the end of days. But if this be the case, once more, why did the early Church go to the Gentiles before the end times? If they had felt that this present mission among the Gentiles was in accordance with the will of Jesus, then we can only but conclude that there still remains a conflict in the sayings.

Another possibility may lie in the thought of the Church Fathers. Jesus envisioned the end of the age and the ushering in of the kingdom as *imminent*. Some may question how this can be, since thousands of years later we are still waiting. As we shall see in our later discussion of the kingdom, the Church sees no contradiction. The "messianic kingdom is still to come. It comes every day and it will come in its fullness 'at the end of times.'"[51] To usher in the kingdom in the *present* is not to contradict the apocalyptic imagery of the messianic banquet at the end of days.

If in the words of Jesus the "kingdom of God is upon you," then the salvation of the Gentiles has been radically *conveyed* to the present. This transformation into the kingdom finds no grander place than in His

---

[49] Matt 12:28.

[50] Schuyler Brown, "The Matthean Community and the Gentile Mission," *Novum Testamentum* 22, 3 (1980): 196.

[51] Lev Gillet, *Communion in the Messiah: Studies in the Relationship between Judaism and Christianity* (London: Lutterworth Press, 1942), 106.

resurrection. In this vein does the illustrious Jerome comment: "The former command was given *before* the resurrection and the latter *after* the resurrection."[52] To Jerome Jesus had come initially for the Jews, knowing full well the eventual place of the Gentiles in the kingdom.[53] But it was only in and through His resurrection—the *very* institution of the messianic banquet—that the salvation of the Gentiles could be enacted. Accordingly, "it is only at the *last*"[54] (after the resurrection) that Jesus instructs the disciples to "teach all nations, and baptize them." And hence for the disciples, they were living in the "last." If we consider the action of the early Church within this context, then there is little conflict. For the apostles, especially Paul, the kingdom was imminent and in some manner had already come. And if it had indeed come, then surely the salvation of the Gentiles was something to be striven for.

For Jesus the matter was extremely clear. Our way into understanding this lies in the *messianic banquet* and its place in time:

> Many *will* come from east and west, and sit down with Abraham, Isaac, and Jacob in the kingdom of heaven. But the sons of the kingdom will be cast out...[55]

In the saying Abraham, Isaac, and Jacob, were seated at the table of the kingdom. This implies that they had risen from the dead. If we also consider the judgment of the "sons of the kingdom," then the saying places the ingathering of the "many" *at* the end of the age, the time of resurrection and judgment.

To this we couple the narrative of the *Syrophoenician woman*, in which a Gentile "dog" outside finds a place inside at the feet of her Master. She remains there till she hears: "Let it be to you as you desire."[56] She is then elevated to sit as an adopted child at the table next to the Jewish patriarch Abraham. Perhaps now we may understand the meaning of John the Baptist's saying: "God is able to raise up children to Abraham from these stones."[57] The children of Abraham, transfigured from stones (lifeless Gentiles), sit with him in the kingdom at the table of the Master. In the messianic banquet of Isaiah when all nations are gathered at the table, a "veil that covers the eyes

---

[52] Jerome, *Commentary on Matthew* 1.10.5-6, CCL 77:65.
[53] Jerome, *Commentary on Matthew*, 2.15.23, CCL 77:132–33.
[54] Tertullian, *Prescription Against the Heretics* 8, ANF 2: 247.
[55] Matt 8:11-2.
[56] Matt 15:28.
[57] Matt 3:9.

of the Gentiles will be forever rent asunder,"[58] and all the nations, Jewish and Gentilic, will behold God with an unveiled face. This table fellowship, which we should remember is the greatest symbol of unity in Judaic thought, is nothing else but the *very* "inauguration of the kingdom of God."[59]

Jesus thus saw the place of the Gentiles in the kingdom not as a rejection of the Jews but rather as a confirmation of their election. This call of the election "has as its fundamental objective the rescue and restoration of the entire creation."[60] Israel's mission was to restore creation through her covenant to God. The salvation of the Gentiles was an avowal, not a denial of Israel's singularly unique calling. In like manner Zechariah's prophetic utterance envisions the grasping by the nations of "the sleeve of a Jewish man" begging the Jewish peoples: "Let us go with you, for we have heard that God is with *you*."[61] If the Jews were not *first* affirmed as "sons of the kingdom," how could they be a light to the Gentiles? Whose sleeve would the Gentiles grasp? It was to this end that Jesus sought to create within Israel a faith that "would transform the life of His own people, and that a transformed Israel would transform the world."[62] He enlightens the Syrophoenician woman: "Let the children be filled first."[63] For if they are not fed, who will be left to bring the bread of life to the nations?

[58] Joachim Jeremias, *Jesus' Promise to the Nations*, 28.

[59] Vesilin Kesich, *The Gospel Image of Christ*, 182.

[60] N. T. Wright, *The New Testament and the People of God*, 268.

[61] Zech 8:23.

[62] T. W. Manson, *Only to the House of Israel*, 24.

[63] Mark 7:27.

CHAPTER NINE

'I did not come to bring peace but a sword'

I think, therefore I am.
—DESCARTES

I am, because we are; and since we are, therefore I am.
—JOHN MBITI

SHOULD WE LOOK FOR A WORD TO SUMMARIZE humanity's history it would inevitably be *oscillation*. Humanity has forever moved back and forth between "peace" and the "sword," never quite being able to say which it prefers. Of course the official preference is for peace, but only when it conveniently achieves a goal. If that goal be unattainable or unsustainable, then the sword would begin to glisten. And when it did glisten a great deal of men looked to the Scriptures for justification (and not instruction). Chief among these "justifications" was the saying of the "sword not peace" uttered by Jesus.

We thus come to the last of the sayings related to the kingdom of God and the *other*. Satan was bound and rejected. Free from his grips, Israel, and through her all the nations, was called to the messianic banquet in the kingdom. But how may the guests sit at the table of the Master if there is division? How may a kingdom without "peace," having been divided by the "sword," stand? And how is it that the Master Himself is the source of this division?

The Church Fathers, and with them two thousand years of Christianity, have struggled with this "dark" saying. For, was not Jesus the Prince of Peace?[1] Did He not tell His disciples: "My peace I give to you,"[2] and that only through Him they "may have peace"?[3] When raised from the dead was not the first thing Jesus said, "Peace be with you"?[4] Surely then He was in fact bringing peace and not the sword. Again, why did He elevate the place of the peacemakers to that of the "sons of God"?[5] Or for that matter, why did the early Church remember their Master in the words: "He Himself is our peace"?[6] And why did they preach "peace through Jesus Christ"?[7] Simply put, how is it that Jesus was remembered as bringing peace if He had said: "Do not think that I came to bring peace on earth. I did not come to bring peace but a sword"?[8]

A MAN'S HOUSEHOLD IS HIS ENEMY

What then did Jesus mean? In the two Gospels where this saying is found, the structure is identical. It is formed of three parts: the *denial* of peace, the *affirmation* that Jesus has come to divide, and finally a paraphrasing of *Micah 7*:

> (1) Do not think that I came to bring peace on earth. (2) I did not come to bring peace but a *sword*. (3) For I have come to "set a man against his father, a daughter against her mother, and a daughter-in-law against her mother-in-law"; and "a man's enemies will be those of his own household."[9]

Luke differs from Matthew in that he introduces the saying with: "I came to send fire on the earth."[10] Luke also has "division" instead of sword: "Do you suppose that I came to give peace on earth? I tell you, not at all,

---

[1] Isa 9:6.
[2] John 14:27.
[3] John 16:33.
[4] John 20:19.
[5] Matt 5:9.
[6] Eph 2:14-18.
[7] Acts 10:36.
[8] Matt 10:34.
[9] Matt 10:34-35. See Micah 7:6 which is almost completely found in this saying of Jesus.
[10] Luke 12:49.

but rather *division*."[11] This indicates that the act of the sword is to divide, and thus in this context it is given in a figurative rather than a literal sense.[12] To further the point, both of the Gospel writers follow the saying with the parable of division: "man *against* his father, a daughter *against* her mother." Luke also adds: "For from now on five in one house will be divided: three against two, and two against three."[13] The two are the mother and the father; the three are the son and his wife, and the daughter. For in first-century Palestine, it was customary that the son's wife would come to live with him, thus accounting for the three. In this way, the sword of Jesus envisioned cuts between the generations, dividing the very essence of the family.

Accordingly the sword is not for killing, but rather for dividing a household. But even if we limit the sword to mere division it would still be against peace, thus returning us to our initial problem. And if we are honest we must recognize that Matthew, though indicating division, sought to convey this meaning through the violent image of the sword. As M. Black notes, "while 'division' may imply 'conflict' but not necessarily 'violence,' the 'sword' has all its associations with violent conflict."[14]

We should also mention that this theme of disunity in the family was taken up by others *before* Jesus. The passage in Micah, "son dishonors father...,"[15] had already been developed by another early Jewish writer in the book of Jubilees:

> And in that generation the sons will *convict* their fathers and their elders of sin and unrighteousness... And they will strive one *with* another, the young with the old, and the old with the young...*on account of the law* and the covenant... And they will stand with bows and *swords* and war to turn them back into the way; but they will not return until much blood has been shed on the earth, one by another.[16]

This early Judaic writer tells of the division in the family not for its own sake, but for the sake of the covenant. The young rise up against their elders to "turn them back into the way" of the law, at times even with the sword! So much so that their return to righteousness will not come until "much

---

[11] Luke 12:51.

[12] M. Black, "Not Peace but a Sword," in *Jesus and the Politics of His Day*, ed. E. Bammel and C. F. D. Moule (Cambridge: Cambridge University Press, 1984), 288. Also see Oscar Cullmann, *The State in the New Testament* (London: SCM Press, 1957), 32.

[13] Luke 12:52.

[14] M. Black, "Not Peace but a Sword," 289.

[15] Micah 7:6-7.

[16] *Jubilees* 23:16-20. Though part of the *Pseudepigrapha*, and thus non-canonical, this work reflects early Judaic thought contemporary with Jesus.

blood has been shed." This is rather striking. Jesus in referring to Micah depicts the division of the house by the sword. Yet, this very same reference, centuries earlier, was taken up by another Jew in the book of Jubilees. The notable addition being that the sword was to be wielded for the *sake* of God and His law.

We do not have to look far for another transformation of the prophecy in Micah. In what is the Jewish Mishnah's "only significant mention of the Messiah,"[17] we hear: "With the footprints of the Messiah...children will shame elders, and elders will stand up before children...the face of the generation in the face of a dog. A son is not ashamed before his father."[18] The advent of the Messiah is thus clearly associated with this *very* same division within the family. Given this is the only "significant" mentioning of the Messiah in the Mishnah, we should listen very closely indeed.[19]

It follows that by depicting the imagery of division, and by indicating that He would personally be its cause, Jesus was delicately revealing that He was and is Israel's Messiah. And it is not coincidental that we recurrently find this division theme of Micah in two of the Gospels, in the Mishnah, Talmud, and in the apocalyptic writings. For this same core structure—the division of families in association with the sword and the coming of the Messiah—to be found in writings distanced in time and thought, there must have been something else at play. What we have before us, in the judgment of Dale C. Allison, is "a chiastic line about conflict between young and old [which] was repeatedly used to depict one aspect of eschatological strife."[20] This familial infighting must have been seen uniformly as a feature of *eschatology* (an event of the end times). Whereas Micah described the historical turmoil, the Jewish works transformed it into a prophecy of the final events that will come "with the footprints of the Messiah."

We should also recall that this was not the first time Jesus had spoken of familial disunity. He had revealed to His disciples that at the end, "children will rise up against parents..."[21] If Jesus spoke of division twice, once as being related to His sword and the other as part of the end of days, then it is fair

---

[17] Craig A. Evans, "Authenticating the Words of Jesus," in *Authenticating the Words of Jesus*, ed. Bruce Chilton and Craig A. Evans (Leiden: Brill, 2002), 13.

[18] *Mishnah Sotah* 9:15.

[19] Some time later, the ancient Rabbi Nehorai echoed once more the same visions of violence surrounding the arrival of the Messiah. See *Babylonian Talmud Sanhedrin* 97a. Also see *Sibylline Oracles* 8:84.

[20] Dale C. Allison, "Q 12:51-53 and Mark 9:11-13 and the Messianic Woes," in *Authenticating the Words of Jesus*, ed. Bruce Chilton and Craig A. Evans (Leiden: Brill, 2002), 293.

[21] Mark 13:12.

to conclude that *His sword would manifest the end of the age.*[22] This saying of Jesus, in the mind of the eminent Catholic scholar John P. Meier, was spoken with the greatest intention:

> [The saying] coheres with the prophetic and especially apocalyptic traditions of Israel, which saw the loosening of loyalty in family units as a prime sign of the tribulations of the last days, tribulations often symbolized by a sword.[23]

Another meaning has often been suggested. For the next three centuries after Jesus' death the Church would be consistently persecuted. Within persecuted minorities, divisions often arise. When forced to side with or against God, a family could all too easily become divided. At an earlier stage we do well to remember that the first Christians were converts. This conversion caused an unrelenting tension within families, especially in a world where religion was life. Choosing to become a Christian was then a "radically divisive decision"[24] imposed by Jesus on His followers. Therefore we find the Apostle Paul granting concessions of separation. If one spouse chose to be baptized whilst the pagan partner was unwilling, then the bonds of marriage could be severed if required.[25] But though this interpretation is rather neat, Jesus seems to be saying more than *just* this. He had come to divide loyalty within the family, persecution or not. By referring to the coming of the Messiah who will incite His people to divide by the sword for the sake of the law, Jesus meant more than simply the strenuous pressures of conversion.

This brings us to a related query: Was Jesus against familial bonds? And if we may dare: What was His attitude to His own family? We are told in the Gospels (at least during His early ministry) that the brothers of Jesus "did not believe in Him."[26] At one point His own "people" sought to silence Him, thinking "He is out of His mind."[27] When told by a woman in the crowd: "Blessed is the womb that bore You," Jesus replied: "More than that, blessed are *those* who hear the word of God and keep it!"[28] Once as Jesus

---

[22] Ferdinand Hahn, *The Titles of Jesus in Christology: Their History in Early Christianity* (Cambridge: James Clarke & Co., 2002), 153. Also see Dale C. Allison, "Q 12:51-53 and Mark 9:11-13 and the Messianic Woes," 299.

[23] John P. Meier, *A Marginal Jew*, Vol. III, 69.

[24] Ben F. Meyer, *The Aims of Jesus*, 213.

[25] 1 Cor 7:12-16.

[26] John 7:5.

[27] Mark 3:21.

[28] Luke 11:27-28.

sat teaching, one came forward and informed Him: "Look, Your mother and Your brothers are outside seeking You." Jesus characteristically replied: "Who is My mother, or My brothers?" and looking around at those seated added: "whoever does the will of God is My brother and My sister and mother."[29] One able scholar thus surmises: "This attitude to His own family was reflected in the shocking demands for family disloyalty that He made on His followers."[30] He who does not "hate his father and mother, wife and children, brothers and sisters, yes, and his own life,"[31] cannot be a disciple of Jesus. Likewise, a disciple who wishes to first bury his father is told: "Let the dead bury their own dead."[32]

If such sayings seem shocking to the modern reader in a society where the family unit is at times devalued and debased, what would be the reaction in the family-centric society of first-century Palestine? It would seem that the family unit, the tightest of bonds, that which a Palestinian Jew would most depend on, was the singular target of Jesus' sword.[33] But can this be the truth of the matter?

In each of the above sayings the rejection of familial loyalty is not without purpose. Jesus did not devalue family, but He did make it a far second to the kingdom of God. Obedience and action upon hearing the will of the Father are for Him immensely more pressing. Preaching the kingdom displaces the obligation to bury one's dead. Commitment to father, brother, land, or even one's life, was not in any sense wrong. But to place it above commitment to the kingdom was. To follow Jesus required the loosening of the strongest of human bonds, the family. It demanded complete freedom, so that one may serve Him wholly.[34]

And had Jesus devalued the family unit, why then do we hear that Peter (after being called) was spending time with his mother-in-law?[35] Peter even took his wife along to a mission.[36] If Jesus had rejected all familial bonds, why were James, John, and their mother so close?[37] It stands to reason that the early Church would not have continued honoring marriage and the place of the family, if Jesus had dismissed it as redundant. Rather Jesus was teaching that if the obligations to family and God were in conflict then, at

[29] Mark 3:32-35.
[30] N. T. Wright, *Jesus and the Victory of God*, 149.
[31] Luke 14:26. Also see Mark 10:29.
[32] Luke 9:59.
[33] John P. Meier, *A Marginal Jew*, Vol. III, 68.
[34] Martin Hengel, *The Charismatic Leader and His Followers*, 13.
[35] Mark 1:29-30.
[36] 1 Cor 9:5.
[37] Mark 15:40; Matt 27:56.

least for the great Jerome, the "forthright rejection of your family may be a higher form of familial loyalty in relation to God."[38] But as powerful as this call to the higher form of loyalty to God was, "it should not be pressed into too sharp a contrast with responsibility to birth-family."[39] For Ambrose it was simply a matter of recognizing the reality of the obligation:

> It is necessary that we should esteem the human *less* than the divine. If honor is to be paid to parents, how much more to your parents' Creator, to whom you owe gratitude for your parents! If they by no means recognize their Father, how do you recognize them? He does not say children should reject a father but that God is to be set *before* all.[40]

Once more we question: If Jesus did not mean the absolute obliteration of the family unit, what exactly was He saying?

THE TWO SWORDS SAYING

Before we continue our examination of this allegedly inflammatory saying, we should consider another which shall perhaps be revelatory. It is a saying that has at times been misconstrued to conclude that Jesus encouraged armed revolution, and that He allowed Christians to bear arms. It was even used to prove the right of the medieval papacy to wield spiritual and material swords.

On the night of His betrayal, Jesus questioned the disciples:

> "When I sent you without money bag, knapsack, and sandals, did you lack anything?" So they said, "Nothing." Then He said to them, "But now, he who has a money bag, let him take it, and likewise a knapsack; and he who has *no* sword, let him sell his *garment* and buy one…" So they said, "Lord, look, here are two swords." And He said to them, "It is enough."[41]

From this saying many misinformed scholars have painted Jesus as a violent political revolutionary.[42] S. G. Brandon, for one, mistakenly claims

---

[38] Jerome, *Commentary on Matthew* 1.0.37, CCL 77:74.

[39] James D. G. Dunn, *Jesus Remembered*, 598.

[40] Ambrose, *Exposition of the Gospel of Luke* 7.134-136, EHG 286-287.

[41] Luke 22:35-38.

[42] See Conrad Noel, *Jesus the Heretic* (London: J.M. Dent, 1939); John Lewis, *Christianity and the Social Revolution* (London: Victor Gallanez, 1935); and recently S. G. Brandon, *Jesus and the Zealots*.

that it was Jesus' political movement that eventually led to His crucifixion, and that it was the sword which would be the instrument of this political Zealotism.[43] Is Jesus, then, commanding His disciples to buy swords and enact a revolution?

Even *if* we took this command literally there would be no claim that this was anything more than self-defense. But this would be admitting too much if we consider that it is only some verses later, when Peter strikes with the sword, that Jesus not only rebukes him: "Put your sword in its place, for all who take the sword will perish by the sword,"[44] but also heals the victim: "He touched his ear and healed him."[45] In doing so, Jesus emphatically distances Himself in word and deed from any use of the sword. To this we add that Jesus had strictly taught non-resistance to violence, commanding that one should turn the cheek if struck.[46]

But if Jesus did not support the *use* of the sword, why did He command its purchase? The disciples were expressly told to sell their "garments" to buy a sword. The outer cloak, in Greek *imation*, was "the most necessary garment of all" for the peasant, serving in a way as a "sleeping bag."[47] Therefore it was that which one would be most reluctant to part with. According to the Mosaic law, if one had another's garment, even as a pledge, one was commanded to return it before sun down: "For that is his *only* covering, it is his garment for his skin. What will he sleep in?"[48] Perhaps now we appreciate the radical nature of the Sermon on the Mount: "If anyone wants to sue you and take away your tunic, let him have your *cloak* also."[49]

It was this "garment" the disciples were called to sell, that which was necessary for life. Jesus was evoking in vivid language the "extreme gravity and danger of the moment."[50] The selling of the necessary garment so that a sword may be purchased was simply a marker of the severity of the coming situation. The time had utterly turned. Once He had sent them out with no possessions so that they should rely on the kindness of those they had been sent to preach.[51] But now no one will take them in and feed them. On the

---

[43] S. G. Brandon, *Jesus and the Zealots*, 20.

[44] Matt 26:52.

[45] Luke 22:51

[46] Matt 5:38-39.

[47] G. W. H. Lampe, "The Two Swords," 337.

[48] Exod 22:26-27.

[49] Matt 5:40. Luke reverses the order, and has: if one wants your *cloak*, give him your tunic as well. This possibly indicates that he was a Greek city dweller, unaccustomed to the necessity of the cloak in the cold Palestinian nights.

[50] M. Black, "Not Peace but a Sword," 291.

[51] See Vincent Taylor, *Jesus and His Sacrifice: A Study of the Passion-Sayings in the Gospels* (London: Macmillan & Co., 1939), 192.

contrary "war will come to them with such unendurable force that nothing shall be able to stand against it."[52] The saying was not concerned with the swords, but with the *tribulation* that was coming. The disciples only caught the surface of His words and thus replied: "Look, Lord, here are two swords." To this Jesus simply responds: "It is enough." What is enough? Are the *two* swords enough for this bitter tribulation that necessitates the selling of the essential garment? In the words of the great Cyril of Alexandria:

> Observe how, so to say, He even ridicules their speech, well knowing that the disciples not having understood the force of what was said, thought that swords were required, because of the attack about to be made upon Himself... [Were] two swords enough to bear the brunt of the war about to come upon them, to meet which many thousand swords were of no avail.[53]

How could two swords meet the battle that even a thousand swords could not? It has often been suggested that Jesus was not telling the disciples that two swords would suffice. Rather it was "this talk" which was enough. Jesus then was not talking of swords, but of the radically different situation that would come after His death. A thousand swords will not help. And should they help, Jesus denies their use. He who takes by the sword "will perish by the sword." Jesus encourages His disciples to see that their words were futile, as Cyril teaches, they had not "understood the force of what was said."

To move from this saying to the conclusion that Jesus was a violent revolutionary then becomes unsustainable. And if we consider the context of the words it becomes ludicrous. At no point does Jesus support violent methods for freedom, not even for a moment.[54] But if Jesus had so categorically rejected the *use* of the sword, why did He come to *bring* the sword?

---

[52] Cyril of Alexandria, *Commentary on Luke*, Homily 145, *CGSL* 579. Ambrose seemingly represents a minority of the Fathers in seeing in the "two-swords" saying a justification of carrying a sword in self-defense: "Perhaps he may command this so that a *defense may be prepared*, not as a necessary revenge, but that you may be seen to have been able to be avenged but to be unwilling to take revenge." *Exposition of the Gospel of Luke* 10.53-55, *EHG* 405-406. It should be noted that this saying of Ambrose sits in the context of other swords such as the "spiritual sword" and the "sword of suffering."

[53] Cyril of Alexandria, *Commentary on Luke*, Homily 145, *CGSL* 580.

[54] See Christopher Rowland, *Christian Origins*, 158; E. P. Sanders, *Jesus and Judaism*, 231; Oscar Cullmann, *The State in the New Testament*, 32.

THE SWORD THAT DIVIDES TO UNITE

To answer this we need to turn to the beginning, when man was created in the image of God the Trinity. If we look at the word closer, it is in fact Tri-unity. Man was thus created in the image of the perfect unity *of* the three co-essential Persons.[55] Placed within man, then, is an unquenchable and infinite need for that unity, for union. In the paradisal fall, man had lost the knowledge of his God. But within him the need for unity would still burn.

When man fell the devil did not seek to create for man another world, as Alexander Schmemann is careful to note, he instead chose to usurp the existing one:

> The devil did not create new, "evil" words, just as he did not and could not create another world, just as he did not and could not create anything. The whole falsehood and the whole power of this falsehood lie in the fact that he made the *same* words into words *about something else*, he usurped them and converted them into an instrument of evil and that, consequently, he and his servants in "this world" always speak in a language literally stolen from God.[56]

A new world was not formed; that which was created by God became corrupted. Words too had fallen and became about "something else." One of these words was *unity*. To Fr. Schmemann, "there is no word in human language more divine—but therefore also more *diabolical*, in that it has fallen and been 'stolen' from God."[57] This word stood for a single and true reality: the manifestation of the divine life *as* unity. It was imprinted upon man in his deepest being. Man was chosen to dwell in unity with his fellow men with the very *same* unity that God had revealed in His divine life. But when man fell, the devil took grasp of what was created and transformed it into evil. Unity, the revelation of life itself, ceased to be the meaning of life with God. Instead, it was reduced to an "end-in-itself or, in the language of faith, an idol."[58] It became its own god.

But unity, having been created by God, would create an insatiable need within man—albeit, a fallen need. Man having rejected God sought

---

[55] This does not of course presuppose the Trinitarian developments of the coming centuries, but it does in a very real way presuppose the ineffable unity of God, in the image of which man was created.

[56] Alexander Schmemann, *The Eucharist: Sacrament of the Kingdom*, tr. Paul Kachur (New York: SVS Press, 2003), 148.

[57] Alexander Schmemann, *The Eucharist*, 150.

[58] Alexander Schmemann, *The Eucharist*, 153.

unity in family, friends, tribe, and nation; all, that in a few words, men live and die for. The *unity from above* had given way to the *unity from below*: "being turned downward—to the earthly and natural, to things below—and regarding flesh and blood as its principle and source, this unity from below begins to divide in the same measure that it unifies."[59] What was created in the image of God, the unity from above, had turned on itself and become the false unity from below. And before long, men sharing in this fallen unity would begin to seek the place of heaven itself:

> Now the whole earth had *one* language and one speech… And they said, "Come, let us build ourselves a city, and a tower whose top is in the heavens; let us make a name for ourselves, *lest* we be scattered abroad over the face of the whole earth." But the Lord came down to see the city and the tower which the sons of men had built. And the Lord said, "Indeed the people are *one* and they all have one language, and *this* is what they begin to do… Come, let Us go down and there *confuse* their language, that they may not understand one another's speech."[60]

Man out of his need for unity sought to "make a name" for himself, lest he be "scattered abroad." This false unity from below sought to build its tower, sought to find its place in heaven as its own god. Therefore God *divides* this false unity! In the words of John Chrysostom, God made an end to "their *evil peace*" by creating among them a "*good* dispute."[61] If the people "meant to reach the heights of heaven,"[62] then God was forced to *divide* their language so that this false unity would not destroy man altogether. For as this fallen unity no longer found its moving principle in God and became a "god-in-itself," it did not in fact bring unity, it brought division, and with it death.

On reading this, many will perhaps ask whether this is simply a matter of mere words, and whether this is the actual and concrete experience of human existence. Let us then think of an individual. What is the natural history of his life? He is born into *a* family, which he defines in *exclusion* of other people. His family is a unit *as* opposed to other units which are *not* his own. Over time this family grows and becomes a tribe which is defined once more in opposition to what is *not* one's tribe. Perhaps later this tribe will unite with a few other tribes and become a nation, as contrasted to *other* nations.

[59] Alexander Schmemann, *The Eucharist*, 153.

[60] Gen 11:1-9.

[61] John Chrysostom, *The Gospel of Matthew*, Homily 35.1, PG 57:405; NPNF 1 10:232.

[62] Jerome, *Commentary on Matthew* 1.0.34, CCL 77:73–74.

Thus in family, tribe, and nation, unity serves to *mark out* who is with us and who is not. Within the family, tribe, or nation, there is indeed unity, but only for the singular purpose of defining who is not part of this unity. Unity, therefore, has become an instrument *of* division. It places one united family in opposition to another united family and so on. This unity from below is then false. It does not unite, tragically and devastatingly, it divides. Men die for their families, tribes, and nations, so that they might fight *another* family, tribe, or nation:

> Everything in the world lives through unity, and everything in the world is divided by this unity and constantly *divided* itself into collisions and struggles of "unities" that have become idols.[63]

If one should look at the history of humanity, every division is the result of this so-called unity. Family feuds result from two "united" families in opposition, civil wars from two opposed "united" tribes, and world wars when nations "unite" against others. This false unity, in its final reality, is nothing else but division. False unity stands against false unity. What was originally intended to bring all things into the *one* united life of God became a debased tool of division and hatred. Dividing not only man from man, as Cyril of Alexandria reminds, but also man from God: "there is sometimes, so to speak, an *unsafe* peace, and which *separates* from the love of God."[64]

It was into this world of false unity that Jesus was sent; a world in which the *unity from below* had rule. It was into this world that He cried out solemnly: "I did not come to bring peace but a sword." He comes not to bring peace to these false "unities," each united against another. He comes, sword in hand, to divide all who "have made a unity against Unity."[65] As God had divided the language of the "united" men as they built their idolatrous tower of Babel, Jesus divides. He brings "a necessary conflict" in order "to *break an evil peace*."[66] He places "man against father" and "daughter against mother" to undo the very bonds that have deceived man into a state of false unity. The family was the fundamental unit of unity in human life. To destroy false unity in its every place, Jesus was required first to remove these most fundamental of bonds. An anonymous Church Father puts it as such:

---

[63] Alexander Schmemann, *The Eucharist*, 153.

[64] Cyril of Alexandria, *Commentary on Luke*, Homily 94, CGSL 380.

[65] Augustine, *Sermon* 12.18, NPNF 1 6:304.

[66] Jerome, *Commentary on Matthew* 1.0.34, CCL 77:73–74. See also Gregory of Nazianzus, *On the Holy Lights*, Oration 29.15, NPNF 2 7:358.

> There is a good peace and there is an evil peace…In this way then God brought a *good disunity* to the earth in order to break an *evil unity*… God [thus] brought a sword *of* disunity among them…[67]

Each and every unity from below, family, tribe, or nation, is to be divided so that man may once more find the *unity from above*. So that man may find a *true* unity in himself, in his family, tribe, and nation. Not in opposition *to* another, but in unity with them as the body of Christ. Jesus comes wielding the sword to destroy all that is false, to destroy each and every false construct that stands between man and his neighbor, so that they might live in Him as *one*, as His body. It is through this sword and division that "the one real (for it is divine) unity enters into the world… Through it every division is overcome and shall be fully conquered, so that God may be all *in* all."[68] With the "footprints of the Messiah" the division prophesized by Micah enters into the world, to set man against man, false unity against false unity, so that men may become one *in* the unity of God.

Had Jesus brought peace and not the sword to these "false unities," man would inevitably have kept dividing. Utterly divided even within himself, man would be decomposed into a single individual "unity" in absolute hatred of all else. This truth is revealed in a mysterious incident of the Egyptian desert. It was said that Abba Macarius the Great whilst walking in the desert saw the skull of a dead man. With his stick he struck the skull. It then spoke to Macarius:

> Macarius then replied: "Who are you to speak to me like this?"
> The skull said to him, "I was a pagan during the time of the pagans. I have been *allowed* to speak with you."
> Macarius then asked, "Are you at peace, or do you suffer?"
> The skull said to him, "I am being punished. Just as the sky is high over the earth, so too is there a river of fire boiling over our heads and underneath us, lapping over our feet. We stand in the middle, unable to *look* at one another because our backs are *joined* to each other. But at the moment when someone offers a great supplication for us, we gain a little peace."
> Macarius asked him, "What is this peace?"
> The skull said to him, "For the blink of an eye we see each other's *faces*."
> When Macarius heard this, he wept and cried out before asking, "Are there worse punishments than yours?"
> The skull said to him, "Yes, for *below* us is punishment whose fire—whose

[67] Anonymous, *Incomplete Work on Matthew*, Homily 26, PG 56:767–68.
[68] Alexander Schmemann, *The Eucharist*, 156.

terrible fire—is even darker and more pitiless... As for us since we did not know God, we were not cast into this punishment below, but those who know God and reject Him have been cast below us."[69]

In hell the poor pagan was tied back to back with other men so that he could not take peace in even a glimpse of their faces. This frightening image is utterly individualistic. Man in the end was in "unity" with other men, being joined "back to back." Man though sitting inches from another, in what seemed to be perfect "unity," was absolutely alone, incapable of even seeing the face of the other. The unity from below that joins man "back to back," then, is the absolute and depraved division which will separate men for all eternity.

It is for this reason that Jesus does not come to bring peace to these false unities, but rather the sword. It is these bonds which He has come to divide, cutting the bonds that join individuals "back to back," families "back to back," and tribes "back to back." The bonds that seem to "unite," in reality, divide us, hindering our ability to behold the face of the other. By dividing with the sword Jesus reveals to us the *true* unity. He reveals what it means to behold the face of the other, what it means to behold the face of God. This is the image of the kingdom, where God is all *in* all.

---

[69] Paraphrased from Macarius the Great of Egypt, *Saint Macarius the Spirit Bearer*, tr. Tim Vivian (New York: SVS Press, 2004), 72-74.

PART THREE:

The Mystery of the Kingdom

CHAPTER TEN

'Say nothing to anyone'

A secret between two is God's secret, between three is all men's.
—SPANISH PROVERB

Those who were possessed came before Him, and the unclean spirits unable to bear His presence cried out: "You are the Son of God." But Jesus *"sternly warned them that they should not make Him known."*

With a word a child is raised from the dead. The parents overcome with amazement sing in ecstasy, yet Jesus *"commanded them strictly that no one should know it."*

Jesus questions once more: "But who do you say that I am?" Peter replies confidently: "You are the Messiah." Jesus then *"strictly warned them that they should tell no one about Him."*

THESE THREE VIGNETTES SKETCH AN INTRIGUING picture of the Gospels. A daughter is healed and her parents are to tell no one. Demons reveal the nature of Jesus and are strictly commanded to silence. Peter calls Jesus the "Messiah" and is immediately sworn to secrecy. These observations have moved many scholars to brand that which was concealed by silence as the "messianic secret."[1] As soon as anyone, human

---

[1] One famous (albeit incorrect) conclusion drawn from the secrecy passages was that of

or otherwise, recognizes the divine nature of Jesus, they are commanded to utter *silence*. But, if we may dare to ask: Why?

If Jesus had come to call all men to knowledge of Himself, why then did He hide such knowledge? What did this command to silence mean? What was it meant to achieve? And that said, why then was Jesus not consistent in commanding secrecy? If the aim was to conceal this truth about His nature, why heal multitudes, and for that matter, why feed thousands miraculously and *publicly*? If anything this "messianic secret" is still a mystery and it is into this mystery that we proceed, taking these three vignettes of silence—exorcism, miracle, and disciple—as our entry points.[2]

SILENCE IN EXORCISM

(1) "Let *us* alone! What have we to do with You, Jesus of Nazareth? Did You come to destroy us? I know who You are—the Holy One of God!" But Jesus rebuked him, saying, "Be quiet, and come out of him!"

(2) Then He healed many who were sick with various diseases, and cast out many demons; and He did not allow the demons to speak, because they knew Him.

(3) And the unclean spirits, whenever they saw Him, fell down before Him and cried out, saying, "You are the Son of God." But He sternly warned them that they should not make Him known.

(4) And demons also came out of many, crying out and saying, "You are the Christ, the Son of God!" And He, rebuking *them,* did not allow them to speak, for they knew that He was the Christ [*Messiah*].[3]

---

the nineteenth century scholar William Wrede who claimed that the messianic secret was a theological retrojection. Allegedly Jesus never claimed to be the Messiah and the belief that Jesus was indeed the Messiah was a post-resurrection belief. It was, for Wrede, an "after-effect of the view that the resurrection is the beginning of the messiahship," and thus Jesus' messiahship was created by the early Church and Mark. See William Wrede, *The Messianic Secret*, tr. J. C. G. Greig (London: James Clarke & Co., 1971), 229. In the words of Martin Hengel, the result is that "today the unmessianic Jesus has almost become a dogma among many New Testament scholars." "Jesus, the Messiah of Israel," in *Studies in Early Christology* (Edinburgh: T & T Clark, 1995), 16. This misconceived hypothesis has been sufficiently disproved by many, for a further discussion see *The Messianic Secret*, ed. Christopher Tuckett (Philadelphia: Fortress Press, 1983). Also see T. W. Manson, "Realized Eschatology and the Messianic Secret," in *Studies in the Gospels: Essays in Memory of R. H. Lightfoot* (Oxford: Basil Blackwell, 1955), 220; James D. G. Dunn, *Jesus Remembered*, 627.

[2] See Ulrich Luz, "The Secrecy Motif and the Marcan Christology," in *The Messianic Secret*, 75. For a survey of the opinions of modern scholarship see James L. Blevins, *The Messianic Secret in Markan Research, 1901-1976* (Washington, University Press of America, 1981); David E. Aune, "The Problem of the Messianic Secret," *Novum Testamentum* 11 (1969): 31.

[3] Respectively Mark 1:24-25; Mark 1:34; Mark 3:11-12; and Luke 4:41.

Of the three categories of silence that we have seen, the most striking is that of the *exorcism*.[4] In a number of cases when Jesus approaches an afflicted person, the scenario fits into a remarkable two-part pattern. The demons cry out in *declaration of the nature* of Jesus: "I know who You are— the Holy One of God," "You are the Christ, the Son of God," "You are the Son of God." Jesus then commands the demons to *silence*: "Be quiet," "He did not allow the demons to speak," "He rebuking them, did not allow them to speak," "He sternly warned them." This command to silence clearly is with a singular intention: "because they knew Him," "they knew that He was the Messiah," "they should not make Him known." It thus is instantly obvious that the demons are immediately commanded to silence upon declaring their knowledge of the nature of Jesus as the Messiah the Son of God. Interestingly, as we shall see later, none of the demons are ever said to have disobeyed this command.

We are accordingly able to appreciate that Jesus sought to silence these declarations, but the question remains as to why? Was Jesus not the Messiah? Was He not the Son of God? With what aim does He then proceed to silence the demons? Was He denying their declarations?

Here we need to make a very precise distinction. It was not so much a matter of Jesus denying the truth uttered by the demons, but rather denying *their* truth. The words proclaimed by a liar, though perhaps true, are not credible. If a pathological liar declares that he is innocent of a particular crime, who would believe him? It may well be that *this* time he speaks truth, but his words are worthless. The same principle holds here. An early theologian, Athanasius, judges: "Although what they said was true, and they did not lie...yet He did not wish that the truth should proceed from an *unclean mouth*."[5] The demons were not the "right" subjects of declaration, and thus they were silenced to "keep them from sowing their own wickedness in the midst of the truth."[6] Had Jesus accepted their declaration, His mission would have been in dire jeopardy. To rely upon Satan for confessing the truth of God would be to place one's faith in the faithless.[7] In the words of Cyril the Great, light may not be recognized by darkness:

---

[4] There is another category that is often suggested. In Mark 4:11, the disciples are told: "To you it has been given to know the *mystery of the kingdom* of God; but to those who are outside, all things come in parables..." This however is unrelated to the messianic secret, and has been argued against sufficiently. For a discussion see Schuyler Brown, "The Secret of the Kingdom of God," *JBL* 92, 1 (1973): 60-74.

[5] Athanasius, *To the Bishops of Egypt* 1.3, TLG 2035.041, 25.544.13-20; NPNF 2 4:224.

[6] Athanasius, *Life of St. Anthony* 26, FC 15:159.

[7] Schuyler Brown, "The Secret of the Kingdom of God," 61 n. 7.

He would not permit the *unclean* demons to confess Him. It was not right
for them to usurp the glory of the apostolic office or to talk of the mystery
of Christ with polluted tongues. Yes, *nothing they say is true*. Let no one
trust them. Light cannot be recognized with the help of darkness...[8]

But the discerning reader of the Gospel will point out that Jesus "seems"
to lack consistency. When the Gerasene demoniac came before Jesus
(strangely, worshipping Him) he cried out: "What have I to do with You,
Jesus, Son of the Most High God?"[9] Is this not an identical declaration to that
of the other demons? Yet we hear of *no* command to silence. More so when
Jesus prepares to depart, the exorcised man begs Jesus "that he might be with
Him,"[10] to which Jesus responds: "Go home to your friends, and tell them
what great things the Lord has done for you."[11] Had Jesus acted neutrally
with this man we might have conceded that some of the details were lost
over the centuries. But Jesus did not simply avoid the command to silence;
instead He commanded the once-demoniac to proclaim the exorcism! Is
this not at entire variance with the command to secrecy? Why were the other
demons silenced, but not he? And why was he sent to proclaim the "secret"?

The matter lies in the careful examination of the passage. The Gerasene
demoniac was never commanded to proclaim the *declaration* of the
demon that had possessed him, rather he was to proclaim the *healing*. In
the previous cases the demons were silenced because of a truth that they
had uttered. In this case what was to be proclaimed was not the satanic
declaration, but the healing itself. There is thus a distinction between the
silencing of the demons—concealing the "messianic secret"—and the
proclamation of the miracle. This leads us intently to the second category of
the *silencing of miracles*.

SILENCE IN HEALING

Within the Gospel of Mark[12] there are four miracles in which there are
commands to silence: The case of a *leper* who is healed and then warned

[8] Cyril of Alexandria, *Commentary on Luke* 12, CGSL 101.

[9] Mark 5:7.

[10] Mark 5:18.

[11] Mark 5:19.

[12] See also their parallels in the other Gospels. In the case of Matt 12:15-21, Peter M.
Head claims that "Matthew associates the public reticence of Jesus with His fulfilling of the
Scriptures." For this discussion see *Christology and the Synoptic Problem: An Argument for
Markan Priority* (Cambridge: Cambridge University Press, 1997), 243.

to "say nothing to anyone;" the raising of *Jairus' daughter* where "He commanded them strictly that no one should know it;" the healing of a *deaf-mute* who was then commanded to "tell no one;" and finally the giving of sight to a *blind man* who was told: "Neither go into the town, nor tell anyone in the town."[13] Of interest, in two of these cases, that of the leper and that of the deaf-mute, the command was disobeyed (unlike the ironic obedience of the demons), so much so that "the more He commanded them, the more widely they proclaimed it."[14]

But these were not the only miracles that Jesus performed. In fact many of the miracles would have been incompatible with secrecy. We find for instance that the healing of a paralytic was tied to the public teaching that Jesus had the authority to forgive sins,[15] and in another place we notice that Jesus heals a man with a "withered hand" after teaching on the true nature of the Sabbath.[16] In these two cases healing is performed in public with no call to secrecy. Indeed it would be impossible to call for secrecy as the healing was coupled with a teaching to the public. Later we are told that as Jesus alighted from a boat at Gennesaret, the crowds became frantic "and as many as touched Him were made well."[17] Here, as elsewhere, Jesus healed "all" who came to Him publicly and yet commanded no one to silence. The only possible conclusion is that the command to secrecy was not concerned with simply concealing miracles, and neither was its chief purpose to hide the authority of Jesus as a miracle worker. The command to secrecy had *another* purpose.

Many scholars upon examining the call for secrecy in the healing and exorcism passages have seen within them the *same* secret. But this seems to miss an awfully important detail. In the silencing of demons, the silence is carefully directed at the revelation of the *nature* of Jesus as the Messiah and the Son of God. Whereas in the case of the miracles (as well as the Gerasene demoniac), the silence has nothing to do with the nature of Jesus. Rather it is directed at concealing the miracle *itself*.

---

[13] Mark 1:44; Mark 5:43; Mark 7:36; and Mark 8:26 respectively.

[14] Mark 7:36. Many scholars have offered explanations for this apparent disobedience by men as contrasted to the obedience of the demons. A common interpretation is that "the stress lies on the fact that Jesus' miraculous deeds cannot remain hidden" (Heikki Räisänen, "The 'Messianic Secret' in Mark's Gospel," in *The Messianic Secret*, 132). That is, the miracles are so powerful that not even a command can prevent their proclamation.

[15] Mark 2:1-12.

[16] Mark 3:1-6.

[17] Mark 6:56.

[These passages] contain nothing about a "messianic secret." It is *not* the messiahship of Jesus, or His divine sonship which is to be kept secret, but the event of healing, the *miracle*.[18]

Put succinctly, the matter of Jesus' identity is never overtly raised.[19] It thus becomes clear that there were two different things at operation. Jesus commanded the demons not to reveal the *messianic secret* of His true nature, and He commanded the healed not to reveal the *miracle secret* of the miracle itself.

But what was the purpose of this miracle secret? We have already touched upon the crucial observation that a survey of the miracles reveals that this command to secrecy was not consistent. Some healings received the command whilst others did not. This suggests that this call for silence did not have a single and consistent motive. In fact, as James D. G. Dunn pointedly notes, "it is highly probable that in different situations there was a variety of motives operative."[20] Whereas in the case of the demons the purpose was singular—to conceal the mystery of Jesus' nature—the same may not be said of the miracle secret. That is to say, each command was a reaction to a *particular* circumstance, three of which (at least) are evident.

After healing the leper, the disobedient patient proclaims his miracle so "freely" that "Jesus could no longer openly enter the city."[21] At one point the crowd became so large that He "could not so much as eat."[22] Jesus' popular reputation clearly hindered His ministry and movement, and thus to avoid this impediment Jesus may have commanded silence *about* the miracles. Secondly, other commands to silence may have been for the sake of the patient. The leper was required to show himself to the priests to confirm his healing,[23] and the raised daughter of Jairus' required something to eat.[24] More dramatically it may even have been for the protection of the patient as in the case of the healed blind man who was "cast out" from the synagogue for proclaiming a miracle of the "hated" Jesus.[25] Thirdly, Jesus was performing large scale miracles in the context of the popular expectation of a political Royal-Messiah. We find that after the miracle of feeding five thousand the

[18] Ulrich Luz, "The Secrecy Motif and the Marcan Christology," 80.

[19] Lewis S. Hay, "Mark's Use of the Messianic Secret," *Journal of the American Academy of Religion* 35, 1 (1967): 21.

[20] James D. G. Dunn, "The Messianic Secret in Mark," in *The Messianic Secret*, 118.

[21] Mark 1:45.

[22] Mark 3:20.

[23] Mark 1:44.

[24] Mark 5:43.

[25] John 9:13-35.

crowds sought to "take Him by *force* to make Him king."[26] To which Jesus reacts by departing to the mountain "by Himself, alone." It would then stand to reason that He saw only too clearly how politically labile the crowd was, and from then on would seek to avoid such popular expectations by commanding silence about the miracles.[27]

We now come to the final command of secrecy, that which was directed at the disciples. Here is a clear situation where the content of the secret *is* the nature of Jesus. What intrigues us is that those sworn to secrecy are not demons; they are the followers of Jesus.

SILENCING OF THE DISCIPLES

> Now Jesus and His disciples went out to the towns of Caesarea Philippi; and on the road He asked His disciples, saying to them, "Who do men say that I am?" So they answered, "John the Baptist; but some say, Elijah; and others, one of the prophets." He said to them, "But who do *you* say that I am?" Peter answered and said to Him, "You are the Christ [*Messiah*]." Then He strictly warned them that they should tell no one about Him.[28]

This passage is rather awkward for two reasons. First, Jesus never affirms nor denies Peter's statement,[29] and secondly, He commands silence for that which is *true*! Unlike in the case of the demons this was not a confession from an "unclean mouth," but from the mouth of a follower of Jesus. If that be the case, why would Jesus prevent this truth from being proclaimed to others? The answer comes some verses later.

Immediately after this command to silence, Jesus begins to teach the disciples "that the Son of Man must suffer many things," to which Peter reacts by taking Jesus aside and rebuking Him. Jesus turns around and looks at *each* disciple before sternly saying to Peter: "Get behind Me, *Satan*! For you are not mindful of the things of God, but the things of men."[30] Jesus is incredibly clear: to subtract the dimension of suffering from the nature of the Messiah is to side with Satan. The Messiah can only be understood as the suffering Son of Man.

---

[26] John 6:15.

[27] James D. G. Dunn, "The Messianic Secret in Mark," 126-127.

[28] Mark 8:27-30.

[29] In Matt 16:15-20, Jesus claims that the Father reveals this to Peter. But in Mark we find no statement, negative or positive.

[30] Mark 8:31-33.

Peter and the disciples were incapable of comprehending how the
Messiah could suffer. It was for this reason that Jesus commands the
disciples to silence. Yes, they had understood that Jesus was the coming
Messiah, but they had misunderstood the nature of the Messiah. Peter's
understanding of the Messiah was not the same as Jesus'. For the disciples,
Jesus was the very same political Messiah that the crowds had envisioned.[31]
It is this incomprehension which explains the necessity of the messianic
secret. Without which, in one scholar's estimation, the consequences would
be tragic and far reaching: "The disciples misunderstood the nature of Jesus'
messiahship; so *a fortiori* would the crowds if it were revealed to them."[32]
If the disciples were to proclaim the messiahship of Jesus, it would be an
inadequate description of who He was. Jesus sought to redefine the messianic
concept, and if the disciples had not perceived this then, as Chrysostom
perceives, they would undoubtedly proclaim what Jesus was *not*:

> Peter had learned that Christ is the Son of God. But he had *not* learned of
> the mystery of the cross and the resurrection. It was as yet not manifested
> to him. It remained *hidden*. Do you see how correct Jesus was in forbid-
> ding them not to declare His identity publicly? For if it so confounded the
> disciples, who were being made aware of it, who knows what the response
> of others might have been.[33]

It could even be said that the command to silence functions more as
an indicator of a messianic misconception and misunderstanding than as
a messianic secret.[34] The content of the messianic secret was the mystery
of Jesus as the Messiah. The reason it was a secret was to prevent its
misunderstanding until Jesus had redefined and transformed the messianic
concept by infinitely deepening it with His suffering.

Nevertheless, after this incident at Caesarea Philippi the disciples
were initiated into this secret, at least on some level. With the declaration
of Peter they became aware of the messiahship of Jesus, but were left
grappling with how such a Messiah could suffer. The significance being
that now the disciples were aware of the messiahship of Jesus *whereas* the
crowds were not. In the words of Ulrich Luz: "the secret remains a secret.

---

[31] Irving M. Zeitlin, *Jesus and the Judaism of His Time*, 118; Also see John Chrysostom,
The Gospel of Matthew, Homily 54.1, PG 58:533; NPNF 1 10:332.

[32] D. J. Hawkin, "The Incomprehension of the Disciples in the Markan Redaction," *JBL*
91 (1972), 499.

[33] John Chrysostom, *The Gospel of Matthew*, Homily 54.5-6, PG 58:536; NPNF 1 10:335.

[34] James D. G. Dunn, *Jesus Remembered*, 649.

But after Caesarea Philippi it is one secret for the disciples and *another* for the rest."[35]

This becomes evident on observing that the Gospel of Mark may in some manner be seen as two parts: that which precedes this incident (Mark 8:30), and that which follows it. The transition point being the revelation that Jesus was the Messiah (as poorly understood as this was by the disciples). After this point the disciples were initiated into *more explicit teaching*. Jesus reveals to them His passion predictions, the transfiguration, the key to exorcisms, and the meaning of rank.[36] Fascinatingly after this point we also observe that the *reactions of the disciples* and the crowds begin to diverge. Both groups before were previously "astonished beyond measure" on hearing the words of Jesus and witnessing His deeds.[37] After the declaration of Peter at Caesarea Philippi, however, though the crowds were still amazed at the actions of Jesus,[38] the reaction of the disciples turns to that of fear.[39] Even the *comprehension of the disciples* begins to change after this point. Previously they lacked understanding of the parables, were unable to comprehend the feeding miracles, and misunderstood the saying on defilement.[40] But now after being initiated into the secret, the focus shines upon the disciples' lack of Christological understanding.[41] Their deficiency of understanding no longer is concerned with food or parables, but now is turned towards the passion, the suffering of the Son of Man, and the resurrection.[42]

And, ultimately, after this key point there is a fundamental shift in those commanded to silence. Before this transition point in the Gospel of Mark the command to silence was only directed to two groups: the healed and the demons. As we have seen, those healed were not to reveal the *miracle secret* which did not directly concern itself with the knowledge of Jesus as the messianic Son of God. But it was the demons that were charged not to reveal the *messianic secret*, not men. This supernatural demonic knowledge stands in amazing contrast to the ignorance of men.[43] Strangely after Caesarea Philippi, Mark pointedly makes no further references to the supernatural

---

[35] Ulrich Luz, "The Secrecy Motif and the Marcan Christology," 83. Also see T. A. Burkill, *Mysterious Revelation: An Examination of the Philosophy of St. Mark's Gospel* (New York: Cornell University Press, 1963), 67.

[36] Respectively Mark 8:31-33, 9:30-32, 10:32-34; Mark 9:1-13; Mark 9:28-29; and Mark 10:35-45.

[37] Mark 1:27, 5:20, 5:42, 6:51, 7:37.

[38] Mark 9:15, 10:32, 11:18, 12:17.

[39] Mark 9:6, 9:32, 10:32. Mark 10:24 is a special reaction to Jesus' proclamation.

[40] Respectively Mark 4:13; Mark 6:52; and Mark 7:18.

[41] Ulrich Luz, "The Secrecy Motif and the Marcan Christology," 85.

[42] Respectively Mark 8:32; Mark 9:32; and Mark 9:10.

[43] T. A. Burkill, *Mysterious Revelation*, 62.

declaration of the demons. Those charged with the secret were now the disciples and not the demons:

> Now after six days Jesus took Peter, James, and John, and led them up on a high mountain apart by themselves; and He was *transfigured* before them... And Elijah appeared to them with Moses, and they were talking with Jesus... And a cloud came and overshadowed them; and a voice came out of the cloud, saying, "This is My beloved Son. Hear Him!"[44]

This "transfiguration" coupled with the words of the Father, "This is My beloved Son," was a revelation of the divine sonship of Jesus and thus fits into the same category of Peter's declaration and the silencing of the demons. As they came down from the mountain, Jesus took Peter, James, and John, and "commanded them that they should tell no one the things they had seen."[45] Once more the revelation of the nature of Jesus is strictly commanded to be kept secret. This time, however, that is not the end of the story. Jesus adds that these things should be kept secret *"till the Son of Man had risen from the dead."*[46]

The gravity of the last part of His statement cannot be emphasized enough. It reveals that the secret is not to be kept *indefinitely*. And more significantly, the "messianic secret" is to be revealed *through* the cross and resurrection. Whereas beforehand the command to silence was indefinite and seemingly without clear purpose, Jesus now speaks with forceful clarity. The content of the secret, Jesus' divine sonship, was to be kept concealed for one reason and one reason alone: His nature may only be grasped through the light of the cross.[47]

If the disciples misunderstood the true nature of the Messiah at Caesarea Philippi, and if they were confused as to "what the rising from the dead meant" at the transfiguration, then clearly the content of the secret was beyond humanity "until the whole plan of the dispensation"[48] had been fulfilled. Had it previously been revealed to the multitudes surely they would have been made to stumble repeatedly as the disciples had and, as Chrysostom notes, "who knows what the response of others might have been."[49] Only after His death and resurrection would (and could) the secret

---

[44] Mark 9:2-13.
[45] Mark 9:9.
[46] Mark 9:9.
[47] Also see Peter M. Head, *Christology and the Synoptic Problem*, 246.
[48] Cyril of Alexandria, *Commentary on Luke* 49, CGSL 221.
[49] John Chrysostom, *The Gospel of Matthew*, Homily 54.5-6, PG 58:536; NPNF 1 10:335.

be revealed. The Golden-Mouthed Chrysostom once more insists that the secret serves to protect the "right" nature of Jesus:

> And why did He charge them [with silence]? That when the things which offend are taken out of the way, the *cross* is accomplished and the rest of His *sufferings* fulfilled, and when there is nothing any more to interrupt and disturb the faith of the people in Him, the right opinion concerning Him may be *engraven* pure and immovable in the mind of the hearers.[50]

The Hidden & Suffering Son of Man

Having seen the nature of the secret in regards to the silencing of the healed, demons, and disciples, we may now press further. There are perhaps two trails that will lead us to the depths of this enigmatic secret. Both unsurprisingly are closely related. The first is the *realignment of the messianic concept* with the suffering Son of Man; the second is the *hidden nature* of the Messiah.

That Jesus did not subscribe to the messianic perceptions of the crowds (or of His disciples for that matter) seems to be certain. But how then did He envision His messiahship? At Caesarea Philippi immediately following Peter's declaration, Jesus began to teach the disciples that the "Son of Man must suffer." He thus takes from Peter a messianic perception and realigns it with the suffering Son of Man. What is of interest is that *very* same thing transpires during the trial of Jesus before the high priest. Jesus is asked: "I put You under oath by the Living God: Tell us if you are the Messiah...."[51] And He replies: "It is as you said.[52] Nevertheless, I say to you, hereafter you will see the Son of Man sitting at the right hand of the Power."[53] Once more Jesus realigns the messianic concept with the Son of Man. In other words, the messianic secret does not serve to hide a truth; it *protects* the truth of the nature of Jesus by not giving into the popular expectations that would render it false.

To be clear, it need be said that it was not that Jesus did not see Himself as the Messiah, but rather that He wished to correct the popular misconceptions and political overtones that were so intensely tied to the title.[54] This deep-seated discrepancy between His messianic conception and

---

[50] John Chrysostom, *The Gospel of Matthew*, Homily 54.4, PG 58:535; NPNF 1 10:334.

[51] Matt 26:63.

[52] We should note that this is not a "Yes, I am." Rather it may be given as "Whatever you say..." or "You might say that."

[53] Matt 26:64.

[54] See Christopher Tuckett, "The Problem of the Messianic Secret," in *The Messianic*

that of His followers meant that He would be forced to resort to commands of silence to avoid fueling such precarious speculation. In the end, as Albert Schweitzer so aptly concludes, "His struggle with the messianic conception could not but end in *transforming* it."[55] And till this transformation took place (when the Messiah was understood as the suffering Son of Man), the messianic secret would by necessity guard its treasure.

This brings us to the second trail into the secret. At the time of Jesus there was an intriguing Jewish belief that the Messiah was to be *hidden* and not recognized for a certain period of time. In a work of an early Church Father, the Jew Trypho comments on the hidden nature of the Messiah:

> But Messiah—if He has indeed been born, and exists anywhere—is *unknown*, and does not even know Himself, and has no power until Elijah comes to anoint Him, and make Him manifest to all.[56]

The Messiah is not manifest until He is anointed by Elijah. Justin the Martyr later responds to Trypho in the same vein: "Now I am aware that your teachers...assert that it is *not* known who He is; but when He shall become manifest and glorious, then it shall be known who He is."[57] The same is seen in the book of Enoch which reflects thought contemporary with Jesus: "And for this reason has He been chosen and *hidden* before Him, before the creation of the world and for evermore,"[58] and again: "For from the beginning the Son of Man was *hidden*, and the Most High preserved Him in the presence of His might, and revealed Him to the elect."[59] In the later work of Fourth Ezra, the Son of Man is "He whom the Most High has been *keeping* [or concealing] for many ages."[60] Indeed, the idea of the hidden Messiah even surfaces in the Gospel of John, when the fact that Jesus is "known" seemingly disproves the possibility that He is the Messiah: "we know where this Man is from; but when the Messiah comes, *no one*

Secret, 9; James D. G. Dunn, "The Messianic Secret in Mark," 128; Ben F. Meyer, *The Aims of Jesus*, 309 n. 119; T. W. Manson, "Realized Eschatology and the Messianic Secret," 216; Vesilin Kesich, *The Gospel Image of Christ*, 162.

[55] Albert Schweitzer. *The Quest of the Historical Jesus*, tr. W. Montgomery (London: SCM Press, 2000), 210.

[56] Justin the Martyr, *Dialogue with Trypho* 8, ANF 1:199.

[57] Justin the Martyr, *Dialogue with Trypho* 110, ANF 1:253.

[58] *1 Enoch* 48:6. Chapters 37-71 have been dated as before 70 AD. In these particular chapters, Son of Man is equivalent with Messiah, Chosen One, and Righteous One.

[59] *1 Enoch* 62:7.

[60] *4 Ezra* 13:25-26; 14:9. This work is commonly dated to 100 AD. Once more the Messiah is identified with Son of Man in this particular work.

knows where He is from."[61] In the rabbinic literature this concept of a hidden Messiah comes radically to the present. The Messiah is said to have already been born but lives *unknown* in an *unknown* place on the earth until He assumes His messianic office at the end of the ages.[62]

Though many of these works were after the time of Jesus, they reflect earlier Judaic thought. And in any case, such conceptions are testified to in the Gospel of John as well as in the book of Enoch which may itself in fact predate the Gospels. We may then conclude that a belief was held by at least some of Jesus' fellow Jews that the Messiah would be hidden *until* He was made manifest in glory. The parallels with the sayings of Jesus that the disciples were to maintain silence about His messianic secret until His death and resurrection are strikingly obvious. Jesus had to remain hidden until His revelation on and through the cross.

In sum, the *miracles secret* though perhaps in some ways related to the messianic secret, differed in that it indicated the power of Jesus that cannot and may not remain hidden. Miracles were to be concealed for various reasons, at times for the safety of the healed, and at others for the sake of Jesus' own movement and mission. The *messianic secret* on the other hand sought to protect the *true* nature of Jesus so that He might only be understood through the ultimate and definitive revelation of the Messiah crucified and glorified.[63] To attempt to understand His nature on any other terms was to place oneself with Satan, as Peter discovered in dramatic fashion. It is for this very reason that the demons were commanded to silence. The demonic and all else (demon or disciple) who sought no part in the cross and resurrection could not confess the mysterious nature of Jesus. The Messiah had to be *hidden* until the crucifixion lest His messiahship cause "*untaught* minds to stumble"[64] upon the offense of the cross. Till the disciples understood Jesus as such and followed Him even to His death, they would not be *truly* His disciples nor would they live in His secret. The same may be said of our present age:

> It is and remains a secret until after the crucifixion and resurrection, simply because no secret is ever so well kept as that which no one is *willing* to discover.[65]

---

[61] John 7:27.

[62] *Babylonian Talmud Sanhedrin* 98a; *Midrash Rabbah* on Exodus 1:31; where the Messiah is thought to be dwelling unknown in Rome. Documents found at Qumran also reflect this view, see *1QSam* ii:II.

[63] John P. Meier, *A Marginal Jew*, Vol. II, 652; Also see Eduard Schweizer, "The Question of the Messianic Secret in Mark," in *The Messianic Secret*, 70.

[64] Jerome, *Commentary on Matthew* 3.17.9, CCL 77:150.

[65] T. W. Manson, "Realized Eschatology and the Messianic Secret," 220.

CHAPTER ELEVEN

'The Kingdom of Heaven suffers violence'

This alone is commendable violence,
To force God, and take life from God by force.
—SAINT CLEMENT OF ALEXANDRIA

I REMEMBER SITTING IN MY ROOM ONE NIGHT attempting to read the Bible. I was twelve and had just been convinced that it was time that I should begin to read the grown-ups Bible. I was told as a matter of course that I was ready, that it would make sense, and that it would be "beneficial." Unfortunately in this summons to biblical manhood, no one had thought to mention that it would be wise to start at the beginning and read through consecutively. Thus I picked up the large Book in my small fingers and did as too many do. I made the sign of the cross, placed my finger towards the end, and picked a page at *random*—the easiest and silliest way to go about the matter. I looked at the page in fear tinged with excitement and was not quite sure what to expect. The words were as follows:

> And from the days of John the Baptist until now the kingdom of heaven suffers *violence*, and the violent take it by *force*.[1]

[1] Matt 11:11-12.

Needless to say, it was some months later before I bothered to open the grown-ups Bible again. The disconcerting thing is that this saying of Jesus remains just as enigmatic in my mind as it was when I was a child. Now I may have a little more appreciation of its context (the saving-grace of reading the Scriptures from beginning to end), and of some possible interpretations, but nevertheless the enigmatic questions remain. The problem is not only mine; scholars of the caliber of John P. Meier have judged the saying as "not easily understood,"[2] others considering that the "problems of this verse are legion."[3] Another, P. S. Cameron, who devoted himself to the study of the interpretation of this saying from the time of the early Church Fathers to the modern day, declared that after two thousand years "the exegetical comedy continues."[4]

In this vein I confess that I can see no clear single solution to the saying. But I can see *two*. Both are convincing; both are logical and historical. One finds unanimous support among the Church Fathers, the other finds its foundation elsewhere. Yet both, though entirely dissimilar, are convincing.

CONFUSED THOUGHTS ON AN ENIGMATIC SAYING

The problems of this saying are of course obvious. The kingdom of heaven is said to "suffer violence." To begin, how can the kingdom "suffer," and all the more "violence"? In what manner is the power of God afflicted with violence? And if that was not sufficiently complex, we hear that the "violent" take the kingdom by "force." Who are the violent and on what grounds, and indeed how, can they take that which is of God by force?

As hinted we need to frame the saying in its context. In Matthew the saying is preceded by a message sent from the *imprisoned* John the Baptist to Jesus: "Are You the Coming One, or do we look for another?"[5] Jesus answers ambiguously, choosing instead to teach the "multitudes concerning John." It is *within* this teaching that we find our enigmatic saying of "violence."

---

[2] John P. Meier, *A Marginal Jew*, Vol. II, 157. For a list of possible meanings see W. D. Davies and Dale C. Allison, *The Gospel According to Saint Matthew* Vol. II (Edinburgh: T & T Clark, 1991), 254-255. For a study of possible underlying Aramaic meanings as well as rabbinic parallels see David Daube, *The New Testament and Rabbinic Judaism*, 285-300. Also see Frederick W. Danker, "Luke 16:16: An Opposition Logion," *JBL* 77, 3 (1958): 231-243.

[3] Christopher Tuckett, *Q and the History of Early Christianity* (Edinburgh: T & T Clark, 1996), 135.

[4] P. S. Cameron, *Violence and the Kingdom: The Interpretation of Matthew 11:12* (Bern: Peter Lang, 1988), 169.

[5] Matt 11:2

And immediately following the saying we hear of the *rejection* of Jesus and John by this "generation": "John came neither eating nor drinking, and they say, 'He has a demon.' The Son of Man came eating and drinking, and they say, 'Look, a glutton and a winebibber, a friend of tax collectors and sinners!'"[6] Thus, we find that the saying is wedged between the imprisonment of John and the rejection of both Jesus and John, a finding that is crucial to the understanding of this saying.

But before we can even consider this question of meaning, we must first consider the kingdom itself. It is no good discussing the "violence" if we remain ignorant of the *subject* of the violence. Although a fuller discussion will be made in the following chapter, a few words may suffice. In simple terms the kingdom is the reign of God over man, in which the power and authority of God are manifest. Of interest is the fact that in the ministry of Jesus this power becomes palpable for Israel. It may be concretely experienced. And thus we hear that some "enter into" and are "within" the kingdom, whilst others are "outside." That is to say, even in the days of Jesus some were able to live in the kingdom under the rule of God. Should we consider the saying at hand another truth emerges. For the kingdom to "suffer violence" it must be within the reach of Israel and as such it must be *present* in some manner. For, properly speaking, only that which is present may be said to suffer.

Armed with its context and its subject (the kingdom) we may now approach the saying itself:

> And from the days of John the Baptist until now the kingdom of heaven suffers violence [*biazetai*], and the violent [*biastai*] take it by force [*harpazousin*]. For all the prophets and the law prophesied until John.[7]

The problem of this saying lies in these three phrases, "suffers violence," "the violent," and "by force."[8] Respectively these are translations from the

---

[6] Matt 11:18-19.

[7] Matt 11:11-13. The saying is also found in Luke 16:16, albeit in a different context. Also we should note that Matthew has it as "kingdom of heaven" whilst Luke has it as "kingdom of God." These two phrases are equivalent and interchangeable as will be shown in the following chapter. For a further discussion of the relation of the Lukan version to the Matthean, see Stephen Llewelyn, "The Traditionsgeschichte of Matt. 11:12-13, Par. Luke 16:16," *Novum Testamentum* 36, 4 (1994): 330-349.

[8] The Greek itself is ambiguous; therefore scholars such as David Daube and Gustaf Dalman have looked to Aramaic in the hope of answers. They offered the Aramaic *peras* as a possibility for the original word that Jesus used for "suffers violence." This particular Aramaic word gives connotations of "breaking with violence" and thus the "kingdom of God breaks out with violence into the world." We should, however, remember that if the translation to Greek from Aramaic was troublesome, why would going in reverse twenty centuries later be less problematic? In any case this meaning is suggested by the middle voice of the Greek and thus

Greek *biazetai, biastai,* and *harpazousin.* These words are the keys to the saying, and their ambiguity is almost solely responsible for its confusion. Thus we shall have to consider the Greek as painful as this may be. But if we proceed slowly, the benefit will far outweigh the detriment.

We begin with *biazetai.* In Greek this verb may be taken in *two* ways. (1) It may be understood in the *passive voice.* If a verb is taken in the passive voice then its subject is "acted upon" or "receives the action" expressed by the verb. For example, if we say "Jimmy will be baptized," then the subject (Jimmy) receives the action (baptism). In like manner, if we take the verb *biazetai* (suffers violence) then the subject (the kingdom) receives the action (violence). And so in the passive voice the kingdom is said to be "violently attacked." (2) Another way of reading this verb is in the *middle voice.* If taken in the middle voice then the subject "performs" or "experiences" the action with the emphasis being upon the subject's participation. Let us take our example of Jimmy once more. If this time we say "Jimmy, have yourself baptized," then the subject (Jimmy) willingly participates in the action (baptism). In this manner *biazetai,* read in the middle voice, would give the meaning of the "kingdom is exercising force" in which the subject (the kingdom) performs and participates in the action (violent force).

To reiterate, depending on which voice we read the verb *biazetai,* the meaning of the verse may either be that the kingdom is *violently attacked,* or that the kingdom is *exercising force.* The NKJV follows the passive voice and thus translates it as: "the kingdom of heaven suffers violence." The NIV on the other hand follows the middle voice and gives it as: "the kingdom of heaven has been forcefully advancing." This distinction has not been seen without purpose. In fact it has produced every possible interpretation of the saying known to biblical scholarship.

Now to the "violent" (*biastai*) who take the kingdom "by force" (*harpazousin*). The subject is clearly the kingdom. Therefore some who are called the violent have been taking the kingdom by force. The meaning of the "violent" thus depends upon their action "taking by force." This action, *harpazousin,* may mean "to plunder." This entails a negative image where one takes something that is not rightfully theirs. But this is not always the case. When Jesus defends His authority to exorcise demons He asks the Pharisees: "How can one enter a strong man's house and plunder [*harpasai*]

---

this is where we begin. See Gustaf Dalman, *The Words of Jesus,* 140-143; *Jesus-Jeshua: Studies in the Gospels* (New York: Macmillan, 1929); and David Daube, *The New Testament and Rabbinic Judaism,* 284-294.

his goods unless he first binds the strong man?"[9] In this case to take "by force" denotes a *righteous action*!

And so finally, if we consider that "suffers violence" (*biazetai*) may be taken in the middle or passive voice, and add to this the meaning of taking "by force" as being negative or positive, then a number of feasible templates of interpretation of the saying become possible:

> In the *passive voice*:
> (1) The kingdom suffers violence as it is attacked by evil and violent men who seek to plunder it.
> (2)The kingdom suffers violence as righteous men seek to plunder its goods violently, i.e. its fruits of salvation.

> In the *middle voice*:
> (3) The kingdom exercises force and is made known, and thus now that it is made known it is attacked by evil men who are against the kingdom.
> (4) The kingdom exercises force and is made known, and thus now righteous men seek to seize it and enter it.

Of course there are other possible interpretations, but all generally follow the same pattern in that either the "kingdom is made known" or that it "suffers violence," and that the act of taking it by force is either negative or positive. Some have taken these two facts and created theories that are better left in works of fiction than in biblical study.[10] That withstanding, should we consider the above four templates of interpretation, two credible interpretations emerge. (1) and (3) are effectively saying the same thing in that the kingdom (whether it suffers or is made known) is being violently attacked by *those who are against it*. (2) and (4), on the other hand, indicate that the kingdom (whether it suffers or is made known) is attacked by the *righteous who seek to enter it*—this sense is also given by Luke's version of the saying where "everyone is *pressing* into it."[11]

These two possibilities of interpretation stand as our suggested solutions to this enigmatic saying.

---

[9] Matt 12:29.

[10] For a survey of the possible options in interpretation see W. D. Davies and Dale C. Allison, *The Gospel According to Saint Matthew*, Vol. II, 254-255.

[11] Luke 16:16: The saying is found in different context to that of Matthew, in the context of a teaching on the law.

First Possibility: The Suffering Kingdom

We begin with the first possibility in which the kingdom suffers violence from those who are against it. In a previous chapter we discovered that the end of days was understood in early Judaic thought to consist of tribulation. As part of this tribulation a predominant theme (if not characterization) was violence. As we have seen, a household would turn upon itself, the sword would be wielded by one generation against another, and nation would war with nation.[12] It needs to be stressed that this link between the final days and violence is paramount in understanding the present saying.

It is not only that at the end of days violence would increase, it prevails: "And unrighteousness shall again be consummated on the earth, and all the deeds of unrighteousness and of violence... And violence in all kinds of deeds increase."[13] But this violence is not an end in itself—it is directed with purpose. Brant Pitre, a Catholic scholar, brings to light two fascinating passages from the *Dead Sea Scrolls* in which the end of days sees the persecution of the righteous *by* the "violent."[14] We hear of the "*violent* ones of the covenant who are in the House of Judah, who plot to destroy those who observe the *law*..."[15] Elsewhere the plight of the righteous is made explicit: "the *violent* men have sought my soul when I relied on your covenant."[16] In the book of Jubilees this violence borders upon graphic:

> And in that generation the sons will *convict* their fathers and their elders of sin and unrighteousness... And they will strive one *with* another, the young with the old, and the old with the young...*on account of the law* and the covenant... And they will stand with bows and *swords* and war to turn them back into the way; but they will not return until much blood has been shed on the earth, one by another.[17]

The parallel is not difficult to draw. The kingdom of God is breaking through into the world and the righteous are afflicted by the "violent ones." The time before the new age—the age where God would reign—was to

---

[12] See the earlier chapter "I did not come to bring peace but a sword." Specifically, also see *1 Enoch 90*, *4 Ezra 9:3*, *2 Baruch 27:4*.

[13] *1 Enoch 91:6-7*. Also see *1 Enoch 91:11, 103:15*.

[14] Brant Pitre, *Jesus, the Tribulation, and the End of the Exile* (Grand Rapids: Baker Academic, 2005), 168-169.

[15] *4QPsalmsPesher 2:14-15*.

[16] *1QHodayot 10:20-22*.

[17] *Jubilees 23:16-20*.

be marked with violence against the righteous of the kingdom. And if the kingdom was in a certain sense *already* here, then the violence against the kingdom of God would be directed at none other than its chief proponents: Jesus and John.[18]

Here we should note the strength of this reading of the saying. Other interpretations (whatever their flavor) fall down when faced with the clause that immediately follows the saying: "For all the prophets and the law prophesied until John."[19] In contrast, this interpretation of eschatological violence, perhaps singularly, does not shy away. And thus we must ask: Why do the law and the prophets last only *until* John? Within the Jewish literature we find that the end of days is not only characterized by violence, it is also marked by *lawlessness* and *false prophecy*. In the Lamentations of Jeremiah we hear of this period of cessation:

> The Law is *no* more,
> And her prophets find *no* vision from the Lord.[20]

Similarly in Ezekiel: "they will *seek* a vision from a prophet; but the law will *perish* from the priest,"[21] and in Zephaniah: "Her prophets are insolent, treacherous people...they have done *violence* to the law."[22] In the wake of such passages the apocalyptic writings also describe the lawlessness and false prophecy to come.[23] In the rabbinic work of the *Mishnah Sotah*, the cessation of prophecy and the law are not only placed in the context of the tribulation, but intriguingly are also placed "with the footprints of the Messiah."[24] Consequently in pointing to the cessation of the law and the prophets, Jesus was essentially claiming in a highly Judaic and scriptural way that "with the death of John, the period of eschatological 'lawlessness' has set in."[25] Jesus may then be understood as such: With John we have passed into the end-time tribulation of lawlessness and false prophecy in which the

---

[18] Dale C. Allison, *The End of the Ages has Come: An Early Interpretation of the Passion and Resurrection of Jesus* (Philadelphia: Fortress Press, 1985), 123.

[19] Matt 11:13. We should not think that this saying implies a radical end to the law. In the version of the saying found in Luke the law is safeguarded immediately afterwards: "And it is easier for heaven and earth to pass away than for one tittle of the law to fail" (Luke 16:17). Rather, the cessation of the law is a marker of tribulation not abrogation.

[20] Lam 2:9. Also see Jer 13:11-22 and Ezek 13:1-7.

[21] Ezek 7:25-26.

[22] Zeph 3:4.

[23] *1 Enoch* 93:9-11; *Jubilees* 23:19, 21; *Psalms of Solomon* 17:11-18.

[24] *Mishnah Sotah* 9:15.

[25] Brant Pitre, *Jesus, the Tribulation, and the End of the Exile*, 171-172. Also see Norman Perrin, *The Kingdom of God in the Teaching of Jesus* (London: SCM Press, 1963), 174.

violent ones persecute the kingdom and its persons. Indeed, Jesus Himself had spoken in clarity of these days:

> Many will say to Me in that day, "Lord, Lord, have we not *prophesied* in Your name, cast out demons in Your name, and done many wonders in Your name?" And then I will declare to them, "I never knew you; depart from Me, you who practice *lawlessness!*"[26]

Should we consider the context of the saying, this interpretation would begin to strengthen. At the time of the saying John was *imprisoned* and had sent a message to Jesus. It was this discussion about John that led to the saying itself. More so, the saying actually comes *within the teaching about John*. And immediately after the saying, Jesus talks of both His *rejection* as well as that of John. Taken in this manner the saying is padded before and after with rejection and imprisonment. Should we cast our minds further along in history we would find that John was decapitated and Jesus was crucified.

Given, therefore, the place of the saying within this chapter of Matthew, along with its apparent context in Jewish apocalyptic thought, one may easily render this interpretation a real possibility. The kingdom was suffering violence through the two who had proclaimed it.[27] John and Jesus had both preached the kingdom, and both suffered on its account. John was imprisoned, and Jesus envisioned nothing less than a *violent* death. Those who stood at the forefront in ushering in the kingdom were now suffering, and thus their suffering was part of the inauguration of the kingdom. This strongly brings to mind the words of Jesus in the Beatitudes: "Blessed are those who are persecuted for righteousness' sake, for theirs *is* the kingdom of heaven."[28] This is also consistent with the suffering Son of Man revealed in the "messianic secret." If the righteous were to suffer on account of the law, and if this violence was necessary for the inauguration of the kingdom, then the Son of Man could only be understood *as* suffering. The kingdom would be afflicted through its Champion.

To conclude, this saying may be understood as revealing the kingdom which *suffers* through those who are ushering it in. This was a marker of the end-time tribulation that would see a period of lawlessness and false prophecy. It follows that the "violent men" are those who have chosen to oppose the kingdom, and are "taking it by force" by persecuting the

---

[26] Matt 7:22-23.
[27] See G. R. Beasley-Murray, *Jesus and the Kingdom of God* (Grand Rapids: Wm. B. Eerdmans, 1986), 94.
[28] Matt 5:10.

righteous. To this we must add that in all probability this saying was spoken in reflection of the impending fate of *both* Jesus and John as a "manifestation of that conflict,"[29] and thus it at once deepens the suffering dimension of the Son of Man.

But who was responsible for this affliction? Who were the violent? Were they the evil forces in general? Perhaps Satan? Others have suggested the Romans or possibly even the Zealots. P. S. Cameron, after surveying the history of this enigmatic saying's interpretation, surmised that all the evidence points to the suffering of John specifically, making it probable that the violent included Herod Antipas (who executed John).[30] It is quite clear, nonetheless, that the saying if meant in this way referred to the suffering of *both* Jesus and John, since both had played a part in ushering in the kingdom. As to the violent ones, all who stood against the kingdom were implicated, be they demons or men.

This interpretation is, however, not without problems. For one, if Jesus had meant that the kingdom was suffering through its persons, why did He not say so? Secondly, we have in part ignored an important observation: On what account may the kingdom *of* God be attacked? We sometimes, in ignorance, envision a world in which Satan is on equal footing with God, in which both are in a constant wrestle for humanity. In reality this could not be further from the truth. Satan has no power in and of himself, and stands as a microbial parasite next to the universe (even then, this would not be a fair comparison). In reality, it is the kingdom of God which is on the offensive:

> …it is the kingdom of God which attacks the kingdom of Satan. Whenever Jesus speaks of the conflict with Satan and his demons, it is always in terms of their defeat… It is contrary to this basic motif to think of the kingdom itself, whether in its eschatological appearing or as an invasion into this age, as actually experiencing violence at the hands of evil spirits.[31]

Put in slightly different terms, within the agenda of Jesus' preaching and mission, there is little room for the practicing of violence against God or His kingdom.[32] That said, the interpretation is not necessarily dismissed.

---

[29] Norman Perrin, *Jesus and the Language of the Kingdom* (Philadelphia: Fortress Press, 1976), 46. Also see Perrin's other work, *Rediscovering the Teaching of Jesus*, 74-77.

[30] P. S. Cameron, *Violence and the Kingdom*, 154.

[31] George E. Ladd, *The Presence of the Future: The Eschatology of Biblical Realism* (Grand Rapids: Wm. B. Eerdmans, 1974), 161.

[32] See W. G. Kümmel, *Promise and Fulfillment: The Eschatological Message of Jesus* (London: SCM Press, 1957), 123.

Just because Jesus did not specifically mention the "kingdom suffering through its persons," does not deny its possibility. As to the second objection, Jesus though always dominant over evil, became a man so that He might *suffer* for men. His suffering does not denote the victory of Satan, but rather the humiliation of evil and the resurrection of good! Nevertheless another equally viable interpretation of this difficult saying presents itself.

SECOND POSSIBILITY: THE VIOLENCE OF REPENTANCE

Earlier we saw that taking "by force" is not always to be understood negatively. In the parable of Jesus, by binding the "strong man" (Satan), the "stronger man" (Jesus) was able to "take by force" the souls of the righteous that were once in the captivity of Satan. If this action, *harpazousin*, may be righteous then the violent men, *biastai*, may also be righteous. This introduces us into the second of the possible interpretations. To consider this we must first examine the relation of John to Elijah:

> And from the days of John the Baptist until now the kingdom of heaven suffers violence, and the violent take it by force. For all the prophets and the law prophesied until John. And if you are willing to receive it, *he is Elijah* who is to come.[33]

This part of the saying that identifies John with "Elijah who is to come" is laden with meaning. The prophet Elijah, though already dead eight hundred years before Jesus, was in many biblical and extra-biblical texts foretold to return.[34] This expectation is found in the Wisdom of Ben Sira[35] as well as in the book of Malachi: "Behold I will send you Elijah the prophet before the

---

[33] Matt 1:12-14. Scholars have often made great discussion about the "timing," whether John was on the side with the law, or with Jesus and the kingdom; whether he was pivotal or transitional; inclusive or exclusive. To me, this is to miss the point of the pericope: John serves to *divide* Israel's history into two. For a discussion of the role of John in the saying see D. A. Carson, "Do the Prophets and the Law Quit Prophesying before John?" in *The Gospels and the Scriptures of Israel*, ed. Craig A. Evans and W. Richard Stegnar (Sheffield: Sheffield Academic Press, 1994), 179-194; Also see Joachim Jeremias, *New Testament Theology: The Proclamation of Jesus* (London: SCM Press, 1971), 46-47; W. D. Davies and Dale C. Allison, *The Gospel According to Saint Matthew*, Vol. II, 253; Joan E. Taylor, *The Immerser: John the Baptist within Second Temple Judaism* (Grand Rapids: Wm. B. Eerdmans, 1997), 313; John of Damascus, *An Exact Exposition of the Orthodox Faith* 4.15, NPNF 2 9:88.

[34] See Joseph Klausner, *The Messianic Idea in Israel*, 451-457, for an analysis of the concept of the return of Elijah, and his role in the messianic age. Also see Deut 19:19.

[35] *Sirach* 48:10-11.

coming of the great and dreadful day of the Lord."[36] In the Gospel of Mark the disciples confirm this expectation: "Why do the scribes say that Elijah must come first?"[37] The *Talmud* also adds that Elijah will return to cleanse the tribes of Israel,[38] and bears a "flask of oil for anointing" the Messiah.[39] The Jew Trypho echoes such sentiments to Justin the Martyr:

> But Messiah—if He has indeed been born, and exists anywhere—is unknown, and does not even know Himself, and has no power until *Elijah* comes to anoint Him, and make Him manifest to all…[40]

This expectation begins to lean upon the interpretation of the "violence saying" when we appreciate the role of Elijah in anointing Jesus. When the imprisoned John sends word to Jesus, he asks: "Are you the Coming One, or do we look for another?"[41] Jesus evades, instead declaring: "If you are willing to receive it, *he is Elijah who is to come*."[42] Elijah was envisioned as coming at the end of times to anoint the Messiah who would remain *hidden* until such a day. But if John had "anointed" Jesus by baptizing Him in the Jordan, and if John was in some sense "Elijah," then who was Jesus? Albert Schweitzer continues: "Jesus unveiled to them almost the whole mystery of the kingdom of God… As two great prophets were not foreseen for the days before the end-time, there could be only *one* answer…"[43] Jesus was the hidden Messiah, and John had come in the "spirit and power of Elijah"[44] to anoint Him. John was not only proclaiming the kingdom, He was anointing and thus manifesting the King Himself. N. T. Wright has rightly observed that "Jesus leaves His hearers no choice. Either He is an imposter, or He is indeed inaugurating the kingdom."[45]

It is from here and from here alone, that we may consider words uttered centuries earlier by Micah in a prophecy of the restoration of Israel:

---

[36] Mal 4:5.
[37] Mark 9:11.
[38] *Mishnah Eduyyot* 8:7.
[39] *Babylonian Talmud Keritot* 5ab.
[40] Justin the Martyr, *Dialogue with Trypho* 8, ANF 1:199.
[41] Matt 11:3.
[42] Matt 11:14.
[43] Albert Schweitzer, *The Quest of the Historical Jesus*, 337.
[44] Luke 1:17.
[45] N. T. Wright, *Jesus and the Victory of God*, 468. Also see R. Steven Notley, "The Kingdom of Heaven Forcefully Advances," in *The Interpretation of Scripture in Early Judaism and Christianity*, ed. Craig A. Evans (Sheffield: Sheffield Academic Press, 2000), 311.

The one who *breaks open* will come up before them;
They will *break out*,
Pass through the gate,
And go out by it;
Their *king* will pass before them,
With the Lord at their head.[46]

This prophecy draws forth from the image of a travelling shepherd. When a shepherd began to tire and sought to sleep, he would erect a makeshift fence of stones and wood, and at times would choose to block the gate with his own sleeping body. In the early morning the sheep would begin to grow agitated. One among them would then charge at the makeshift fence attempting to "break out" by knocking over the stones. The others, now encouraged, would likewise charge at the wall in the *same* place, thus making the hole larger and larger.

From this passage in Micah it becomes clear that the "one who breaks open," first makes an opening, and then the others who "break out" follow in his wake. Recall that the Greek word for "suffers violence," *biazetai*, if read in the middle voice can mean "to exercise force" or "to *break* forth."[47] And hence the kingdom breaks into the present forcefully. The same is to be said of the "violent men," *biastai*, who may be understood to be the "breakers." If the parallel is not yet obvious, an anonymous and ancient Midrash found in the *Pesiqta Rabbati* makes the matter explicit.[48] According to this Jewish commentary, Elijah is the "one who breaks open," the Messiah-redeemer is the "king," and the Lord is God. If we also recall that Jesus said of John the Baptist that "he is Elijah," then this passage in Micah becomes critical. For if John is in some way Elijah then he takes upon himself the role of him who "breaks open."

Seen in this light, the kingdom breaks forth violently among men. One among these men, the "one who breaks open" (John who comes in the spirit of Elijah), violently "breaks" into the kingdom. Those who "break out," the violent men, follow after him into the kingdom. To put it plainly, the kingdom has been made known violently since the beginning of John's ministry, and since then men have followed his charge in storming the kingdom. This is no unauthorized assault. Looking to the passage in Micah, the king passes before the violent men and God is at their head! But how does John "break open" the gates of the kingdom?

[46] Mic 2:13.

[47] See Brad H. Young, *Jesus the Jewish Theologian* (Massachusetts: Hendrickson Publishers, 1995), 52.

[48] *Pesiqta Rabbati* 161a.

The evangelist Luke is quick to reveal that John went into the entire region around the Jordan "preaching a baptism of *repentance* for the remission of sins."[49] The "one who breaks open," thus breaks through with *violent repentance*. If the kingdom had "suffered violence" since the days of John the Baptist, then does this not coincide with John's preaching of repentance? And if after that point the violent had taken the kingdom by force, is there not a parallel with all those who had heeded John's summons to repentance? The first sheep had stormed the gate so that others may enter: "[John] called them to follow him in acts of repentance and righteousness... Jesus' statement, therefore, 'those who break through take hold of it' is an affirmation of John's message and of those who responded in faithful obedience."[50] In this case, unlike our former interpretation, the violence is symbolic, not literal.[51] It indicated the painful degree to which one was called to enter the kingdom. The imminent presence of the kingdom demanded a radical change of mind. Men were called to pluck out their eyes for the sake of the kingdom, were called to leave their families, and to despise their possessions.[52] In short, they were called to the sword; to divide all that hindered them from the kingdom.[53]

Also it should be noted that the mere fact that John is "Elijah" places this "breaking open" in the context of the end of times when Elijah was to return, and hence aligns it with the ushering in of the kingdom.[54] That "Elijah," the "breaking," and the "kingdom," should all be included in the one saying of Jesus is extraordinarily significant and strongly parallels early Judaic thought. Jesus is revealing that the kingdom is so present and so palpable that it can be "taken by force" by those "who will take every risk and make every sacrifice in order to have their share."[55] The violence that the kingdom suffers is thus *repentance*. Indeed the key to the kingdom is repentance so violent that the gates of heaven cannot withstand its force. And it is here that the early Church Fathers stand unanimously, a rarity which testifies to the strength of this interpretation.[56]

---

[49] Luke 3:3.

[50] R. Steven Notley, "The Kingdom of Heaven Forcefully Advances," 310.

[51] B. E. Thiering, "Are the 'Violent Men' False Teachers?" *Novum Testamentum* 21, 4 (1979), 295. Though Thiering is correct in seeing this, he goes onto conclude that the saying refers to ideological attacks against the kingdom by false teachers—a conclusion I find to be unlikely.

[52] Respectively, Mark 9:43; Luke 14:26; Mark 10:21.

[53] Matt 10:34.

[54] R. Steven Notley, "The Kingdom of Heaven Forcefully Advances," 281.

[55] T. W. Manson, *The Sayings of Jesus*, 134. Also see Gerd Theissen and Annette Merz, *The Historical Jesus: A Comprehensive Guide* (London: SCM Press, 1998), 380; James Dunn, *Jesus Remembered*, 452.

[56] Only the early Greek and Latin Fathers will be surveyed, as the later Fathers such

The Fathers unlike scholars were not generally concerned with the meaning of the word *biazetai* (suffers violence), but rather concentrated on the *biastai* (violent men) who take the kingdom by force. And so we find that Iranaeus understood the violent to be "those who by strength and earnest striving axe on the watch to snatch it away on the moment."[57] Gregory of Nazianzus, on the other hand, whilst identifying the saying with repentance also sees within it the repentance of those sinners who were seemingly beyond salvation:

> Therefore do not delay in coming to grace, but hasten, lest the robber outstrip you, lest the adulterer pass you by, lest the insatiate be satisfied before you, lest the murderer seize the blessing first, or the publican or the fornicator, or any of these violent ones who take the kingdom of heaven by force. For it suffers violence *willingly*, and is tyrannized over through *goodness*.[58]

John Chrysostom discerns the violent to be those who approach the kingdom with "earnestness of mind," and act as thieves in scheming for the kingdom.[59] If passion or lust disturbs such an aim then he enjoins "let us do violence to our nature."[60] Here the dimension of renunciation or *asceticism* becomes apparent. The image of violence is repentance to the extent of denying the needs of the flesh. In provoking the faithful to violently seize the kingdom by doing violence to their nature, Chrysostom combines the approaches of all the Fathers who went before him. This theme of violent asceticism unto the flesh for the sake of the kingdom is taken on and intensified by John Cassian: "For not the slothful, or the careless, or the delicate, or the tender take the kingdom of heaven by force, but the violent. Who then are the violent? Surely they are those who show a splendid violence not to others, but to their *own* soul..."[61] It is only through such anguish that one may seek "to enter within the hope" of the kingdom.[62]

---

as Gregory Palamas and Simeon the New Theologian, and their Latin counterparts, seem to repeat their arguments of the earlier Fathers—which to me does not show a lack of originality but rather a sense of reverence to these ancient theologians!

[57] Iranaeus, *Against Heresies* 4.37.7, ANF 1:520.

[58] Gregory of Nazianzus, *Oration on Holy Baptism* 40.24, NPNF 2 7:368.

[59] John Chrysostom, *The Gospel of Matthew*, Homily 37.4, NPNF 1 10:245.

[60] John Chrysostom, *The Gospel of John*, Homily 54.4, NPNF 1 14:196. The same thoughts may be seen in his other homilies, see *The Second Epistle to Timothy*, Homily 9, NPNF 1 13:517.

[61] John Cassian, *Conferences* 3.24.26, NPNF 2 11:545. This concept of violence in asceticism is seen in a story of the Desert Fathers where the overcoming of the temptation to sleep is identified with taking the "kingdom by storm." See Benedicta Ward, *The Desert Fathers: Sayings of the Early Christian Monks* (London: Penguin Classics, 2003), 74-76.

[62] Cyril of Alexandria, *Commentary on Luke*, Homily 110, CGSL 448.

Whilst still strictly in the same class of interpretation Hilary of Poitiers introduces another element into the saying. The violent men—*biastai*—are those who usurp the legal rights of another. In other words the Gentiles take to themselves the rightful inheritance of the Jews: "Earlier expectations are being torn apart. The glory that was pledged to Israel by the patriarchs, which was announced by the prophets and which was offered by Christ, is now being *seized* and carried off by the Gentiles, through their faith."[63] The kingdom suffers violence by those who "illegally" take it by force from the legal heirs, the Jews. But for another early theologian, Jerome, it was not so much the manner in which men seized the kingdom as it was the sheer violent audacity of humanity in even considering entry into the kingdom at all: "Is it not truly violence, think you, when the flesh desires to be as God and ascends to the place whence angels have fallen to judge angels?"[64]

This *new* situation was marked in Augustine's estimation by the very same violence with which Jacob employed in wrestling with God: "Jacob learnt from God, who made him to *wrestle* with an Angel; under the guise of which Angel, God Himself wrestled with him…he exerted *violence* to hold Him, he prevailed to hold Him: [God] caused Himself to be held, in mercy, not in weakness."[65] It is only in this violent desire for the kingdom, and thus for God, that man may reach the kingdom. And as such, this violence and this violence alone, is that which is commendable. As in the case of Jacob this was not contrary to will of God, rather "God was at the head" of these violent men and mercifully made His kingdom vulnerable for their sakes. Far from displeasing God, Clement of Alexandria enlightens, it is in this violence that God inexplicably takes utmost pleasure:

> For this alone is commendable violence, to *force* God, and take life from God by force. And He, knowing those who persevere firmly, or rather violently, yields and grants. For God *delights* in being vanquished in such things.[66]

Put succinctly, the violent men in some way may be performing a righteous action, similar to the violent action (*harpazousin*) of Jesus in plundering the souls captive by Satan. If we couple the expectation of the return of Elijah who would anoint the Messiah, with Jesus' claim that John

---

[63] Hilary of Poitiers, *On Matthew* 11.7, SC 254:260. This was perhaps the most influential of the interpretations of the Fathers, and has been echoed time after time by modern scholars.

[64] Jerome, *Letter to Eustochium*, NPNF 2 6:40.

[65] Augustine, *On the Psalms* 147.28, NPNF 1 8:672.

[66] Clement of Alexandria, *Who is the Rich Man that Shall Be Saved* 21, ANF 2:597. Also see Clement of Alexandria, *The Stromata* 5.3, ANF 2:448.

"is Elijah," along with the prophecy in Micah of the "one who breaks out" (long understood by some of the rabbis to be Elijah), then this possibility becomes all the more sustainable. John was in the spirit of Elijah. He came to reveal Jesus the Messiah, and to *break* into the kingdom through his preaching of repentance. All who hear and react to such preaching through their incessant and violent repentance break through the very same opening made by John, forcefully entering the kingdom of God.

Having seen these possible interpretations it is difficult if not impossible to conclude which is more satisfactory or convincing (if any). But we may at the very least say that two interpretations tower above the rest. Their points of resemblance scatter when faced with their dissimilarities. One places the suffering of the kingdom on the shoulders of Jesus and John as part of the *eschatological tribulation*, the other upon the righteous who through *violent repentance* may enter the kingdom by force. In the end, however, I suspect that the mystery of this saying will likely remain concealed till the kingdom is made manifest at the end times, till it suffers violence—whatever that may eventually (or already) mean.

CHAPTER TWELVE

Present or Future: 'Thy Kingdom come'

There are two sides to every question.
—PROTAGORAS

I F YOU WERE TO TAKE A QUICK GLANCE AT THE GOSPELS you would inevitably find that Jesus spoke of the kingdom of God as coming at some point in the *future*. Should you doubt this, simply look to the Lord's Prayer: "Thy kingdom come...." But if you took the very *same* Gospels, you would also inevitably find that Jesus spoke of the kingdom as if it were already here in the *present*. So then: Has it come or is it coming? The next thing you would undoubtedly notice is the frequency of the word "kingdom" at the mouth of Jesus. It stood at the core of His message. After His resurrection He evidently spoke of nothing else.[1]

But these two details (the ambiguity of the timing and the centrality of the kingdom in Jesus' thought) are to a major extent lost on the modern Christian. Rarely in our day is the kingdom seen as a significant agenda of Jesus. And then, even when one gives thought to the kingdom it is rarely *the*

---

[1] Acts 1:3.

kingdom that Jesus envisioned. By identifying the "kingdom of God" with *only* the utopian heaven after death, humanity becomes lost to the central message of Jesus. The kingdom once "at hand," once "near," once already "come," in the words of Jesus, is relocated to an indefinite future, or at best to the time after personal death. Indeed, the kingdom was dispatched so far away that we have become content with our present day, with our present world. It was so far relegated that *this* world became the "kingdom." The kingdom of Jesus that was "not of this world" was exchanged for another. This world, Alexander Schmemann laments, "which for the early Christians was transparent to the kingdom, reacquired its own value and existence independent of the kingdom of God."[2]

In short, the kingdom of God for Jesus was not simply part of His teaching. It was His only teaching. It was not only a futuristic utopia of rest after death. It was the eternity of God breaking into the present of humanity. It is this "kingdom *of* God," a rarely considered yet essential message of Jesus, to which we now turn. Our aim is to consider the *timing* of the kingdom, to search out whether it has come or whether it is coming. Hopefully this in itself will secure the kingdom of God in our minds in *as* central a place as Jesus gave it in His message. But before doing so we do best by asking a simple yet crucial question: What exactly is the kingdom of God?

THE NATURE OF THE KINGDOM

Before Jesus, the phrase "kingdom of God" was rarely used.[3] The concept itself, however, was prevalent. But it should be warned that its structure was not neatly defined, nor was its definition exact. And thus we will try to discern its nature by making a number of generalized points.

The first is that the early Jewish understanding rather than focusing on the kingdom instead looked to the "*king*."[4] Ultimately, this king would be God alone, or as the Psalmist put it: "The Lord shall reign forever."[5] Over time, however, this hope was vested in a human king. This obviously preconditioned the establishment of universal or at least local rule. The relevant problem being that Israel never had the first, and seldom had the latter. We need to remember that Israel for a staggering part of its history was

---

[2] Alexander Schmemann, *The Eucharist*, 43.
[3] For a survey of modern perspectives on the kingdom see Wendell Willis ed., *The Kingdom of God in 20th-Century Interpretation* (Massachusetts: Hendrickson Publishers, 1987).
[4] Psa 103:19, 145:13.
[5] Psa 146:10; Also see Psa 24:7-10, Isa 52:7.

oppressed by other nations (the Babylonians, Assyrians, Persians, Greeks, Egyptians, Seleucids, and Romans, to name a few). In fact, the "kingdom" of Israel rarely existed. For the seven hundred years before Jesus, Israel hardly even had its own king.

If Israel scarcely had effective and autonomous rule, then we should appreciate that for the kingdom of God to be actually present on earth it would require a fairly powerful upheaval of the current circumstance. The second point that concerns us is then this: Israel would necessarily need to look to the *future* for the inauguration of the kingdom.[6] And it was precisely this that was envisioned. We hear in the prophecies that the scattered and dispersed Jews would be *gathered from their exile* and thus there would be an ingathering of the "preserved ones of Israel."[7] Once gathered in the kingdom, a *messianic banquet* with a messianic figure would be enacted.[8] Closely tied to the restoration of Israel was the *fate of the Gentiles*, which would either take the form of servitude to Israel or in many other cases salvation through Israel.[9] But this restoration of the kingdom could only come after the "birth pangs of the new age," after the great *tribulation* and *defeat of Satan*.[10] Following which there would be the *final judgment* of the nations as well as Israel.[11] But here we need to be very careful. This future enactment of salvation should not lead us to think that the expectation looked to some surreal place or land. The stress was on God's might in gathering, restoring, defeating, judging, and saving. The stress was not on the *kingdom*, it was on *God*.

In other words the kingdom of God means just that: it is *God's* kingdom. It is the manifestation of God's power and authority "in the world of human experience."[12] That is to say, it is the sphere or scope where God exercises His reign *in* power. We should not see in this a realm, place, or domain. What is at play is the kingdom as manifest in authority, *not* location. In the words of the Orthodox scholar Vesilin Kesich, it refers to "God's act of reigning or ruling, rather than God's realm, to God's dominion rather than

---

[6] We should also note that if the kingdom was placed within an eschatological context in that it would only be realized in the final days, then it would also be irrevocably and inextricably tied to the role of the Messiah who would, as we have seen, *also* come at the end.

[7] Isa 49:5-6; Also see Deut 30:1-10; *1 Enoch* 90:33.

[8] Isa 25:6.

[9] Isa 2:2-4; Mic 4:1-3.

[10] Isa 24:21-22; *Jubilees* 5:6; *1 Enoch* 90:23.

[11] Isa 66:15-16; Mal 4:1; *1 Enoch* 90:20-27.

[12] C. H. Dodd, *The Parables of the Kingdom* (Glasgow: Collins, 1978), 32. Also see John Riches, *Jesus and the Transformation of Judaism* (London: Darton, Longman & Todd, 1980), 92; E. P. Sanders, *Jesus and Judaism*, 127; also see his other work *The Historical Figure of Jesus* (London: Penguin Books, 1993), 169-204.

to God's domain."[13] Above all, as Alexander Schmemann indicates, "the kingdom of God is unity with God, the source of all life, indeed life itself."[14] And thus it should by now be apparent that the kingdom is not a "pleasant *place*" that we go to after death, it is infinitely more. This then is the third point that we need to keep in mind when considering the kingdom: It is God's *reign* not domain.

We now come to our fourth and final point. All along we have seen that the early Jew yearned for this future kingdom. But if we look to the Gospels an obvious problem declares itself: To *which* kingdom exactly do we refer?

In the Gospel of Matthew many of the kingdom sayings refer to the "kingdom of *heaven*" as their subject, but in the other Gospels we find that it is the "kingdom of *God*." Are these identical or do they differ? Two things strike us in this question. The first is that Matthew in his Gospel uses the phrase "kingdom of heaven" (*basileia ton ouranon*) thirty-two times, the phrase "kingdom" (*basileia*) by itself fifty-five times, and the phrase "kingdom of God" (*basileia tou theou*) only four times.[15] The second thing that strikes us is that Matthew, and he alone, uses "kingdom of heaven." That is, with the singular exception of Matthew, every other New Testament writer instead uses the "kingdom of God." Many on observing this have sought to prove that there is a distinction between that "*of* heaven" and that "*of* God." But if we look at one particular usage the matter becomes clear:

> ...it is hard for a rich man to enter the kingdom of *heaven*...it is easier for a camel to go through the eye of a needle than for a rich man to enter the kingdom of *God*.[16]

The two phrases are used interchangeably within the same saying, "making any real distinction in meaning nigh impossible."[17] The two terms are thus almost certainly *identical*. We may then ask: If it meant the same thing, why did Matthew use "kingdom of heaven" instead of the more common usage? To answer this we need to remember that Matthew's community (his audience) was predominantly Jewish. Pious Jews were inclined to avoid mentioning the word "God"[18] and hence we may understand Matthew's

---

[13] Vesilin Kesich, *The Gospel Image of Christ*, 183.

[14] Alexander Schmemann, *The Eucharist*, 40-41.

[15] The four instances of "kingdom of God" are Matt 12:28; 19:24; 21:31, 43.

[16] Matt 19:23-24.

[17] John P. Meier, *A Marginal Jew*, Vol. II, 239. The terms are likely to have become related first in the Book of Daniel, where "the *God* of heaven" will establish a "kingdom which shall never be destroyed" (Dan 2:44).

[18] For a discussion on the Name of God, and Jewish attitudes towards it, see Daniel

insistence on giving the phrase as the "kingdom of heaven" instead of "kingdom of God."

In conclusion, then, the kingdom of God (or heaven) was not a neatly defined entity; it held within it a *multiplicity of meaning*. In it were vested not only the rule of God, but also tribulation, not only judgment, but also future restoration. That said, the "kingdom of God" as a phrase is only found four to six times in the entire Old Testament.[19] In contrast it is found over one hundred times at the mouth of Jesus. And so, if the kingdom in the early Jewish texts was mentioned on only a handful of occasions and yet carried within it varied meanings, the matter becomes infinitely complex when one turns to Jesus. He used it not only frequently but also variously, placing it in multiple settings and contexts. He even placed it at varying times. The "kingdom of God" then, at least for Jesus, "was forced to carry a very wide range of meaning."[20] So wide that we may now appreciate the difficulty of the original questions posed: What exactly is the kingdom? And when will it come?

If Jesus resorted to parable after parable, saying after saying, all in the hoping of communicating to humanity what "the kingdom of heaven is like,"[21] then it should be clear that the task at hand is not as simple as one would perhaps hope.

THE FUTURE: THE KINGDOM IS COMING

The kingdom is still to come. If we were somehow capable of finding for ourselves a first-century Jew and asked when the kingdom would come, the answer would not surprise us: It would be at the *end* of the age.

Though the "kingdom of God" may have been infrequent in Jewish literature before the time of Jesus, when it did occur, it referred to the future.[22] This is quite logical. If you were to hope for a restoration and obviously things were not restored at the present moment, then you would be quite wise to

---

Fanous, *The Person of the Christ*, 114-125.

[19] Its usage increased slightly in the intertestamental period and more so in the rabbinic literature (albeit in different contexts). For the "kingdom of God" in rabbinic literature see Geza Vermes, *The Religion of Jesus the Jew* (London: SCM Press, 1993), 131-135.

[20] E. P. Sanders, *Jesus and Judaism*, 152.

[21] Matt 13:44 for example. Matthew's version of Jesus' parables generally begin with the aforementioned pattern: "The kingdom of heaven is like…"

[22] Besides the other references from the Scriptures already given, this expectation was also held by other Jewish writings contemporary with Jesus, see *Assumption of Moses* 10:1; *Sibylline Oracles* 3:40-48; *Targum Zechariah* 14:9; *Targum Obadiah* 21.

conclude that the restoration was still to come. If you also expected that this restoration would be *physical* and so tangible that your people would rule the world, then this hope for the future becomes all the more plausible. An indissoluble connection therefore exists between the kingdom *and* the end-time hopes of ancient Judaism. And as such, Jesus speaking of a kingdom in the future "would not have been strange to a typical Jewish audience in first century Palestine."[23] Far from strange, it would be expected. Thus it is here that we begin; in the future.

The first thing that strikes anyone in considering the kingdom is the Lord's Prayer: "Thy kingdom *come*."[24] One of the disciples draws near to Jesus and asks: "Lord, teach us to pray..."[25] The response is the central prayer of all who came after Jesus. In this distinctively Jewish[26] prayer the *first* petition—this is crucial to see—the disciples are commanded to seek is the coming of the kingdom. One does not pray for something that is present. One may give thanks for that which is present, but one would hardly ask for it. In other words, if the kingdom has already come why does Jesus instruct His disciples, and with them all Christianity, to pray for the kingdom to come? Quite clearly this is a "decided reference to the future."[27] It is a plea for the coming kingdom, a plea for God to manifest His rule in the life of His people.

The following three petitions likewise look to the future. "*Give* us this day our daily bread" looks forward to the future satiety, for the bread is not yet here; "*forgive* us our debts as *we* forgive" points to purification and unity, the very indications of the kingdom; and "*lead* us not into temptation [*peirasmos*]" where temptation is the eschatological tribulation or "birth pangs" that usher in the new age. This is incredible. The only prayer that Jesus taught His disciples places at its *first* petition "not a need or problem of this present world" but the call for the future kingdom![28]

We do not have to look far for confirmation. When Jesus declared the faith of the Gentile Centurion, the kingdom once more was situated in the future:

---

[23] James D. G. Dunn, *Jesus Remembered*, 392.

[24] Matt 6:9-13.

[25] Luke 11:1.

[26] For the background of the Lord's Prayer within its first-century context see J. Heinemann, "The Background of Jesus' Prayer in the Jewish Liturgical Tradition," in *The Lord's Prayer and Jewish Liturgy*, ed. J. J. Petuchowski and M. Brocke (London: Burns & Oates, 1978), 11-89.

[27] Dale C. Allison, *The End of the Ages has Come*, 102.

[28] John P. Meier, *A Marginal Jew*, Vol. II, 302.

> I say to you that many *will come* from east and west, and sit down with
> *Abraham*, Isaac, and Jacob in the kingdom of heaven.[29]

The nations "*will* come." The very fact that Abraham is sitting at the table is indicative of his rising from the dead, once more an intensely end-time or eschatological event. Few thus could argue credibly that Jesus did not expect a future coming of God's kingdom. In this public declaration Jesus was encouraging the nations (along with Israel) to set their eyes and hearts upon the table in the *future* kingdom of God.[30] To this we add the kingdom parables and sayings in which the judgment is expressly placed in the future: "So it will be at *the end of the age*. The angels will come forth, [and] separate the wicked from among the just."[31] The judgment will take place "*when* the Son of Man comes in His glory,"[32] when the wise and foolish virgins will be separated, one taken into the kingdom, the other left outside the gates crying for all eternity: "Lord, Lord, open to us…"[33] But when exactly would the kingdom come? How far along in the future: Is it near or delayed?

Although still undoubtedly in the future, a number of the sayings of Jesus paint the kingdom as imminent. At times, even seemingly within a lifetime:

> Assuredly, I say to you that there are some standing here who will not taste death till they see the kingdom of God *present* with power.[34]

If we consider the average life expectancy in first-century Palestine, this would indicate that the kingdom would arrive in twenty to thirty years at most. Mark, however, understood this saying very specifically, for he situates the *transfiguration* immediately after it: "Now after *six days* Jesus took Peter, James, and John, and led them up on a high mountain *apart* by themselves; and He was transfigured before them."[35] Therefore, at least for Mark, the saying was fulfilled "six days" later. Today it is rare to find scholars who subscribe to this interpretation, perhaps to their detriment.[36]

---

[29] Matt 8:10-12; Also see Luke 13:25-30.

[30] Dale C. Allison, *The End of the Ages has Come*, 102.

[31] Matt 13:49; Also see 13:24-30; 24:42, 43-44, 45-51.

[32] Matt 25:31-46.

[33] Matt 25:11.

[34] Mark 9:1; Also see Matt 16:28.

[35] Mark 9:2.

[36] G. R. Beasley-Murray, *Jesus and the Kingdom of God*, 188. Scholars have often resisted this interpretation on the basis that it occurred only "six days" later and thus is hardly a prophecy, and that the implication of some will see it before they "taste death" is that some will actually die beforehand.

For one, the fact that Mark saw the connection is deeply significant
(unless we understand more than he). Secondly, the parallel is clear. Jesus
said "some" would not taste death and *only* "some" (Peter, James, and John)
were witnesses to the transfiguration. Thirdly, Jesus was careful to indicate
that they would "see" the kingdom, and on the mountain they saw a vision.[37]
Fourthly, as we have seen, the kingdom was always tied to the end times.
The fact that Jesus "appeared in glory" along with Moses and Elijah, both of
whom were eschatological figures, clearly is indicative of something related
to the kingdom. Fifthly, the declaration of the Father: "This is My beloved
Son. Hear Him,"[38] reveals not only the transcendence of Jesus, but also the
presence of power. Finally, this interpretation of the saying is also that of the
esteemed Church Fathers. Interestingly, many of the Fathers paused here
to query: Is the kingdom that is revealed in the transfiguration manifested
absolutely or only in *part*? And if the transfiguration is the "kingdom of God
present," then does that mean it has already come?

John Chrysostom, whilst affirming that the kingdom was present "six
days" after the saying, quickly qualifies that it was only a "taste" of the
kingdom: Jesus had shown the three disciples the "*kind* of glory"[39] which was
to come. John of Damascus puts it in another way: the transfiguration was
a "*parable*"[40] of the future kingdom. In this case the "glory of the heavenly
kingdom is *prefigured*" and is not absolutely present.[41] The transfiguration
was a taste, a kind, a parable, a prefiguration of the glorious kingdom that
would come in the future. It was "present in power," yet was only a taste of
that to come.

But still we question: When will it come? A taste may come now, but
when will it come in its fullness? This is not only our question. Before it was
ours, it belonged to the disciples. Four chapters *after* the transfiguration, four
of the disciples (three of whom witnessed the transfiguration) approached
Jesus and asked Him "privately": "Tell us, when will these things be?" Jesus
responds: (1) when you hear of *tribulations*; (2) when you are *persecuted*;
(3) when there is *familial division*; (4) when you hear of *false messiahs*; then
you shall see the Son of Man coming in power and glory.[42] Jesus then clearly
adds: "learn this parable from the fig tree," from its signs one may deduce
the coming of summer. Likewise, when you see the above tribulations, know

---

[37] Mark 9:9.
[38] Mark 9:7.
[39] John Chrysostom, *The Gospel of Matthew*, Homily 56.1, NPNF 1 10:345.
[40] John of Damascus, *Sacra Paralleia* 73, PG 96:497-498.
[41] Hilary of Poitiers, *On Matthew* 17.2, SC 258:62.
[42] Mark 13:3-27.

that the end "is near—at the doors…"[43] Lest we think that now a timeline had been revealed, Jesus continues: "But of that day and hour no one knows… Take heed, watch and pray; for you do not know when the time is."[44]

Place side by side with this, the radical call of discipleship. If Jesus called the disciples to give up land, possessions, family, and even one's life; then the kingdom cannot be far. If Jesus gave radical warnings of the tribulation to come, so much so that one must prepare now; then it must be near. Jesus would hardly tell the disciples to "watch and pray" if the kingdom was not imminent. His sayings and actions implied the "expectation of an imminent event of climactic and crucial importance."[45] Simply stated, one does not radically change one's life unless a radical circumstance is impending. So, yes, the kingdom is not yet, but it cannot be far, it is even "at the doors." This is also the very content of the parables. The kingdom is so near that it is *urgently* imminent: "Watch therefore, for you know neither the day nor the hour in which the Son of Man is coming."[46] At one point the imminence of the kingdom in the parables became so concrete, so *real*, that Jesus' hearers were almost brought to panic and ecstasy: "Now as they heard these things, He spoke another parable…because they thought the kingdom of God would appear *immediately*."[47] The parables thus, in some sense, served to heighten the expectations of the kingdom to the extent that some thought it was in the here and now. The crucial distinction being that *they* thought it had come.

Jesus on the other hand was unmistakably clear that the kingdom had not yet come. And if as we have considered, the disciples were called to pray for the kingdom *to come*, the salvation of the Jews and Gentiles was still *to come*, the parables placed the kingdom at the end of times, and the transfiguration was a "taste" of the kingdom *to come*, then we cannot but conclude that Jesus understood the kingdom to be in the *future*. But at the same time do not the disciples pray for the future kingdom in the *present*, does not the Gentile Centurion experience a miracle in the *present*, and do not those who "taste" the kingdom taste it in the *present*? If something is so near that it can be tasted, so close that it is at the doors, so imminent that it demands radical self-denial, then can it not be said to be already here?

---

[43] Mark 13:28-29.
[44] Mark 13:32-33.
[45] James D. G. Dunn, *Jesus Remembered*, 436.
[46] Matt 25:13.
[47] Luke 19:11.

CHAPTER THIRTEEN

Present or Future: 'The Kingdom of God has come'

In rivers, the water that you touch
Is the last of what has passed
And the first of that which comes;
So with present time.
—LEONARDO DA VINCI

MANY YEARS AGO ON AN ODD VENTURE into an even odder village, a young man came across a lovely, albeit slightly senile, little old lady. As he wondered aimlessly through ambiguously cobbled streets, she gestured that he should take a seat beside her. Before even introducing herself or her purpose, she started to say something in excessively broken English. I say something because at that point he really could not make sense of her abrupt speech. Moments later it dawned on him that she was relating advice. It went something along these lines: Whilst you walk there are but three options. You may either stare at the ground, or you may look ahead, or you may simply close your eyes. Stare at the ground and you will never get anywhere. Look straight ahead and you will trip over a rock or stairs or whatever may lie in your path. Close your eyes and you rest your fate in the hands of others. The trick, she quietly whispered, is to know when to do each of the three—when to look up, when to look down, and when to trust in others. After this she immediately took her walking stick, stood up, and left the young man all alone on the cold bench. At first he knew not what to make of this strange behavior till he remembered that minutes earlier he had been walking aimlessly.

This somewhat odd advice is fairly useful when it comes to walking. It is of far greater worth when one considers the kingdom. If we were to spend our lives staring at the present (the ground) we would never approach our future in any meaningful way. In like manner if we were to look only to the future (looking straight ahead) we would exist in a fantastical state, constantly stumbling upon the reality of our present. And if we did neither and closed our eyes to both the future and the present, not only would we not get anywhere, we would in all certainty be victim to great harm. The difficulty is in keeping our eyes open to both the present *and* the future. We have previously looked to the kingdom in the future, and whilst our eyes must constantly maintain this in vision, we now turn to the present which, in the words of Leonardo da Vinci, is "the *first* of that which comes."

THE PRESENT: THE KINGDOM HAS COME

"Jesus came to Galilee, preaching the gospel of the kingdom of God, and saying, 'The time is fulfilled, and the kingdom of God is *at hand* [*engiken*].'"[1] This saying of Jesus is recorded on at least four occasions, each with the exact same wording. But what precisely does "at hand" mean? Is it here or is it coming?

In Greek "at hand" is given as *engiken* which is from the verb *eggizo*. Ordinarily it may be understood to mean "draw near," "at hand," or "approach." But in the perfect tense, as it is here, its meaning is far more subtle. It "indicates an action *already* performed and resulting in a state or effect which *continues* into the present."[2] In other words, something was completed in the past but its effect continues into the present. And thus by saying that the kingdom "draws near" in the perfect tense, Jesus indicates that "it has *already* drawn near" and thus now it is in the state of "being near."

Does this suggest that the kingdom "draws near" (either as a state or as an action) or does it indicate that it is so imminent that it is bursting in? It would seem that it stands ambiguously in both courts: future in that it is near, and present in that it is so imminent that it is *as if* it is already here. Can it then be both?

[1] Mark 1:15; Matt 4:17, 10:7; Luke 10:9, 11.
[2] James D. G. Dunn, *Jesus Remembered*, 407.

If a train pulls into a station and has not yet come to a perfect halt, one passenger may say that the train "has arrived," whilst another will confidently and stubbornly argue that it is "still to arrive." Both in a certain sense would be correct. For imminent nearness and actual arrival often intersect—so much so that it is extremely difficult, if not exhausting, to speak of one without the other.[3] A reality, whether it be a train or the kingdom, in our understanding of time and space "can approach so close that it is practically, if not literally and technically, present."[4] Jesus, therefore, would be indicating that the kingdom was in some manner present, or at the very least that it was so near that it was imminently arriving. In either case, we should note the significance. The kingdom was not simply a general-always-available power, but rather comes at a *time* (presently or imminently) into human existence. Put in slightly different terms, the divine life breaks into the human condition, infinity reaches out and touches space, and eternity becomes manifest in time. With Jesus, and only with Him, does that which is *of* God break into that which is *of* man. Nowhere is this more apparent than in the Beelzebub controversy:

> But if I cast out demons by the Spirit of God, surely the kingdom of God has *come* [*ephthasen*] upon you.[5]

Here, Jesus identifies His exorcisms with the coming of the kingdom of God. In Greek *ephthasen* ("come") is from the verb root *phthano* which may mean to "anticipate," "precede," "come," or "arrive." In this specific case most scholars would have it to mean "has come." Others have disagreed on varying grounds of varying credibility.[6] But we can say almost certainly that Jesus (at least in this saying) was claiming that the kingdom was in the present. This point gains clarity when we consider its context.

Jesus was accused of casting out demons by the power of Satan. He reacts by claiming that He casts out demons by the power of God, and if it be by the power of God, then the kingdom in its *power* "has come upon you." If Satan was being bound, then the power of God's rule had displaced that

---

[3] See R. F. Berkey, "Eggizen, Phthanein, and Realised Eschatology," *JBL* 82 (1963): 181.

[4] John P. Meier, *A Marginal Jew*, Vol. II, 433. Also see C. H. Dodd, *The Parables of the Kingdom*, 40.

[5] Matt 12:28.

[6] E. P. Sanders, for one, offers an interesting (though perhaps not applicable) parallel as a counter-argument: "it seems to me obviously dubious to lean so heavily on the meaning of the verb *ephthasen*... When the author of the *Testament of Abraham* wrote that the 'cup of death' came (*ephthasen*) to Abraham, the patriarch still had more than nineteen chapters to live." See E. P. Sanders, *Jesus and Judaism*, 134. Though fascinating, this parallel is weak. For a discussion of the argument see John P. Meier, *A Marginal Jew*, Vol. II, 413.

of Satan. And if Satan's kingdom was displaced, then the "final exercise of God's rule was already in effect."[7] Each exorcism was thus a manifestation of the kingdom in the present life of Israel.[8] The kingdom was made manifest when the blind saw, the lame walked, the dead raised, and the demons exorcised. In each and every act of God's power, Israel was being wrestled from the grips of Satan. These were far more than divine interventions, as Vesilin Kesich notes, these were "the signs of God's presence in the world He created."[9] God may have *always* been enthroned, but now His enthronement was being *made known* in forceful power through Jesus.[10]

We should also bring to mind the difficult saying of the "kingdom suffering violence."[11] Only that which is *present* and within the reach of humanity, may suffer violence at the hands of humanity. The kingdom could hardly suffer from "the days of John the Baptist" if it were not in some manner present. The very idea that it suffers, as John P. Meier so eloquently comments, "implies that what is in essence transcendent, eternal, invisible, and almighty—God's kingly rule—has somehow become immanent, temporal, visible, and vulnerable in Jesus' ministry."[12] Whether, as we have seen, the kingdom was "breaking forth" or was being "violently attacked," it still must have stood in the present for it to be afflicted. The kingdom, then, is no longer imminent; it is here. Once more our confusion increases: How can it be in the future, but at the same time be present? Perhaps out of this very same confusion the Pharisees felt compelled to ask: "When will the kingdom come?" Jesus brings no peace to their confusion or ours:

> The kingdom of God does *not* come with observation; nor will they say, "See here!" or "See there!" For indeed, the kingdom of God is *within* you [*entos hymon*].[13]

These words, *entos hymon*, may mean "within you" or "in your midst." A case may be made for the latter. In the first place, Jesus rejects the observation of time and place, for the kingdom is in the *here* and *now*—it is in your midst. Secondly, it is difficult (though not impossible) to imagine that Jesus would say to the Pharisees that "the kingdom is within you," especially since He is never recorded as saying the same to His followers. It should also be

---

[7] James D. G. Dunn, *Jesus Remembered*, 461.
[8] Norman Perrin, *The Kingdom of God in the Teaching of Jesus*, 76.
[9] Vesilin Kesich, *The Gospel Image of Christ*, 189.
[10] Augustine, *Our Lord's Sermon on the Mount* 2.6.20, PL 34:1278; NPNF 1 6:40.
[11] Matt 11:11-13.
[12] John P. Meier, *A Marginal Jew*, Vol. II, 403.
[13] Luke 17:20.

noted that though the Church Fathers generally understood it as "within you,"[14] there are some notable exceptions. Many of these early theologians compared "within you" to a saying in the book of Deuteronomy: "[the] word is very near you, in your mouth and in your heart."[15] The kingdom is as close to you as the word you speak is to your mouth and mind. Tertullian goes on to say that the kingdom is of such proximity that it is "in your hand, within your power."[16] It is so imminent that it is within *your* reach, and, as Cyril of Alexandria warns, "it depends on your own will...whether or not you receive it."[17]

Whatever the case may be, whether as "within you," "in your midst," or "within your reach," at least one consequence is the same: the kingdom is in the here and now. Here, however, one must pause and question: If the kingdom is in the here and now (in a word, present) then why was Jesus careful to mention that the kingdom will come *without* "observation"? If by "present" we mean that the earth ceased to exist and that the Son of Man appeared on a cloud in glory, or perhaps for the more historically minded, that the Romans were ousted by Jesus who ushered in the *new* kingdom of Israel—then quite obviously the kingdom was and is not present. But just as obviously, on the other hand, Jesus stressed that the kingdom had come.

If we consider that Jesus spoke of the kingdom a great deal more than the entire Old Testament, then we may begin to fathom His purpose. If I were to "take over" a particular colloquial phrase, how would I go about transforming its meaning? I would repeat it day and night to my audience in various yet specific contexts, each with the intent of conveying *my* meaning of this particular phrase as opposed to the common and known meaning. And thus in the same manner that Jesus redefined the messianic concept, He now *redefines* the kingdom. It was "without observation" for it was not the kingdom of men, but of God. In its redefinition the kingdom was directed away from a political movement and was transformed into a radical means of sharing in the power and life of God. The kingdom was indeed present, but "not like Israel had *thought* it to be."[18]

---

[14] For instance, Origen, *On Prayer* 25.1, GCS 3:356–57.

[15] Deut 30:14.

[16] Tertullian, *Against Marcion* 4.35, ANF 3:409.

[17] Cyril of Alexandria, *Commentary on Luke* 117, CGSL 467-468. Modern scholars have reiterated such an interpretation; see G. R. Beasley-Murray, *Jesus and the Kingdom of God*, 102.

[18] N. T. Wright, *Jesus and the Victory of God*, 472. Also see C. H. Dodd, *The Parables of the Kingdom*, 40-41.

A LOGICAL CONTRADICTION

That Jesus spoke of the kingdom in the present is a fact. That He at other times spoke of it in the future is also a fact. Any attempt to give meaning to the kingdom must therefore reconcile the two.

Remarkably the early Church itself was uncertain as to the timing of the kingdom. When Jesus was raised from the dead, the disciples asked Him: "Lord, will You at this *time* restore the kingdom to Israel?" Evidently, there are two possible reasons for their question. Either the kingdom has come and they are mistaken, or, it is still to come. In both cases, despite all the teaching of Jesus it would seem that the disciples still envisioned a worldly kingdom. Characteristically the answer of Jesus evades the question at hand: "It is not for you to know..."[19] The disciples were not alone. Paul (at least in his earlier ministry), and with him the Gentilic Church, hoped for the imminent restoration of the kingdom, even within their lifetimes.[20] Paul at one stage had to call for calm when some became mentally stricken for fear that the day had already come:

> Now, brethren, concerning the coming of our Lord Jesus Christ and our gathering together to Him, we ask you, not to be soon *shaken in mind* or troubled, either by spirit or by word or by letter, as if from us, as though the day of Christ *had* come.[21]

But if our analysis thus far has told us anything, it is that difficulty arises on taking the kingdom as solely present *or* as solely future. A solution must therefore lie in both the present *and* in the future. In other words, rather than doing away with the future or the present, we do best by holding both and recognizing that Jesus *meant* both. And if Jesus spoke of them both, then "the two were, we must assume, linked."[22] Consequently, we need to discern the indelible rope that ties the two together. A rope that in my estimation has three different yet related threads running through it.

The first thread is that of the *non-contradictory paradox*. Contradiction to the modern mind is illogical. The ancient Jewish mind differed entirely. It was hardly concerned with the principle of non-contradiction, as revered as that principle may be in Western logic.[23] To speak of something in the future

---

[19] Acts 1:6.
[20] Rom 8:23; 1 Thes 4:15-17; 1 Cor 15:51. See Richard H. Hiers, *The Historical Jesus and the Kingdom of God* (Gainesville: University of Florida Press, 1973), 109.
[21] 2 Thess 2:1-3.
[22] E. P. Sanders, *Jesus and Judaism*, 154.
[23] John P. Meier, *A Marginal Jew*, Vol. II, 399.

did not prevent one from speaking about the same in the present. To the ancient Jew it was this very paradox that brought out meaning. By holding two things that may contradict in such close proximity one could describe things that did not readily lend themselves to clear and logical formulation. The paradox therefore indicated that which "cannot be said otherwise, at least not so effectively or so well, possibly not at all."[24] Enter the idea of the kingdom of God as present *and* future.

If we look at the sayings of Jesus as a whole it becomes evident that He approached the concept of the kingdom of God from a multitude of angles. In fact a favorite opening of Jesus was: "The kingdom of heaven is *like...*"[25] He employed all manners of rhetorical devices to give a picture of the kingdom. To then take any *one* of these sayings, parables, or analogies, and deny the rest would be a severe mistake. For if one meaning or saying were sufficient, then Jesus would have left the matter there. But as an ancient Jew, He held multiple ideas in close unison to reveal something that simply could not be defined. And here a pressing note must be made: We should not expect these parables, metaphors, and sayings to harmonize concisely. Indeed, we should be surprised if they did harmonize, for what need would there have been for the metaphor in the first place?

For instance, in my bid to describe a particular dessert to a friend I might make use of various images. I might say it was like diving into a wave *as well* as being like the sunlight on my face on a cold winter's day. Both of these metaphors reveal something about the dessert. If we take either one of the images *alone* it would be difficult to imagine the dessert. On the same account, trying to draw a link between diving into a wave *and* sunlight on my face would result in anything but my particular dessert. The same may be said of the kingdom. Jesus brought to the forefront of His hearer's mind a multiplicity of meaning. To rush off with any one of these images and take it as a definition of the kingdom would then be just as silly as saying that diving into a wave is the same thing as eating dessert. Likewise to take *all* the images of the kingdom and expect them to harmonize in non-contradiction would be just as ludicrous as expecting "diving into a wave" and "sunlight on my face" to sit logically side by side.

And thus each image related by Jesus has to be seen in the *context* of the rest of the images.[26] No one image may be taken by itself, and the images

---

[24] James D. G. Dunn, *Jesus Remembered*, 486.

[25] See Matt 13.

[26] Norman Perrin famously termed this idea a *tensive-symbol* as contrasted to a *steno-symbol*. The latter reflects a one-to-one representation, for example the symbol *pi* always

themselves have to be seen in the light of the kingdom. In other words, to get anywhere near what the kingdom is and when it will come, we need to hold each and every metaphor, parable, and saying about the kingdom tightly together. Only then will we appreciate what the "kingdom of heaven is like." For the kingdom as understood by Jesus is "such that no single formula can do justice to it."[27]

When it comes to the timing of the kingdom specifically the same findings hold true. If there is a multiplicity of meaning then it is not difficult to appreciate that time (present or future) may also evade definition—and indeed it does. This brings us to the second thread that ties the present and future dimensions of the kingdom inextricably together: the *nature of the kingdom* itself. The kingdom is not a time nor a place. More precisely, it is not identifiable in time nor space, as other subjects may be. Rather it is the coming of God *as* King, manifesting His power over Israel, and through her over the nations. It is a description of an indescribable reality, unlike anything humanity has ever experienced or even imagined. Accordingly, Jesus' sayings on the timing of the kingdom do not fall into any categories known to humanity. It is somehow in the *future*, whilst *imminent*, and in some manner *here*.[28] All the while it is the same reality.

On this point, we do well to consider time itself. Time as an idea is elusive. As children we spent nights discussing time travel and the fated "what if." As adults, time remains just as incomprehensible; the difference being that now we find relief in ignoring its plaguing questions. If we were then to cast our minds to that which is *beyond* time, the matter at hand nears impossibility. But let us consider a possible line of argument. If God exists, then He must be supernatural. If supernatural, then He is not limited by natural laws. If not bound by natural laws, then it stands to reason that He is not bound by time. And if not limited by time, then quite obviously He exists in the past, present, and future. Or more accurately, He exists in *our* past, present, and future; for He exists beyond ("supra") time. Put differently,

---

equates to the same number. A *tensive-symbol* on the other hand reflects multiple meanings, and does so in order to describe something that is difficult to define. Jesus then, according to Perrin, would have spoken of the kingdom as a tensive-symbol. However, this does not mean that the kingdom is symbolic in that it is not a reality. Rather the "symbol" is meant as something which refers to something else. In other words the symbol refers to an undefinable reality, but in no way denies it. For a discussion see Norman Perrin, *Jesus and the Language of the Kingdom*, 29-34.

[27] G. R. Beasley-Murray, *Jesus and the Kingdom of God*, 145.

[28] For a discussion of the tension between the "already" and the "not yet," see Oscar Cullmann, *Salvation in History* (New York: Harper & Row, 1967), 166-185; G. B. Caird, *The Language and the Imagery of the Bible* (London: Gerald Duckworth & Co, 1980), 12; E. P. Sanders, *Jesus and Judaism*, 150-151.

we stand on the earth within a timeline (a beginning and an end), but for God who "stands" *over* our reality there is no beginning or end.

Take this and place it side by side with the proper understanding of the kingdom as the reign of God and not as a domain, as power not place. In this case, wherever God is so will be His reign and hence His kingdom. If He is in *our* past, present, and future, then in the same manner so is His kingdom. It then should become clear that the nature of the kingdom itself explains its paradoxical timing.

But if Jesus had meant us to retain both images, future and present, then we would expect Him to describe the two as being related. A quick glance at the parables reveals that this was in fact precisely what He did. Jesus begins by asking: "To what shall we liken the kingdom of God?" He answers that it is like a small mustard seed that is planted in the *present* and grows into a majestic tree in the *future*.[29] The same thing (a seed) is at once a small seed and yet soon *will* be a tree. The present thus is organically linked to the future. One may not be taken without the other. A learned scholar puts it as such: "He who reckons only with the future hope must come to terms with God's royal working in the present if that hope is to be realized."[30] In the same way that the future tree cannot exist without the present seed, the future kingdom is inextricably tied to its present manifestation. So much so, that unless it is known in the present it may not and cannot be known in the future. Or to look at it in the opposite direction, the future climax of the kingdom transforms the present moment.

This brings us to our third and final thread. Our approach is by way of analogy. Imagine that a child returns from school one evening. Before he even enters the house he smells all kinds of wonderful delight. Once inside he hears the workings of a dinner in the kitchen, the banging of pots and the clanging of dishes. But as he waits in anticipation in the living room, his father suddenly appears from the kitchen. In hand is a small piece of lamb, just enough for one pre-dinner mouthful for our hungry child. This one mouthful, as we know from experience, does not serve to satisfy the hunger of the small child but intensifies his desire all the more, spurring him on to the future dinner. Let us now observe the reality of this analogy.

The first thing to note is that the table is *being prepared*. The second is that the child has *already* been invited to the dinner. The third is that the father who is the *master* of the table takes from the dinner that is being

[29] Mark 4:30-32. Also see for other parables of growth Mark 4:26-29; Matt 13:3-9, 24-30, 33, 47-50.
[30] G. R. Beasley-Murray, *Jesus and the Kingdom of God*, 103. Also see Norman Perrin, *Rediscovering the Teaching of Jesus*, 204.

prepared, from that which is *"near,"* and gives it to the child. The morsel given to the child is hence the very *same reality* as the dinner to come, in that it comes from the dinner itself. But though it is of the same reality as the dinner, the dinner is still *yet to come.* Put in another way, one is a "present" taste of the dinner; the other in the "future" is the dinner proper. The future banquet then comes to the present "in the midst" of the child. It has come "within" the child. Yet though it has "come upon" the child, it still remains "near" and "will come" in the future. And though the morsel is *of* the dinner, it is *not* the dinner in its fullness. The child therefore eats and knows the dinner, he partakes in its reality, all the while knowing and yearning for the dinner which will be set before him in its fullness at the end time.

In like manner the kingdom has become manifest in the present through the Master of the kingdom, Jesus. In exorcising a demon, by healing, by teaching, by His entire life—word and deed—the power of the kingdom is brought to the present. Humanity partakes in the very reality of the kingdom, yearning all the more for the kingdom in its fullness. Jesus therefore enacts in the present the kingdom to come. Its manifestation in the present does not detract from the future glory; it makes it "all the more truly convincing and inevitable."[31] To "underline this organic link"[32] between present and future is to see the kingdom in the eyes of Jesus, as a *single* majestic reality. In the words of the great Orthodox scholar Georges Florovsky, this is an *inaugurated eschatology*:

> It renders accurately the Biblical diagnosis — the crucial point of the revelation is already in the past. "The ultimate" (or "the new") had already entered history, although the final stage is not yet attained. We are no more in the world of signs only, but already in the world of reality, yet under the sign of the cross. The kingdom has been *already* inaugurated, but *not yet* fulfilled.[33]

The *eschatological* kingdom of the future was *inaugurated* in the present. We should note that this differs from other understandings of the kingdom. Those who would have the kingdom already manifest in the present, so much so that it is no longer in the future, term it a *realized eschatology* in that the end times have been realized in the present. Whilst others have chosen to subscribe to *futurist eschatology*, in which the kingdom remains only in

---

[31] W. G. Kümmel, *Promise and Fulfillment*, 154.

[32] John P. Meier, *A Marginal Jew*, Vol. II, 453.

[33] Georges Florovsky, *Bible, Church, Tradition: An Eastern Orthodox View* (Massachusetts: Nordland Publishing Co, 1972), 35-36. Also see Vesilin Kesich, *The Gospel Image of Christ*, 185.

the future. The truth lies closer to the understanding of Georges Florovsky: The kingdom though manifest in the present comes in its fullness in the future. This then is the third thread that runs between the present and the future, binding them as one. The kingdom is thus fulfilled within history, and consummated at the end of history.[34] But for those who have "tasted" its future glory, even today the kingdom is "more obvious than any of the realities surrounding [them]."[35] And as a child will not be content with a single taste, neither should we be content with the present for only the future will manifest the absolute realization of the kingdom.

These three threads that form the rope that organically links the future and present dimensions are the keys to the timing of the kingdom. Only by realizing that the kingdom is a *non-contradictory paradox* that envelops a *multiplicity of meaning* may we appreciate that Jesus reveals an *inaugurated eschatology*. The significance of which is inestimable.

By Jesus' life and death, a long lost path to the kingdom was resurrected—a path that potentiates the partaking of man in the kingdom of the divine. If Jesus does not stand irrevocably holding present and future in union, if He does not hold man and God in union, man could *only* look towards a future glory. But now the future glory is made known in the present, descending via the path resurrected by Jesus. Man may live and know the glory even *now*, all the while in impetuous anticipation and hunger for the kingdom that will come in its fullness with the return of its King. For what is a kingdom without its king? I cannot but look to the words of Cyprian, the illustrious martyr and bishop of Carthage:

> Christ Himself, dearest beloved, *is* the kingdom of God, whom we day by day desire to come, whose advent we crave to be quickly manifested to us. For since He is Himself the resurrection, since in Him we rise again, so also the kingdom of God may be understood to be Himself, since *in* Him we shall reign.[36]

---

[34] George Ladd, *The Presence of the Future*, 218.

[35] Alexander Schmemann, *The Eucharist*, 41-42. Also see Lev Gillet, *Communion in the Messiah*, 106.

[36] Cyprian, *Treatises on the Lord's Prayer* 13, CCL 3a:97; ANF 5:450-51.

PART FOUR:

The Master of the Kingdom

CHAPTER FOURTEEN

'Son of God': Human or Divine

For a good work we do not stone You, but for blasphemy...
Because You, being a Man, make Yourself God.
—JOHN 10:33

IT IS OFTEN SAID THAT WHEN IT COMES TO JESUS there are only two options. He either was the Son of God, or else He was a great man. At least that is what the common man, the scholar, and even major religions will tell you. But is that really the case? Some years ago the famed intellectual, C. S. Lewis, took issue with the second of these options. The very notion that Jesus was *only* a great man was, at least in Lewis' mind, a logical absurdity if not impossibility.

C. S. Lewis' argument took for granted a singular fact, namely that Jesus "claimed" to be the Son of God, and then proceeded to ask how He could make such a claim. Lewis suggested that there were only three answers to this question. Jesus was either lying, else He really did think He was the Son of God but was in all respects delusional, or He was in fact divine.[1]

---

[1] This argument was presented in C. S. Lewis, *Mere Christianity* (London: Collins, 1952), 54-56.

What became clear, at least for the likes of C. S. Lewis, was that the original suggestion—that Jesus was a great man but not God—did not square with the data. For if Jesus was *only* a great man (or even a prophet for that matter) then He could not also be a liar or psychotic, and thus whatever He claimed to be was true. In other words, unless one is willing to claim and accept that Jesus was a pathological liar, or clinically insane, the only other coherent possibility is that He was the divine Son of God. And since few would admit the first two possibilities (unless one be inherently irrational or singularly obtuse), we are left with the last.

This logical argument is, however, not without problems. We may be agreed that *if* Jesus claimed to be the Son of God, then He is who He claimed to be. But did Jesus ever claim to be the "Son of God"? And if He did, is calling Jesus the "Son of God" as a matter of course to say that He is divine? Put in another way, if Jesus did indeed claim to be the Son of God, what exactly did He mean by this? Did He claim that He was on the same footing as the God of Israel in heaven? Was it the case in first-century Palestine that "Son of God" was synonymous with God? And if "Son of God" did not originally mean to be divine as God is divine, how then did Jesus go from "Son of God" to God? Needless to say what is at stake is the very core of Christian belief. These questions will thus introduce us into the final part of this present study which concerns itself with what Jesus revealed of *Himself* in the difficult sayings.

The 'Son of God' Title Before Jesus

What would a first-century Jew have thought on hearing the words "Son of God"? To answer this we do well to remember that there were two main influences on early Judaic thought. The first is that of Greek culture.[2]

Greeks in such times (as well as anyone influenced by Greek thought) would have brought to mind some very specific ideas on hearing the words "son of god." They primarily would have recollected the heroes of Greek mythology who were often called the "sons of god." We know, for instance, that Dionysius and Heracles were allegedly the sons of the god Zeus by mortal mothers. We also know that Zeus was often called the father of all men in Stoic philosophy, a fact that the Apostle Paul capitalized upon

---

[2] For an examination of the Greek and Hellenistic parallels to the Son of God notion see Martin Hengel, *The Son of God: The Origin of Christology and the History of Jewish-Hellenistic Religion* (London: SCM Press, 1976), 23-41.

when preaching to the philosophers in Athens.[3] Some philosophers such as Pythagoras and Plato became so esteemed that they were somehow thought to have been "begotten by god."[4] Even human rulers in the ancient world were called "sons of god." The mother of Alexander the Great was apparently struck by lightning from Zeus before ever consummating her marriage to Phillip, and "suddenly" fell pregnant with the future Emperor. Elsewhere, the Ptolemies thought it no great problem to fancy themselves divine. Even at the time of Jesus, after Caesar was murdered, Augustus was called (or rather called himself) *divi filius*, the "son of the divinized."

That said, it is extremely rare to find the exact words "son of god" in such literature, and it was almost never used as a title. This is, of course, not surprising since the Greeks had many gods and therefore had many names for their gods, and thus one would not be called "son of god," but rather, for example, "son of Zeus."[5]

The second influence upon thought in first-century Palestine was that of the Jewish Scriptures (canonical and extracanonical). An early Jew would have heard "son of God" in a way that varies radically from the modern mind. In the Old Testament, it referred to various subjects, none of which were divine. Time after time *angels* are called "sons of God." The angels are the "sons of God [who] came to present themselves before the Lord,"[6] some of whom (or perhaps humans depending upon one's interpretation) lusted over the daughters of men: "the sons of God came in to the daughters of men and they bore children to them."[7] Of interest is the peculiar incident related in the book of Daniel. After casting three young men into the furnace, king Nebuchadnezzar was astonished and exclaimed: "I see four men loose, walking in the midst of the fire; and they are not hurt, and the form of the fourth is like the Son of God."[8] In the fourth-century a Rabbi by the name of Berekiah claimed that for such a bold statement, Nebuchadnezzar was delivered over to Satan by God for blasphemy in that he said a "Son of God"

---

[3] Acts 17:28.

[4] Many have sought to superimpose the Hellenistic construct of the "divine man" (*theios aner*)—deriving from classical legend and mythology—on New Testament Christology. Even Geza Vermes proclaims it "bound to prove awkward and difficult" (*Jesus the Jew*, 200), and I would add speculative.

[5] Adela Yarbro Collins, "Mark and His Readers: The Son of God among Greeks and Romans," *The Harvard Theological Review* 93, 2 (2000): 86.

[6] Job 1:6. Also see Job 2:1, 38:7; Psa 89:6-7.

[7] Gen 6:4. I am not in any way claiming that this is the proper meaning of "sons of God," but rather am presenting the way in which early Judaic thought would have understood it. Also see Gen 6:2; Deut 32:8 in certain manuscripts.

[8] Dan 3:25. It is often suggested that "Son of God" in this passage is better translated as "son of the gods."

was in the furnace, whereas in fact it was only an angel.[9] Whether such a rabbinic interpretation was free of Christian thought is difficult to say, but what remains is that in early Judaism the fourth figure was understood to be an angel or heavenly being.

At other times it is the *nation of Israel* which is the son: "Israel is My son, My firstborn,"[10] God is the Father of Israel,[11] and the people of Israel are explicitly called the "sons of the living God."[12] This honor of sonship later is bestowed upon the *kings of Israel*: "I will be his Father, and he shall be My son."[13] The king is thus placed in a unique relationship with the God of Israel. In another place, the nature of this relationship is made more dramatic: "You are My Son, today I have begotten You."[14] Both of these references to the sonship of the kings would become the basis upon which the understanding of the Anointed king (*Masiah* in Hebrew) as the Son of God would be built.

In later Jewish thought, in the intertestamental period (a period that is reflective of first-century Palestinian thought), the "son of God" title is further developed. Angels are called "sons of heaven,"[15] as well as "sons of God,"[16] and Israel once more is called God's son.[17] We also hear that any Jew who cares for the needy is called "son of the most High,"[18] and that the Maccabean martyrs are the "children of heaven."[19] In the Hellenistic-Jewish work of *Joseph and Asneth*, Joseph is called a "son of God" by the Egyptians.[20] But perhaps the most significant usage is that of the famed righteous man of the *Wisdom of Solomon* who suffers on account of his claim to be the son of God:

> He professes to have knowledge of God,
> And calls himself a child of the Lord...
> And boasts that God is his father...
> For if the righteous man is *God's son*, he will help him,
> And will deliver him from the hand of his adversaries.[21]

---

[9] *Midrash on Exodus Rabbah* 20:10.
[10] Exod 4:22; Jer 31:9, 20; Hos 11:1.
[11] Deut 32:6.
[12] Hos 1:10.
[13] 2 Sam 7:14; 1 Chr 17:13, 22:19, 28:6.
[14] Psa 2:7, 89:26.
[15] *1 Enoch* 13:8.
[16] *1 Enoch* 69:4-5, 71:1, 106:5.
[17] *Wisdom of Solomon* 9:7; *Jubilees* 1:25.
[18] *Sirach* 4:10.
[19] 2 Macc 7:34.
[20] *Joseph and Asneth* 6:2.
[21] *Wisdom of Solomon* 2:13, 16, 18; also see 5:5. It should be noted that this is a Deuterocanonical work, and hence is part of the canonised Scriptures in the Orthodox and

This brings us to the strange stories of two celebrated holy men (contemporary with Jesus) that are depicted in the early Jewish literature. In the first, a heavenly voice is said to have declared that the entire world was fed on account of Hanina ben Dosa, one who was declared by the mysterious voice to be "*My son*."[22] Stranger still is the case of Honi the Circle-Drawer. He is said to have drawn a circle in the dust, stood in the middle of it, and prayed to God "like a *son of Your house*," and proceeded to threaten that he would not move till it rained. For such a threat he was almost excommunicated, that is, till it was acknowledged that Honi was simply acting as a son with his father:

> Rabbi Simeon b. Shatah said to him: "If you were not Honi, I should decree a ban of excommunication against you. But what am I going to do to you? For you importune before God, so He does what you want, like a son who importunes his father, so he does what he wants."[23]

But though each and every Jew was in a certain sense a son of God, over time the title came to be given especially to the "just man," chief among whom was the messianic son of David.[24] In the book of Fourth Ezra, God clearly describes His relationship to His chosen One: "*My son* the Messiah shall be revealed."[25] Elsewhere the "Son of Man" (a title often associated with the Messiah) is also identified as "My son."[26] If we then recall that in second Samuel and in the second psalm,[27] the king is expressly called "son," then it becomes evident that sonship and the messianic concept were closely related. So much so that the Qumran writings (dated 150 BC to 70 AD), by taking up the theme of sonship in second Samuel, proclaim that a mighty King will arise who is the "Son of God."[28] These very same writings in another place are unmistakably explicit in revealing a time when God will have begotten a Messiah.[29] No longer is this mysterious king only *a* son of God, He now is *the* messianic Son of God. It should be cautioned that even though this connection of the messianic concept to the "Son of God" title is often disputed, we may say that at worst it was just coming into usage

Catholic Churches. For an analysis of this work see Brendan Byrne, *'Sons of God'—'Seed of Abraham'* (Rome: Biblical Institute Press, 1979), 38-48.

[22] *Babylonian Talmud Taanit* 24b.

[23] *Mishnah Taanit* 3:8.

[24] Geza Vermes, *Jesus the Jew*, 195.

[25] *4 Ezra* 7:28.

[26] *4 Ezra* 13:37.

[27] 2 Sam 7:14, Psa 2:7.

[28] *4QpsDan A*ᵃ.

[29] *1QSamuel* 2:11-12. Also see *4QFlorilegium* 1:10-12.

as a messianic association in early Judaism,[30] and at best, in line with the Qumran scrolls, "the expected royal Messiah was also thought of as God's son."[31] But whatever the case may be, the messianic connotations associated with the "Son of God" concept should not be altogether dismissed.

From this brief survey it is evident that the language of divine sonship was "confusingly varied and very obscure"[32] by the time of Jesus. It could stand for a righteous or holy man who enjoyed an intimate relationship with God as his father, or in the case of angels as a mark of their proximity to God, or in the case of the kings as a bestowal of honor as God's representative among His people. It would seem that an angel, nation, emperor, king, philosopher, or righteous man, in essence anyone who by nature or virtue attained a nearness to God, could be called a son of God. But in the very least it should be clear that the title did *not* in any way denote one who was divine as God is divine. And though similar, the Jewish writings never went as far as the Hellenistic writings in claiming that a human could *actually* be the offspring of God as in the case of Zeus' many children. That is to say, the Jewish authors were at pains to show that there still remained an exceedingly great chasm between God and man:

> The point to be underlined is that Jewish apologists in and before the first century AD could use extravagant language attributing deity in some sense to particular individuals and yet not intend it to be taken *literally* and without wishing to diminish the distinction between God and man.[33]

It was one thing to declare a man a "son of God," it was drastically another to identify him with the one God of Israel. In the early Judaic understanding of the title "any idea of physical descent [was] strictly excluded,"[34] and the relationship was "never one of true paternity,"[35] or of identification of essence, but rather one of relation. To be clear, there was

---

[30] R. H. Fuller, *The Foundations of New Testament Christology* (New York: Scribner, 1965), 32.

[31] James D. G. Dunn, *Jesus Remembered*, 709.

[32] Martin Hengel, *The Son of God*, 63.

[33] James D. G. Dunn, *Christology in the Making: A New Testament Inquiry into the Origins of the Doctrine of the Incarnation* (London: SCM Press, 1980), 19. For a more in depth discussion of the Judaic background to the title as well as its relation to the Gospel of Mark specifically, see Adela Yarbro Collins, "Mark and His Readers: The Son of God among Jews," *The Harvard Theological Review* 92, 4 (1999): 393-408.

[34] Walter Kasper, *Jesus the Christ* (New York: Paulist Press, 1976), 109; Also see Also see I. Howard Marshall, *The Origins of New Testament Christology* (Leicester: Apollos, 1990), 112-113.

[35] Brendan Byrne, *'Sons of God'—'Seed of Abraham,'* 13. Also see Oscar Cullmann, *The Christology of the New Testament*, (London: SCM Press, 1959), 275.

but one God of Israel and the Son of God title before Jesus never encroached upon this. But that said, leaping from "Son of God" to God would hardly be possible had not the seeds already been present in the deep and dynamic wells of early Judaism.[36]

The question thus becomes: If Jesus did indeed claim to be the Son of God; did He imagine this to be in the same way that the title was understood at His time? And if the Son of God title never denoted that one was necessarily divine, then how did the title become a marker of divinity?

JESUS AND GOD: SON OF THE FATHER

To answer these questions is not as simple as it may initially appear. In the first place, to speak of the self-consciousness of a man is difficult; let alone a man who lived two thousand years ago; let alone a Man who is worshipped by the Church as God. Therefore we must proceed humbly, cautiously, and with the knowledge that our advances will be limited. Nevertheless in so far as Jesus "emptied Himself" and became truly human, something may be said. So what then did Jesus say of Himself? Did He claim that He was the Son of God? And if He did, what did this really mean?

If you were to take the Synoptic Gospels (Matthew, Mark, and Luke), you would inevitably be taken aback by a most striking observation: Jesus *never* calls Himself "Son of God"! Not even a single time. And only twice does He call Himself "Son." This begs the inquiry: If Jesus never used such titles, from where did such titles originate?

In the Synoptic Gospels there are three different groups of people or beings who declare that Jesus is the Son of God—the demons, the heavenly hosts (including God Himself), and humans. In the chapter concerning the messianic secret we saw that the *demons* on being exorcised would often cry out, "You are the Son of God."[37] The same declaration was found at the mouth of Satan during the temptations of Jesus: "If you are the Son of God..."[38] They were not, however, the only incorporeal creatures to reveal the divine sonship of Jesus. When Mary first conceived she was told by an *angel*: "[the] Holy One who is to be born will be called the Son of God."[39] And at two recorded points in Jesus' life, during His baptism and transfiguration, a

---

[36] James H. Charlesworth, *Jesus within Judaism: New Light from Exciting Archaeological Discoveries* (London: SPCK, 1989), 152.

[37] Mark 3:11. Also see Mark 5:7, Matt 8:29, Luke 4:41.

[38] Matt 4:3, Luke 4:3; Matt 4:6, Luke 4:9.

[39] Luke 1:35.

Voice is heard from heaven declaring: "This is My beloved Son, in whom I am well pleased."[40]

This brings us to the third group of *human* declaration. Sometimes this declaration was of belief and at other times it was of accusation. The disciples worshipped Jesus as "Son of God,"[41] the centurion after witnessing the crucifixion cried out: "Truly this Man was the Son of God,"[42] and Peter confessed: "You are the Christ, the Son of the Living God."[43] On the other hand, the high-priest at the trial pressed Jesus: "Tell us if You are the Christ, the Son of God,"[44] and the crowd mocked: "If You are the Son of God, come down from the cross."[45] These declarations must, of course, be taken in the context of Jesus' reply. Surprisingly, whenever Jesus is declared to be the "Son of God" by others, His response is often a sharp command to silence, else is ambiguous, and at best is reluctant.

If Jesus was reluctant to refer to Himself as the "Son of God" in the Synoptic Gospels, the same may not be said of the Gospel of John. Following the other evangelists, John records six occasions in which Jesus is called the "Son of God" by others.[46] What sets John apart is that for the first time Jesus personally gives Himself out as the "Son of God."[47] Even then, we need to admit that He only does so four times, though He does refer to Himself as "the Son" frequently.[48] It is here, however, that John introduces a transforming dimension into the title. Jesus is not simply the "Son of God," rather He is the *"only-begotten* Son of God."[49] So unique that He is unlike any man before or after Him. So unique that He was in some manner with the Father before the creation: for John He was the pre-existent[50] Son who

---

[40] Matt 3:17, 17:5. This brings to mind the Jewish notion of the *bath kol*. In the intertestamental and rabbinic literature there was a held opinion that a voice from heaven had taken the place of prophecy in declaring the righteousness of God's elect (*Tosephta* 13:2), that is, to testify to their righteousness. An interesting prophecy from the *Testament of Levi*, undoubtedly betraying its Christian editing, goes as such: "The heavens shall be opened, and from the temple of glory shall the sanctification come upon Him with the *Father's voice*, as from Abraham the father of Isaac. And the glory of the Most High shall be uttered over Him, and the spirit of understanding and of sanctification shall *rest upon Him in the water*" (*Testament of Levi* 18, ANF 8:16).

[41] Matt 14:33. Also see Mark 1:1.

[42] Mark 15:29, Matt 27:54.

[43] Matt 16:16.

[44] Matt 26:63, Luke 22:70, Mark 14:61.

[45] Matt 27:40, 43.

[46] Four times by the disciples (John 1:34, 49; 6:69; 20:31), once by Martha (11:27), and once by the Jews as an accusation (19:7).

[47] John 3:18, 5:25, 9:35, 11:4.

[48] For example, John 3:16, 3:35, 5:19, 6:40.

[49] John 3:18. Also see John 1:14, 18.

[50] John 17:5, 6:62, 8:38, 10:36. Also see C. H. Dodd, *The Interpretation of the Fourth Gospel*

descended[51] from heaven on the authority of His Father.[52] Nowhere is this more powerfully and strikingly seen than in the saying, "Before Abraham was, *I am*."[53] And yet, the fact still remains that despite John's frequent heavenly images of Jesus, Jesus only calls Himself "Son of God" four times. A fact that weighs heavily on the background of the seeming silence of Jesus as revealed in the Synoptic Gospels.

It is no great leap, then, to suggest that Jesus showed no special affinity for the title "Son of God" (at least when compared to other titles). And if this be the case why did others refer to Him as such, and why did it become the principal confession of the Church?

The answer lies in the observation that though Jesus did not explicitly or consistently give Himself out as "Son of God" or "Son," He most definitely understood God as *Father*. Not merely as "Father" in the sense of the sonship of Israel to God, but rather Jesus knew God as "*My* Father." Indeed if you consider the language used in the Gospels, the characteristic address of Jesus for God was *Abba*, Father.[54] This Aramaic noun, *Abba*, conveyed familial intimacy whilst also maintaining a level of respect.[55] It is this intimacy which marks Jesus' usage. In the Gospel of John, for instance, Jesus uses "Father" more than one hundred times. Intriguingly, it is only at the cross that we hear Jesus for the first time address God as "My God," for till then it was always "My Father," "Father," or "the Father." This stood in stark contrast to the prayers of Jesus' day in which God was customarily addressed as the "Lord of heaven and earth." This is seen in the prayers of first-century Judaism that have survived to our day (for example, the Kaddish and the eighteen Benedictions) which functioned on a characteristically formal level.

It need be said, however, that Jesus was neither the first nor the last to call God "Father." But whilst others may have on occasion called God "Father," or even rarely *Abba*, no one did it as consistently or as forcefully as Jesus. And thus though perhaps not unheard of, it was at the least "quite unusual for a Jew" to address God as such.[56] It was this which specifically differentiated Jesus from His contemporaries. Jesus was able to refer to God as His Father, simply because He understood Himself to be in a relationship

---

(Cambridge: Cambridge University Press, 1953), 262.

[51] John 3:13, 6:38, 58.

[52] John 3:31, 9:39, 8:42, 16:27, 12:46, 18:37.

[53] John 8:58.

[54] Mark 14:36. Paul's reference to *Abba* gives an impression that it was a special address that was not in common usage (Rom 8:15, Gal 4:6). See Martin Hengel, *The Son of God*, 63.

[55] In spite of today's popular thought *Abba* did not mean "daddy," though it did convey familial intimacy.

[56] Martin Hengel, *The Son of God*, 63.

with God that was in every way unique. To call God "Father" was to express "a sense of sonship,"[57] and to reflect a "filial consciousness."[58] In other words, Jesus may not have consistently given Himself out as the "Son of God," but we may certainly say that *He understood Himself to be the Son of the One He called Father.* And it was this, perhaps singularly, that set Him apart.[59] But did Jesus view His sonship as different to the sonship of others, of His disciples for example? Were they not also called to pray to God as "our Father"?[60]

It was not simply the fact that Jesus referred to God as Father that marked Him out from His fellow Jews; it was the *way* in which He did so. Jesus repeatedly speaks to the disciples of "*your* Father,"[61] but in His prayers to God it is always "*My* Father."[62] Even when Jesus teaches the disciples to pray "our Father," He is teaching *them* how *they* should pray. He is never recorded as praying as such, for Jesus knows God intimately and uniquely as "*My* Father." This point of distinction is made brilliantly clear when Jesus tells Mary Magdalene to go and tell the disciples, "I am ascending to *My* Father and *your* Father."[63] And thus the Father is the same but the relationship is not. Jesus distinguishes His unique sonship from the universal Fatherhood of God. By His consistent usage of Father and by setting that usage in contrast to the rest of Israel, Jesus was claiming "a special relationship to God as His Father beyond the general relationship postulated in contemporary Judaism."[64] Plainly, in the words of Gregory of Nazianzus, Jesus is called Son for the "manner of His sonship is peculiar to Himself."[65]

A number of incidents reaffirm this distinction of Jesus' sonship. One such incident, though often dismissed as *only* a parable, is that of Jesus' parable of the rejection of the only son:

> Now at vintage-time he sent a *servant* to the vinedressers, that he might receive some of the fruit of the vineyard from the vinedressers. And they

[57] James D. G. Dunn, *Christology in the Making*, 28.

[58] I. Howard Marshall, *The Origins of New Testament Christology*, 117.

[59] John P. Meier, "Reflections on Jesus-of-History Research Today," 98-99; James D. G. Dunn, *Christology in the Making*, 27. Also see Eduard Schweizer, *Jesus Christ: The Man from Nazareth and the Exalted Lord* (London: SCM Press, 1989), 49-50; Vesilin Kesich, *The Gospel Image of Christ*, 164.

[60] Matt 6:9.

[61] Matt 5:16 for instance.

[62] Luke 2:49-50.

[63] John 20:17.

[64] Raymond E. Brown, *Jesus God and Man: Modern Biblical Reflections* (London: Geoffrey Chapman, 1968), 89. Also see his other work, *An Introduction to New Testament Christology* (New York: Paulist Press, 1994), 80-88. Also see David Flusser, *Jesus* (Jerusalem: Magnes Press, 1998), 118.

[65] Gregory of Nazianzus, *Orations* 30.20, NPNF 2 7:316.

took him and beat him and sent him away empty-handed... And again he sent another, and him they killed; and many others, beating some and killing some. Therefore still having *one son, his beloved*, he also sent him to them last, saying, "They will respect my son." But those vinedressers said among themselves, "This is the heir. Come, let us kill him, and the inheritance will be ours." So they took him and killed him and cast him out of the vineyard.[66]

Here, then, is an obvious and striking contrast between the "only beloved son" and the "many servants." The only possible conclusion is that Jesus thought Himself to be a Son of none other than the owner of the vineyard. And if the owner of the vineyard is God, then He is none other than God's Son. But the crucial difference is that He is a Son, in a way that the other "many servants" were not, and therefore Jesus was and is the "*only* begotten Son." A fact that is illustrated in the two "Son"[67] sayings of the Synoptic Gospels:

...of that day and hour no one knows, not even the angels in heaven, nor the *Son*, but only the Father...[68]

All things have been delivered to Me by My Father, and no one knows the Son except the Father. Nor does anyone know the Father *except the Son*, and the one to whom the Son wills to reveal Him.[69]

In the first saying the "Son," though apparently "limited" in knowledge, is still placed in distinction to the angels and the *rest* of humanity.[70] The second of the sayings draws, in the estimation of one scholar, "on the maxim that a father and son know each other intimately and a son is the best one to reveal the innermost thoughts of the father."[71] If Jesus is the *sole* revealer of

---

[66] Mark 12:2-8.

[67] Scholars have often claimed that Jesus could not have really spoken these two sayings, since they are too dissimilar to the rest of their respective Gospels. One such scholar, Geza Vermes has claimed they are "representative of the latest stage of the doctrinal evolution and consequently out of place in a historical investigation of Jesus" (Geza Vermes, *Jesus the Jew*, 200). Needless to say, the easiest and most insensible approach to a difficult saying is to dismiss it, though this would hardly be a "historical investigation."

[68] Mark 13:32.

[69] Matt 11:27.

[70] This difficult problem of the apparently limited knowledge of Jesus, whilst not addressed directly or fully, will be examined at least in concept in the chapters, "My Father is Greater than I," and "My God, Why Have You Forsaken Me."

[71] Raymond E. Brown, *Jesus God and Man*, 90. Also see Vincent Taylor, *The Names of Jesus* (London: Macmillan, 1953), 60-65.

the Father, then He clearly is laying claim to an exclusive kinship with God that hereto is unknown to Israel.[72] Not even Abraham or Moses had ever dared to claim such a status. Gustaf Dalman puts it succinctly:

> Jesus never applied to Himself the title "Son of God," [besides in John] and yet made it indubitably clear that He was not merely "*a*" but "*the* Son of God." The position assumed shows itself in the preference He manifested for the designation of God as "His" Father, in the use of which never includes the disciples along with Himself.[73]

Quite clearly, if we may dare to speak of His thoughts, Jesus understood Himself to be in a radically different relationship to God. And if we consider the declaration from heaven at His baptism and transfiguration, then evidently so did God.[74] According to the Gospels Jesus also understood Himself to be not only a son of God, but exclusively the *only* "Son of God" which in some manner He had always been.[75] It is of no surprise, then, that the New Testament writers perceived Jesus to be the "Son of God" in a way that no other Jew had or would ever be, and subsequently reserved the title for Him *alone*.

Finally, we need to understand that twenty centuries later we have in some respects made a messianic title out of words that were not originally titular.[76] To say that someone is a son of God means just that: they are a son of the God of Israel. Therefore if Jesus claimed to be in a relationship of Son to the Father, then it follows that He would be understood as the Son of God. In other words, the aim is not to see Jesus taking upon Himself the messianic title "Son of God" (though according to the Qumran literature such a title may have had messianic overtones) but rather Jesus simply understood Himself to be the unique Son of the God who was His Father. The crucial point being that unlike other titles such as "Son of Man" or "Messiah," the phrase "Son of God" was more so a description of a relationship between Father and Son than an already existent title.

We may then comfortably say that though Jesus may not have consistently given Himself out as the "Son of God," He most certainly depicted Himself

---

[72] M. de Jonge, *Jesus, the Servant Messiah* (New Haven: Yale University Press, 1991), 74; Also see I. Howard Marshall, *The Origins of New Testament Christology*, 115.

[73] Gustaf Dalman, *The Words of Jesus*, 280. Also see Martin Hengel, *The Son of God*, 63.

[74] Matt 3:17, 17:5.

[75] John 17:5.

[76] For this reason I have often called "Son of God" a title though acknowledging that it may not have been a messianic title in the proper sense. Perhaps it would have been more accurate to refer to it as the "Son of God" relationship.

as *the* Son of *the* Father in a way that radically differed from other Jews. But nowhere, so far, has this implied that He is divine as God is divine. How then did the early Church move from referring to Jesus as the "Son of God" to worshipping Him as God?

JESUS AND GOD: GOD FROM GOD

It should be clear by now that the real issue at hand is what Jesus *meant* when He claimed to be uniquely in relation to God as Son. Did He imply that the relationship was one of nature? Or, more to the point, did He claim to be God?

The problem with such a question is that to Jesus' fellow Jews, this would really be asking: Did Jesus claim to be the God of Israel in heaven? The answer to which is a most certain no. To the first-century Jew there was but *one* God of Israel. This was an unalterable fact in the life of the Jew. For a fellow Jew to then claim *anah elah* ("I am God"), he could only be heard as a fool at best and a demon at worst. In the words of a Catholic scholar: "For the Jew 'God' meant God the Father in heaven; and to apply this term to Jesus who was not the Father and who had come down to earth made no sense."[77] It is impossible to imagine how absurd such a claim would sound, for it would threaten the very "monotheism which, as Jews, they instinctively professed."[78]

Clearly, then, Jesus would not and could not have ever said the words "I am God" given the constraints of His context. But though Jesus may not have explicitly laid claim to the title of God, He definitely said and did things that indicated that He was indeed divine. Only when the early Church had begun to penetrate the mystery of who God really was, could it also claim that Jesus was God without displacing the divinity of the Father. Since to the ancient Jew God could only refer strictly to the God to whom Jesus prayed, it follows that the divinity of Jesus could only be maintained once a Jew could envision both Jesus and God His Father as both being *one* God. For any claim otherwise, that Jesus was somehow taking over or laying claim to the throne of the God, would be pure heresy to the Jew. This acute problem (that there was one God of Israel, and yet Jesus also was somehow divine) could only be worked out in the coming centuries of Christianity.[79]

---

[77] Raymond E. Brown, *Jesus God and Man*, 87. Also see Joseph A. Fitzmyer, *A Christological Catechism: New Testament Answers* (New York: Paulist Press, 1991), 98.

[78] A. E. Harvey, *Jesus and the Constraints of History*, 167.

[79] I. Howard Marshall, *The Origins of New Testament Christology*, 123.

This serves to remind us that we should not expect an explicit statement of divinity from the mouth of Jesus in the pages of the Gospels. But at the same time something led the early Church from the claim that Jesus was the Son of God, to the conviction that He was divine in the very same way that God was divine.[80] What then were these foundations or stepping stones on which such a conviction stood? In other words, why did they claim with such certainty that Jesus really was God?

Though John spent an entire Gospel attempting to answer such a question, there are perhaps *five* indisputable things (among many others) that Jesus said or did that mark Him out as divine.

The first is that Jesus took upon Himself a divine prerogative and *forgave sins*.[81] To forgive sins is nothing especially great or divine. Any man is endowed with the authority to forgive sins that have been committed against *him*. But to forgive the sins that have been committed against *God* is an altogether different status. And if this were not a sufficient enough claim to divinity, Jesus not only forgives sins but does so without the requirements of the law. E. P. Sanders, for one, has mistakenly argued that Jesus did not in fact forgive sins but merely pronounced God's forgiveness, which in itself was nothing new since it had always been the right of the priesthood.[82] This seems to miss some rather important details: namely that Jesus was not a priest, and that the acts of sacrifice required for forgiveness were not commanded. Despite the protestations of such scholars, the reactions of the scribes and Pharisees on witnessing Jesus forgiving sins gives the matter away: "Why does this Man speak blasphemies like this? Who can forgive sins but God *alone*?"[83] Precisely. So who then is Jesus?

Secondly, Jesus spoke with the *authority* that was only the privilege of God.[84] As we have seen Jesus would often begin His statements with *Amen*.[85] There is nothing peculiar about such a word in and of itself, but to use it at the beginning of a statement was "unfamiliar to the entire range of Jewish literature."[86] Simply put, Jesus had no need for anyone to confirm His words: He spoke on His own authority. And it was with such authority that Jesus

---

[80] For two fascinating suggestions (each is more convincing when read with the other), see N. T. Wright "Jesus' Self-Understanding," in *The Incarnation*, ed. S. T. Davis (Oxford: OUP, 2002), 47-61; and L. W. Hurtado, *How on Earth Did Jesus Become a God? Historical Questions about Earliest Devotion to Jesus* (Grand Rapids: Wm. B. Eerdmans, 2005), 13-30.

[81] See Mark 2:5, 10; Luke 5:20, 7:48.

[82] E. P. Sanders, *Jesus and Judaism*, 240.

[83] Mark 2:7, Luke 5:21.

[84] For example Matt 21:23, Luke 4:32, 36.

[85] For example Matt 5:18.

[86] Gustaf Dalman, *The Words of Jesus*, 226.

made clear to Israel that His interpretation of the law was not merely *an* interpretation among others, but rather the *only* interpretation. "In short, Jesus did not think of Himself as just another prophetic spokesperson for God: He spoke as if He were divine."[87] Jesus' authority came not from His social status, learning, or descent. It came from within as a marker of His relationship to God as Son.

Given this authority of speech, we should also mention a third indication: the particular *language* of Jesus. In the Gospel of John, Jesus uses the words "I am" (in Greek *ego eimi*) in three very particular ways: with an explicit predicate, "I am the bread of life"; with an implied predicate, "I am He"; and finally without any predicate, or absolutely, "before Abraham was, I am."[88] The significance of these sayings, especially the latter, lies in their Old Testament background. In the book of Exodus during the "burning bush" passage, God reveals His name:

> ...And God said to Moses, "I am who I am [in Hebrew, *ehyeh asher ehyeh*]." And He said, "Thus you shall say to the children of Israel, 'I am [*ehyeh*] has sent me to you.'" Moreover God said to Moses, "Thus you shall say to the children of Israel: 'The Lord [*Yahweh*] God of your fathers...has sent me to you. This is My name forever...'"[89]

Though much can be said about this intense passage, it is important to at least notice that the "sacred" name for God is "I am" (*ehyeh*) and that its third person form is given as "Lord" (*Yahweh*).[90] When we consider the Greek translation of the Old Testament (the Septuagint) that was used by Greek speaking Jews and the early Christians, the parallels become undeniable. The Hebrew name of God, *ehyeh*, is translated to Greek as the absolute *ego eimi*—the very same absolute "I am" used by Jesus in the Gospel of John. We should also bear in mind that this name was sacred and reserved only for God in early Judaism, so much so that pronouncing or even writing it was forbidden and punishable by death. This, then, is one of the highest claims for Jesus' divinity in the Gospels. When Jesus declares in the absolute: "before Abraham was, I am," He not only utters the sacred name of God, but ineffably and unequivocally makes it His own. Indeed, the first-century reaction was clear enough: "they took up stones to throw at Him."[91]

---

[87] Stephen T. Davis, "Was Jesus Mad, Bad, or God?", in *The Incarnation*, ed. Stephen T. Davis, Daniel Kendall, Gerald O'Collins (New York: Oxford University Press, 2002), 242.

[88] John 6:35; 18:5; 8:58 respectively.

[89] Exod 3:14-15.

[90] See Daniel Fanous, "I am who I am," in *The Person of the Christ*, 114-125.

[91] John 8:59. It is not surprising that this idiom of Jesus resulted in the Gospel writers

This brings us to our fourth indication: that Jesus revealed a *unique sonship* to God of which no other human or angel could ever dare to claim. We have at length sought to show this. Whilst perhaps referring to God as *Abba*[92] was not unheard of in first-century Palestine, Jesus' sheer consistency and specificity in differentiating between "My Father" and "your Father" places Him in a unique relationship with the Father. A claim which "would have fallen on Jewish ears" as at least an indicator that Jesus was more than a man.[93] Perhaps the simplest reason for this is to consider what the "Son of God" relationship is actually supposing, even though it must be admitted that the title in its earliest context never went so far. Plainly, what does it mean to be a son, other than to be of the same nature as one's father? The very meaning of son is to be of the same generic class as one's father. If this be the case, then the claim (that Jesus as the Son of God was of the same nature and hence divinity as God His Father) was not a far logical leap.

The fifth and final indication looks to the hope that the prophets had placed in the One who was to come. The idea of a *pre-existent redeemer* was well attested to in ancient Judaism and found its roots in the book of Micah: "But you, Bethlehem Ephrathah...out of you shall come forth to Me the One to be Ruler in Israel, Whose goings forth are from of old, *from everlasting*."[94] In the book of Enoch we are told of this mysterious redeemer that He has "been chosen and hidden before Him [God], *before the creation* of the world and for evermore,"[95] and again: "For from the *beginning* the Son of Man was hidden, and the Most High preserved Him in the presence of His might."[96] In the later work of Fourth Ezra, the redeemer is "He whom the Most High has been keeping [or concealing] for *many ages*."[97]

---

transferring the title of God, "Lord" (in Hebrew *Yahweh*, Greek *Kyrios*), to Jesus. This inevitably would have meant placing Jesus on the same level as God. For a thorough discussion of this title, see Joseph A. Fitzmyer, *The Gospel According to Luke* Vol. I (New York: Doubleday, 1986), 200-204.

[92] Joachim Jeremias (*New Testament Theology*, 61-68) has become famed for claiming that in calling God *Abba*, Jesus was addressing God in a manner that was thereto unknown in pre-Christian Judaism. Whilst perhaps overstating the point, it most definitely stands that Jesus used it consistently and characteristically in a manner that was in stark contrast to His day. For scholars that maintain such a unique usage see John P. Meier, *A Marginal Jew*, Vol. II, 358-359; Joseph A. Fitzmyer, *The Gospel According to Luke* Vol. II (New York: Doubleday, 1985), 898; B. Witherington, *Christology of Jesus* (Minneapolis: Fortress Press, 1990), 215-220.

[93] Joel Marcus, "Mark 14:61: 'Are You the Messiah-Son-of-God?,'" *Novum Testamentum* 31 (1989): 141.

[94] Mic 5:2. Also see Psa 110:3.

[95] *1 Enoch* 48:6. Chapters 37-71 have been dated as before 70 AD. In these particular chapters, Son of Man is equivalent with Messiah, Chosen One, and Righteous One.

[96] *1 Enoch* 62:7.

[97] *4 Ezra* 13:25-26; 14:9. This work is commonly dated to 100 AD. Once more the Messiah

But what has this to do with Jesus?

If we recall that Jesus was *also* often referred to, by his fellow men, as the "Messiah" and as the "Son of Man"—both of whom were concretely related to the idea of pre-existence—then it begs the conclusion that the unique sonship of Jesus as the "Son of God" would inevitably be associated in some way with pre-existence. It should be noted that the "Son of God" conception in no clear way was *originally* associated with such pre-existent notions. But if Jesus was the "Messiah" and the "Son of Man" in the minds of at least some of His fellow Jews, then the claim to sonship would be indelibly marked with pre-existence from then on.[98] For the esteemed scholar Martin Hengel, this association was inevitable: "there was an *inner necessity* about the introduction of the idea of pre-existence into Christology."[99]

Consequently, should we honestly take into account these five "stepping stones" that we have seen (as well as Jesus' entire life), then it is not too difficult to see the path to the conviction that He was indeed divine. Jesus' enemies, it would seem, were already aware of such a path. Though Jesus may not have explicitly given Himself out as God, we do well to remember that at Jesus' trial,[100] as well as at various points during His ministry, He is effectively accused of such:

> For a good work we do not stone You, but for *blasphemy*, and because You, being a Man, make Yourself God.[101]

Therefore at the very least, something Jesus said or did (and I would argue that it was primarily His assertion of unique sonship) forced His opponents to accuse Him of blasphemy. The violent reaction of Jesus' enemies compels us to conclude that Jesus was not understood to be saying that He was simply chosen by God as any other man may be, but rather that He was in some way divine. Evidently the blasphemy charge reflects the impression that Jesus had declared "that He was somehow on par with Yahweh."[102] What astounds

---

is identified with Son of Man in this particular work.

[98] See Daniel Fanous, *The Person of the Christ*, 135-232.

[99] Martin Hengel, *The Son of God*, 71.

[100] For instance Mark 14:64.

[101] John 10:33. It should be noted that Jesus' response to this accusation is doubly indirect in that He first asks concerning the reference to the Judges who were called "gods" by God, and then asks: "do you say of Him whom the Father sanctified and sent into the world, 'You are blaspheming,' because I said, 'I am the Son of God'?" Therefore, Jesus does not respond to their claim that He "made Himself God," but rather asserts that claiming to be the "Son of God" is not blasphemy in so far as being called a "god" is not blasphemy in its context. In short, Jesus is not explicitly claiming to be God here. Also see Mark 2:7.

[102] Joseph A. Fitzmyer, *A Christological Catechism*, 98.

is that Jesus is never recorded as correcting His hearers and saying perhaps, "this is not what I mean." If His opponents were so enraged that Jesus had overstepped the boundaries as a man, then it follows that His followers must have likewise pondered such thoughts.

If Jesus was understood (at least by some) to be pre-existent with the Father before all ages, if He was the sole revealer of the Father, if He stood where no man has ever stood as the unique Son of God, and if He acted and spoke at times as though He were divine, then there is but one possible answer. Faced with such a claim to authority, the famed Jewish scholar, Jacob Neusner, was pressed to ask in exasperation: *"Who do you think you are? God?"*[103] The answer to which, at least for me, is undeniably clear.

---

[103] Jacob Neusner, in an interview following the publication of his book *A Rabbi Talks with Jesus: An Intermillenial Interfaith Exchange* (New York: Doubleday, 1993). Cited in N. T. Wright, "Jesus and the Identity of God," *Ex Auditu* 14 (1998): 52 n. 37.

CHAPTER FIFTEEN

'My Father is greater than I'

To become truly great, one has to stand with people, not above them.
—CHARLES DE MONTESQUIEU

EACH AND EVERY SAYING THAT WE HAVE SCRUTINIZED is for some reason or another problematic. Some are difficult in that they deal with complex subjects or because they point to a context more ancient than ours. Others, still, challenge us not in concept but in their call for change (to which our humanity reluctantly reacts). Other sayings are problematic, if for nothing else, simply because they offend our much practiced sensibilities. But few, if any, of the sayings have sparked as much controversy and so plagued Christianity as the saying to which we now turn.

Jesus in speaking to His disciples for one of the last times declared: "My Father is *greater* than I."[1] These words would go on to echo for centuries, if not millennia.

One who heard such words in the early fourth-century was an ascetic and apparently charming Alexandrian clergyman by the name of Arius.

---

[1] John 14:28.

His line of thinking may have started in this manner: "If God (the One Jesus calls Father) was greater than the Son (Jesus), then it logically follows that the Son is *less* than the Father." So far, few would be overly concerned since this seems to be the point that Jesus is making. The infamous priest then went on to suppose: "And if God was a Father, then in order to become a Father, He must have at some point had a Son. Which if we admit, then we must also admit that the Son had a beginning of existence when He was born. It can only then be that there was a time when God the Father was alone by Himself without the Son." What this "priest" was really saying then becomes clear: "If the Son was less, and if as a Son He had a beginning of existence, then it logically stands to reason that Son is *not* the same nature as God the Father, but rather is a secondary creation in that the Son came *after* the Father."[2] In short, the Son cannot be God in the same way that the Father is God. It was at varying points during the evolution of such thought that warning sirens began to sound throughout the entire Christian world. Within decades this heresy threatened the unity of both Church and empire.

Soon after lighting this theological inferno that would burn throughout Christendom for the coming centuries, this "priest" was seized by a "violent relaxation of the bowels":

> ...and being directed to the back of Constantine's Forum, he [Arius] hastened there. Soon after, faintness came over him, and together with the evacuations his bowels protruded, followed by a copious hemorrhage, and the descent of the smaller intestines: moreover portions of his spleen and liver were brought off in the effusion of blood... The scene of this catastrophe still is shown at Constantinople, as I have said behind the shambles in the colonnade: and by persons going by pointing the finger at the place, there is a perpetual remembrance preserved of this extraordinary kind of death.[3]

This ancient and gruesome account of the death of Arius is not reproduced here without purpose. First and foremost, it is a reminder of the severe truth that theology is not a mere matter of academic technicalities and debate, but rather the very line between life with God and life without Him: between life and death. Here, then, is an example of the effect of a saying carried down a false path to its most grave and tragic end. Secondly, though it is well and good to claim that Arius severely misunderstood the

---

[2] It should once again be noted that this is a paraphrase of Arius' thought.

[3] Socrates Scholastcius, *Ecclesiastical History* 1.38, NPNF 2 2:34. Some scholars have offered that Arius died from poisoning rather than the attested miraculous death—a position that is historically unverifiable.

words of Jesus, it does nothing to explain what Jesus actually meant. Arius, though often portrayed as depraved and sinister in the literature, simply took the words of Jesus to *one* logical (albeit catastrophic) conclusion. For how could Jesus be less than the Father, and yet at the same time be equal to Him? Mathematically, logically, and sociologically, if something was less, then, by definition it could not be equal to the thing to which it was being compared. So in what manner could Jesus be less than the Father, and yet still be God? How can such a glaring contradiction be explained? It is no real wonder that it is this saying, in my experience above all others, which most vexes the ordinary Christian.

REJOICE FOR THE FATHER IS GREATER?

One thing that always seems to be characteristic of past approaches to this saying is that it is isolated not only from the rest of the Gospels, but even from its immediately preceding verses. In effect it is taken out of context. So much so that if one were to look for a singular reason why Arius misunderstood this saying, it would probably be this. If you should doubt this, try to think of what Jesus was saying before He spoke these words. This would be challenging even for a well-versed Christian. What then was its context?

The saying is found in the fourteenth chapter of the Gospel of John, and stands as a part of the great farewell discourse in which Jesus exhorts His disciples to joy not fear:

> Peace I leave with you, My peace I give to you; not as the world gives do I give to you. Let not your heart be troubled, neither let it be afraid. You have heard Me say to you, "I am going away and coming back to you." If you loved Me, you would rejoice because I said, "I am going to the Father," for *My Father is greater than I.*[4]

The point of the passage is clear. The disciples had begun to grow agitated that Jesus had consistently talked of suffering and His imminent departure. Jesus therefore comforts them in a six part statement: (1) I have given you My peace; (2) So do not be troubled; (3) I am going away; (4) I am coming back; (5) If you loved Me, you would rejoice; (6) because My Father is greater than I. If we were given license to paraphrase, the statement would be heard as such: Do not be troubled, for I have given you My peace, and if

---

[4] John 14:27-28.

you really knew that I was going to My Father, you would rejoice *because* My Father is greater than I.

A few things become obvious. In the first place, Jesus granted to His disciples not simply peace, but *His* peace—a peace which is "not as the world gives." In other words, the peace is not one of circumstance. Jesus is not promising an idyllic world without tension, strife, or suffering. It is a peace that cannot be found atop mountains, or in serene temples. Rather it is *His* peace that is not dependent upon one's external environment. The point being that even to the depths of suffering, the disciples are not to be troubled, for their peace is from Jesus and not from the tranquility of external circumstance, or lack thereof. The second thing to notice is that Jesus is exhorting His disciples to *rejoice* in the knowledge that He will shortly leave them. This is counter-intuitive. The disciples had literally given up their lives to follow the One they had intimately known as their Master. Now He was not only telling them that He would imminently depart (without in their minds really changing the world as they expected), but also that this was a good and beneficial thing. Thirdly, it should be mentioned that Jesus was not denying the love of His disciples. Instead He was reminding them that to return to His Father was His very purpose and reason of being. "Any love that would fail to recognize and respect that is not true love."[5] True love that is not possessive must recognize that only by returning to His Father could Jesus "be glorified with that glory that He had with the Father before the world existed."[6] And though it was to the advantage of the disciples for Jesus to remain among them, it was as Cyril of Alexandria notes, not so for Jesus:

> ...it was clearly not to His advantage, so long a time to choose to abide in the guise of humility, which He had taken for our advantage, through His love to us, as we just now said: rather was He bound, when His dispensation towards us had been already suitably accomplished, to ascend to His own glory...[7]

It quickly becomes clear that "in the context everything is focused on His departure."[8] And this brings us to our last point—and this really is the

---

[5] Raymond E. Brown, *The Gospel According to John xiii-xxi*, Vol. II (New York: Doubleday, 1970), 654.

[6] Raymond E. Brown, *The Gospel According to John*, Vol. II, 655.

[7] Cyril of Alexandria, *Commentary on John*, Book 10, LFC 48:345. On the other hand John Chrysostom posits that the disciples should be joyful because though Jesus is to suffer, He goes to His Father who is "able to undo all dangers." *The Gospel of John* 75.4, NPNF 1 14:276.

[8] Herman N. Ridderbos, *The Gospel According to John: A Theological Commentary*, tr. John Vriend (Cambridge: Wm. B. Eerdmans, 1997), 512.

crucial thing to see—that it is *because* the "Father is greater" than Jesus, that the disciples should rejoice. This subtle and vital point has inevitably been either missed, or else dismissed by scholarship as unimportant. But Jesus is clear: "If you loved Me, you would rejoice because I said, 'I am going to the Father,' *for* My Father is greater than I." The disciples are not to rejoice only because Jesus will return to His Father; they are to rejoice *because* the Father is greater.

In sum, whatever its interpretation may be, the saying needs to be seen not only in the context of Jesus' imminent departure and glorification, but also as a primary reason as to why the disciples should rejoice. Jesus did not speak such words haphazardly. There was something in the statement, "My Father is greater than I" that called for joy, not only for the disciples, but more so for greater humanity. Essentially, the question is not how can Jesus be less than the Father (though this certainly needs to be addressed), but rather why we would rejoice in such a thing?

The Idea of Agency

Before we begin to look for a way through this difficult saying, a cautionary note must be made. We need to remember that our principal guides in understanding this saying, the Church Fathers, were speaking and writing three to four centuries after Jesus. The problem being that they did so with language, thoughts, and concepts that reflected centuries of theological development. In the words of one scholar: "It is anachronistic to imagine that John had Jesus speaking to His disciples of inner Trinitarian relationships."[9] Peter or James, for example, would hardly have thought: "Well, as the Incarnate Logos, Jesus is less than the Father who is the source of the Trinity." We should not project the terminology or thought of the fourth century onto the first-century Palestinian mind.

This in no way detracts from the fact that the disciples would have understood Jesus in the *same* fundamental way that we do; only, that we should not expect that the first-century hearers of Jesus would have thought about such a saying with our language or concepts. And though John was perhaps not "thinking in the categories the later church used to express the relation between the Father and the Son," we should not doubt that the fundamental mystery of who God is, "the reality itself, is here revealed."[10]

---

[9] Raymond E. Brown, *The Gospel According to John*, Vol. II, 654.
[10] R. A. Whitacre, *John* (Illinois: InterVarsity Press, 1999), 367.

For instance, imagine two children playing with a battery. If you were to watch as they connected wires between the battery and a small motor, and then sought to ask them about the principles of electromagnetic fields, current, and torque, you would inevitably elicit blank and dumbfounded expressions. But though this may be the case, the two children would still know (with the same certainty as a physics professor) that if they connected the wires to the right leads on the battery and the motor, then the motor would spin. Similarly, though Peter, James, and the other disciples (not to compare any of them with children), may not have been privy to the theological developments that came with Cyril of Alexandria or Gregory of Nazianzus, they could still assert the same truth. Albeit, not in the same way that we may express it twenty centuries later.

The aim, then, is to attempt to hear the saying as authentically as the disciples would have heard it, whilst simultaneously recognizing that we need to rely on later terminology which developed out of the very need of expressing something that could not be described in the language and ideas of the first-century. In a bid to do so we shall first turn to the often overlooked idea of *agency*.

It is no good examining the saying "My Father is greater than I" without taking into account its core, namely the relationship of the Son to the Father. If we should look to John's Gospel we would find that this relationship is frequently phrased in what one may term the "saliahic" language of the sender and the one who is sent.[11] This agent, *saliah* in Hebrew, is according to rabbinic law given authority to act for the one who sent him (often his master, or even his father). This idea of agency developed from a number of simple queries. If a master sent his servant to kill a neighbor, then, the rabbi's would ask: Who is responsible for the murder, the master or the servant? Or suppose a master was due to present evidence as a witness, could he send his agent to represent him? Questions similar to these moved the rabbis to conclude: *"A man's agent is as himself, he ranks as his own person."*[12] This ancient Jewish principle of the agent may be summarized in three statements: The agent was *empowered* to speak and act with the authority of his sender, he was to be *treated* as though it were his sender that was present, and of interest, a sender's *chief* or most exalted agent was his eldest son.[13]

---

[11] For a fascinating discussion on the notion of agency as a key to Johannine Christology see P. Borgen, "God's Agent in the Fourth Gospel," in *Religions in Antiquity* (Leiden: Brill, 1968), 137-148.

[12] *Babylonian Talmud Kiddushin* 43a.

[13] See B. Witherington, *John's Wisdom: A Commentary on the Fourth Gospel* (Louisville: Westminster John Knox Press, 1995), 140.

But what has this to do with Jesus declaring that His Father was greater? Consider one of the many sayings of Jesus regarding the idea of agency: "Most assuredly, I say to you, a servant is not greater than his master; nor is he who is sent *greater* than he who sent him."[14] This very same principle was also testified to by the early rabbis: "R. Simeon said: 'Who is greater: the sender or the sent? ...the *sender* is greater than the sent.'"[15] Therefore the one who is sent is always less than the sender. But though the agent is less than the sender, according to rabbinic law, "a man's agent is as himself." It then follows that the agent who is sent is in some respect *less* than his sender, but in some other respect is *equal* to his sender, in that he acts and speaks as if he were the sender himself.[16] We are, however, still left with our original problem. Even if it can be shown that John had this legal idea of agency in mind (which I believe he does), why would the fact that Jesus is sent—and is therefore less than the Father—be something for the disciples to rejoice in? One possible answer to this is the simple flip side of the problem. If one is sent, then eventually he will return to his sender after completing his set task. Likewise, if Jesus is less because the agent is less than his sender, then by returning from His mission He would return to the glory which He had before being sent. This undoubtedly would be an occasion for joy.

A subtler answer may lie further still. In rabbinic thought, as we have seen, when you happened to meet an agent it was *as if* you in fact met the sender. If the disciples were able to fathom that the saying, "My Father is greater than I," was actually indicating Jesus' relation to the Father as the *One who is sent*, then perhaps the cause of their rejoicing would dawn. By meeting the agent, Jesus, the disciples had unspeakably come face to face with His sender, the living God of Israel! A point made astonishingly clear by Jesus Himself. When Phillip questions: "Show us the Father?" Jesus replies: "He who has seen Me has seen the Father."[17] Once more the words of Jesus echo: "*Rejoice*, for My Father is greater than I."

I do not, however, think we can stop here. Jesus may be less than the Father in that He is sent. And He may be speaking and acting as if God Himself were present. But is this really the same as saying that Jesus is indeed God as the Father is God? Arius, I suspect, would not be satisfied.

---

[14] John 13:16. Also see Matt 10:40, 15:24, 21:37; John 3:34, 5:23, 37, 7:16, 8:42, 12:45.

[15] *Midrash Rabbah* 58.1 on Genesis 32:7.

[16] See Raymond E. Brown, *The Gospel According to John*, Vol. II, 632. We should, however, carefully note that though such legal terminology may be behind much of John's writing, it needs to be qualified that in the special case of Jesus, though He is less in that He is sent, He is still equal to the Father in essence.

[17] John 14:9.

The Economy of the Incarnation

Any solution proposed to this saying will inevitably fail unless it adequately satisfies three requirements. It must be first shown that Jesus is of the *same* divinity as the Father. Secondly, it must also be simultaneously affirmed that He is in some genuine way *less* than the Father. Finally it should be shown that this is something to *rejoice* in. To answer these prerequisites, the Church Fathers offered two broad suggestions.

One of these suggestions focused upon the second fact: that Jesus was in a certain sense less than the Father. The esteemed theologians of the early Church were able to show this by taking as a given that Jesus was indeed God. If you like, they began with the fact that Jesus was God, and proceeded to show how He could be less than the Father. Their claim was simple: If the Son of God had become the man Jesus, then does it not follow that as a man He would be less than the Father?

Imagine that there were two brother-kings who shared the throne of Denmark, and that one of these kings was one day to find himself *by choice* on some dignitary mission in Sudan. The people of Sudan given their geographical location would hardly have heard of Denmark, let alone its king. And even if we allowed for the news of such a visitation to have been made public, it still stands that our Danish king would not be a king in Sudan. In other words, his authority would be meaningless outside of his jurisdiction, namely Denmark. To be fair, as a royal dignitary the Danish king may have been given some special privileges, perhaps even diplomatic immunity. But he certainly would not dare to lay claim to the throne of Sudan, and never would the Sudanese honor him as such. Would it then not make sense to hear the now travelling Danish king say (no doubt reluctantly) of his brother who is still in Denmark: "Now my brother is more powerful and greater than I, for I am in a foreign land and am unable to exercise my authority"? Both are kings, but the current status of one king is that he is less powerful, and in some respects, the *lesser* king.

In technical terms, this first suggestion of the Church Fathers is known as the *economy of the Incarnation*. Jesus being God was equal to the Father, but now that He had left His glory and had taken upon Himself finite flesh, He was less than the Father. Amphilochius, the fourth century bishop of Iconium, speaking in the place of Jesus, explains:

> When I sometimes call Myself equal to the Father and sometimes the Fa-
> ther greater [than I], [I am] not contradicting Myself, but [am] showing
> that I am God and human, for God is of the lofty, humanity of the lowly;

but if you wish to know how My Father is greater than I, *I spoke of the flesh and not of the Person of the divinity.*[18]

As a man, the Incarnate Son of God was less than the Father since He "spoke of the flesh." As God Jesus was limitless, but as man, He willingly took upon Himself limits. One of these limits was that Jesus was now as real a man as we, and as such was less than the Father. But this needs to be very cautiously qualified. The celebrated Amphilochius had claimed that Jesus spoke of "the flesh and not of the *Person* of the divinity." This according to the insurmountable master, Cyril of Alexandria, is somewhat inadequate and inaccurate. Cyril teaches that we should not imagine that Jesus spoke some sayings solely from His humanity and others solely from His divinity. Rather each and every saying or act of Jesus came from His single Person:

> ...the one and only Christ is not two fold, even though He is understood as compounded out of two different elements [divinity and humanity] in an indivisible unity, just as man is understood as consisting of soul and body...we must maintain that both the manly as well as the Godly sayings were uttered by *one Subject.*[19]

In other words the divinity of the Son was united perfectly with His humanity in the one Person of Jesus Christ. Therefore whatever was spoken cannot be attributed to either the humanity or the divinity, but rather to the one Person of God-enfleshed. This is no doubt a difficult point to grasp, and as such we will meet with it more fully in the following chapter. If, however, this qualification is admitted, that Jesus speaks as the One Person of God-enfleshed, then, for Cyril, the saying may be understood as Amphilochius originally proposed: "[Jesus] says that He [the Father] is greater, not because He sat down on the right hand as God, but as He was still with us, that is, in *human* shape."[20] Didymus the Blind did not hesitate to assert the same: "He indicates that His divinity can be equalled to that of the Father, since He is of the same substance with Him, but the Father is greater because the Son *accepted a body.*"[21] For as we shall soon see, only by becoming less, could Jesus redeem humanity: "This is why the Son is less than the Father; for your

---

[18] Amphilochius, *My Father is Greater than I*, Florilegium 1:47, PG 83:96.

[19] Cyril of Alexandria, *Third Letter to Nestorius* 8, SCA 271.

[20] Cyril of Alexandria, *Commentary on John*, Book 10, LFC 48:349.

[21] Didymus the Blind, *Fragments on John 17*, JKGK 184-185. Also see Augustine, *On Faith and the Creed* 18, NPNF 1 3:329. Augustine repeats these arguments elsewhere, specifically that the Son is less than the Father after the Incarnation in that He has "emptied Himself" and become a man, see *On the Trinity* 14, NPNF 1 3:24.

sakes He was made dead to free you from death..."[22]

Gregory of Nazianzus on the other hand, whilst accepting such a solution, claims that it does not entirely clarify the meaning of the saying: "to say that He [the Father] is greater than the Son considered as *man*, is true indeed, but is no great thing. For what marvel is it if God is greater than man?"[23] With this insightful question we arrive at the second suggestion proposed by the early theologians of the Church.

LIKE FATHER LIKE SON

If the first suggestion (the economy of the Incarnation) began with the fact that Jesus was God, and then sought to show how He could be less than the Father, a second group of Church Fathers attempted to go in reverse. They opted not to take the fact that Jesus was God as a given. Instead they began with the fact that Jesus was less than the Father, and proceeded to show how He could *still* be God even though He was in some sense less. In effect they sought to take the logic of the heretic Arius head on by asking plainly: What is the relationship of a son to his father?

To answer this we first need to make a note about ancient patriarchal society. In early Judaism, and to a certain degree even within modern society, the central relationship was that of father and son: Honor, birthrights, inheritance, and even kingdoms, were passed on from father to son. The very pride of the Jews at the time of Jesus laid in their claim of descent from the patriarchs Abraham, Isaac, and Jacob. A Jewish king was only really ever respected as a true king, if he could revel in the fact that he was a "son" of the great king David. We therefore need to understand the respect that a Jew held for his father, and that said, even for his greatest grandfather. And thus no matter how great or lofty the descendant, one would always remain subordinate to one's ancestor. In the words of Albert Schweitzer: "According to Eastern patriarchal notions it is inconceivable that he can attain a rank which puts him above his ancestor."[24] Put in different terms, *genealogy overshadows achievement*. In such times, and perhaps now, a father was always greater than his son. The most natural sentence a son could utter would simply be: "My father is greater than I." And since the son took everything that he had from his father, both nature and nurture, it would be absurd for a son in early Judaism to claim otherwise.

---

[22] Basil the Great, *To the Caesareans* 8.5, NPNF 2 8:118.
[23] Gregory of Nazianzus, *Orations* 30.7, NPNF 2 7:312.
[24] Albert Schweitzer, *The Quest of the Historical Jesus*, 258.

It was upon this notion that the Church Fathers stated their case.[25] Once again we return to our question: What does it mean to be a son? The Fathers responded with two meanings in the case of Jesus. The first is that it means to be less since *the Son is begotten*. For Tertullian the saying, "My Father is greater than I," was simply a reflection of the relationship between Father and Son: "the Father is distinct from the Son, being greater than the Son, inasmuch as He who *begets* is one, and He who is *begotten* is another."[26] And, as John of Damascus pointedly notes, it is not the other way round:

> And we mean by this, that the Son is begotten of the Father and not the Father of the Son, and that the Father naturally is the cause of the Son: just as we say in the same way not that fire proceeds from light, but rather light from fire. So then, whenever we hear it said that the Father is the origin of the Son and greater than the Son, let us understand it to mean in respect of *causation*.[27]

That is why Jesus is less. Who is greater, the generated, or the generator? In the Godhead, the Son is necessarily less since He is begotten; and likewise is the Father greater, since it is He who begets. By clearly indicating Jesus' "generation from the Father without beginning,"[28] it becomes clear that the saying, "My Father is greater than I," in reality reflects the distinction in Person between the Father and the Son. At this point, however, it should be mentioned that there is a chief difference between the sonship of Jesus, and the sonship of the ordinary man. A son is begotten at a point in time. The same cannot be said of Jesus. He is begotten eternally, without any beginning. There essentially never was a time when the Father was without His eternal Son.

But if the Son knew Himself to be less than His Father, then it was with the very same conviction that He knew that He was of the *same nature* as His Father. This, then, is the second meaning of what it means to be a son. Indeed this is the simplest and fullest meaning of the word "son." When a man begets a son (of course through a woman), another man is born who shares the father's genetic material specifically and his manhood generally. It would be truly ridiculous for a man to give birth to an elephant for instance, or an angel for that matter. A man in the ancient or modern world would

---

[25] For an example of a later Orthodox approach to the saying see Hilarion Alfayev, *St. Symeon the New Theologian and Orthodox Tradition* (Oxford: Oxford University Press, 2000), 143-150.

[26] Tertullian, *Against Praxeas* 9, ANF 3:604.

[27] John of Damascus, *An Exact Exposition of the Orthodox Faith* 1.8, NPNF 2 9:9.

[28] Alexander of Alexandria, *Epistles on the Arian Heresy* 1.12, ANF 6:295.

necessarily infer that if his father was a man, then likewise would he be a man. Just as a chimp would by necessity infer that he was a chimp since his father was a chimp. Accordingly, the Church Fathers, with the great Athanasius at their head, would exclaim that "greater" does not refer to nature, but to relationship:

> And hence it is that the Son too says not, "My Father is *better* than I," lest we should conceive Him to be foreign to His Nature, but "*greater*," not indeed in greatness, nor in time, but *because of His generation* from the Father Himself...[29]

Dionysius bar Salibi, a prolific Syrian writer of the twelfth-century is remarkably clear: "the Father is not greater than the Son in nature...because it is the nature of the one who begets and the one who is begotten *to be the same*."[30] In other words, for the same thing to be at once "greater than" and "equal" is impossible. For how can Jesus be equal to the Father and at the same time be less than Him? Quite obviously then, as Gregory of Nazianzus teaches, the "greater refers to origination, while the equal belongs to the nature."[31] If we then take the two meanings of sonship together (that a son is less, whilst also being of the same nature as his father), then the saying becomes clear. Jesus as the Son is less than His Father in *relationship* in that He is begotten, but is equal in *nature* since as a Son He shares in the nature of His Father.

There is also another intriguing way around this problem. The very fact that Jesus dares to compare Himself to the Father, itself says something of tremendous importance. If you were to take a puppy and a man and place them side by side, it would be fairly ludicrous for the puppy (if it could speak) to claim that the man is greater. If we then took the analogy a stage further—though even then it would fall short—and placed a single bacterium side by side with the entire universe, and said that the universe is greater than the bacterium, it would verge on insanity. The common point being: only things in the *same class* or genus may be compared. To claim that I am smarter than a turtle, proves nothing; whereas to claim that I am smarter than another man, proves something. For Jesus to then claim, "My Father is greater than

---

[29] Athanasius, *Discourses Against the Arians* 1.58, NPNF 2 4:340. Also see Council of Sardica, *Ecclesiastical History of Theodoret* 2.6, NPNF 2 3:71.

[30] Dionysius bar Salibi, *A Response to the Arabs*, tr. Joseph P. Amar (Belgium: Peeters Publishers, 2005), 64. Interestingly, he also mentions the second interpretation of the Son being less in that He is incarnate.

[31] Gregory of Nazianzus, *Orations* 30.7, NPNF 2 7:312. The same is made explicit in *Orations* 40.43, NPNF 2 7:375.

I," He would in fact be placing Himself in comparison to God.[32] Basil the Great saw the consequence of this only too clearly:

> I believe that even from this passage the consubstantiality of the Son with the Father is set forth. For I know that comparisons may properly be made between things which are of the *same nature*. We speak of angel as greater than angel, of man as juster than man, of bird as fleeter than bird. If then comparisons are made between things of the same species, and the Father by comparison is said to be greater than the Son, then the Son is of the same substance as the Father.[33]

If the "Son has proved that He may properly be compared with God the Father in the plainest language,"[34] then must not the Son have the same nature as the Father? If Jesus claims that the Father is greater, then in actual fact He is not arguing (as Arius thought) that He is not of the same nature as the Father, but that in actuality, by the very principle that He can be compared, He is of the very *same* nature as the Father. This comparison then serves to ironically counter any claim that Jesus was not divine. One simply does not compare oneself to another of a different class or genus.

In view of this we may conclude that in a sense both of these approaches (that the Son as Incarnate is "economically" less; and that the Son is less in relationship since He is begotten) are necessary. Each asserts a different emphasis of the same truth: Jesus though a man, is divine in the very same way that God is divine. It is in this which the disciples are to rejoice. It is only because the Father is greater, that humanity is to break forth in joy. Humanity is to rejoice for *One of their own*, who is less than the Father, has returned to His glory, and in doing so has glorified humanity. Humanity is to rejoice, for now its King will be enthroned. Humanity is to rejoice, for in seeing the One who is sent, it has seen the Greater who sends Him. Humanity is to rejoice, for it has come face to face with the Living God who previously declared: "no man shall see Me, and live."[35] Humanity is to rejoice for through Jesus it still lives.

---

[32] We should bear in mind that the idea of comparison is not as simple as comparing a man to a man for example, because what is being compared is not of a corporeal nature, as Dionysius bar Salibi reminds us: "the Father is not greater than the Son [in] the same way that a mountain is greater than a hill *because the two of them are incorporeal*." See Dionysius bar Salibi, *A Response to the Arabs*, 64.

[33] Basil the Great, *To the Caesareans* 8.5, NPNF 2 8:118.

[34] Cyril of Alexandria, *Commentary on John*, Book 10, *LFC* 48:356.

[35] Exod 33:20.

CHAPTER SIXTEEN

'My God, why have You forsaken Me'

God has been murdered...
O strange murder, strange crime!
—SAINT MELITO OF SARDIS

That which He has not assumed, He has not healed...
—SAINT GREGORY OF NAZIANZUS

O N THE BANKS OF THE NILE RIVER an old and weary monk knelt in prayer. Each morning since he was a child, he had done the same. This morning, however, he was reluctantly distracted. In the corner of his eye, he saw something that commanded his attention. A small scorpion was entangled in the reeds of the river bank. The more it struggled to free itself, the more it became entangled. And with each second that passed, the scorpion was immersed in deeper and deeper water. For a while the monk simply stared, caught somewhere between "O' Lord Jesus Christ, Son of God..." and this sight of a scorpion drowning. Suddenly the old frail monk reached out to save the drowning scorpion. Imagine his surprise when it stung him. For a few awkward moments the monk retreated in anguish, before reaching out once more to save the creature. But each time he tried, the scorpion stung him more ferociously, till his hands were bloodied and swollen.

A young novice came upon this incredible sight, and half-laughing cried out to the elderly monk: "Foolish old man, do you wish to die in order to save a creature that only desires to inflict pain upon you?" The now faint old monk meekly looked down at the drowning scorpion and replied: "My son, if the nature of a scorpion is to sting, why should I not be loyal to my nature to save?"

This elderly and aching monk was faithful to his nature, irrespective of the cost. In the same way, despite humanity's sting, Jesus would forever reach out to redeem humanity from its entanglement in death. This was and is His nature. But here we should pause. Had it been solely physical anguish that was required of Jesus we could perhaps understand, for a man (though not often) may die for another out of love. And had it only been the monstrous and scandalous act of God becoming man, we could offer that this was an infinite act of sacrifice. But what if, inexplicably, the Father was to turn away from His Son in the final moments of His undying fidelity to His nature? What if the Father was to remain absent as His Son cried out in abandonment on the cross: "Eli, Eli, lama sabachthani?" that is, "My God, My God, why have You forsaken Me?" Unspeakably, what if God *abandoned* God?[1]

In considering this query let me suggest something, as I did at the very beginning of this book, at the risk of sounding just as ridiculous. Though this saying is for some the depth of shameful disappointment in the life of Jesus who seemingly died as a "failed messiah," for me, it is the theological highpoint and glory of the Gospels. In short, this saying is what it means to be *taught by God*. In the Gospel of John, when Jesus sought to silence the "murmurings" of the people as they doubted His authority, He quoted: "They shall all be taught by God."[2] This citation came from the fifty-fourth chapter of Isaiah. (Intriguingly, it follows perhaps the most famous chapter in the entire Old Testament: the *suffering servant of Isaiah*.[3]) This often overlooked chapter tells of a woman who was rejected, humiliated, and ultimately widowed on account of her barrenness. Now, however, she is told to rejoice by the God of Israel:

---

[1] This difficult saying was no doubt the most challenging from a research perspective. Surprisingly, there is a paucity of secondary sources—perhaps indicating the saying's very difficulty.

[2] John 6:45. See Isa 54:13.

[3] Isa 53.

For a mere moment I have *forsaken* you,
But with great mercies I will gather you.
With a little wrath I hid My face from you for a moment;
But with everlasting kindness I will have mercy on you...[4]

This in itself is nothing strange. A woman who was barren in ancient times, especially in Israel, would have felt the burden of anguish to the depths of her being. She would have felt forsaken not only by husband and family, but also by God. What is of interest here is that it is not said that she *felt* forsaken, but rather God Himself is revealing that He had genuinely "forsaken" her. But as a sign that this momentary abandonment would soon be replaced with everlasting mercy she is later promised: "All your children shall be *taught by God*, and great shall be the peace of your children."[5] Remarkably, this passage relates a strange bond between "abandonment" and being "taught by God." Even more remarkably, Isaiah places this passage only a few verses after depicting the passion of the One who will suffer to redeem Israel! What then makes up this strangest of bonds, and what relates it to the passion of the suffering servant?

THE CONTEXT OF THE SAYING

Once more, for a final time, we return to the first-century:

Now when the sixth hour had come, there was darkness over the whole land until the ninth hour. And at the ninth hour Jesus cried out with a loud voice, saying, "Eloi, Eloi, lama sabachthani?" which is translated, "My God, My God, why have You *forsaken* Me?" Some of those who stood by, when they heard that, said, "Look, He is calling for *Elijah!*" Then someone ran and filled a sponge full of sour wine, put it on a reed, and offered it to Him to drink, saying, "Let Him alone; let us see if Elijah will come to take Him down." And Jesus cried out with a loud voice, and breathed His last...[6]

After three hours of darkness over the entire earth, at three in the afternoon, Jesus cries out. This cry—"My God, My God, why have You

---

[4] Isa 54:7-8.
[5] Isa 54:13. Note that in the NKJV it is given as "taught by the Lord," whereas the original meaning (that Jesus Himself cited) is "taught by God." This may be seen in any Septuagint translation of the Old Testament.
[6] Mark 15:33-37.

forsaken Me"—is found only in the Gospels of Matthew and Mark.[7] Both accounts tell us that Jesus cried out in a "loud voice." They also relate that immediately after the cry, some had thought that Jesus had called out for Elijah and thus ran to offer Him sour wine. And before breathing his last, Jesus cries out once more with a loud voice (what He said in this second cry remains a mystery).

If you read this passage intently you would notice three strange things: (1) Jesus questions His *abandonment* by God; (2) the call for God was somehow misunderstood as a call for Elijah; and (3) the misheard call for Elijah in some manner was a cause for offering Jesus wine. Needless to say, the link between each of these incidents is not clear at first.

But before we examine these incidents we need to ask a few questions. The first is: Why did Jesus feel that He was abandoned? Though simple, this query is crucial in coming close to the meaning of the saying. We do well to remember that Jesus would have been in significant pain and respiratory distress. He would have struggled with each breath, and thus to cry out with a loud voice would have been a maximal effort. Such a cry would not have been unfamiliar to the cruelty of crucifixion where "the screams of rage and pain, the wild curses and the outbreaks of nameless despair of the unhappy victims" would have flooded the atmosphere.[8] We also need to recall that Jesus at this point had just been abandoned by His disciples, had been rejected by His own people, and that those who dared to come to the cross were only there to mock Him. Even the earth was darkened at an unnatural hour. How then is Jesus abandoned? He is nearing death, He has been rejected and mocked by men and nature, and all the while God is *silent*.

The next thing we need to question is why these particular words? Jesus was in fact quoting from the twenty-second psalm:

My God, My God, why have You forsaken Me?
Why are You so far from helping Me,
And from the words of My groaning?
O My God, I cry in the daytime, but You do not hear...[9]

The point is clear. The psalm begins with desperate urgency. God has forsaken the Victim by ignoring His plea for help. For a first-century Jew to hear such a quotation, it would be difficult, if not impossible, to avoid

---

[7] Matt 27:46; Mark 15:34.

[8] Josef Blinzler, *The Trial of Jesus: The Jewish and Roman Proceedings Against Jesus Christ* (Westminster: Newman, 1959), 261.

[9] Psa 22:1-2.

drawing the parallels with the suffering of Jesus (if one of course knew the Scriptures, which we cannot assume). Indeed Tertullian went so far as to claim that this psalm contained "the entire passion of Christ."[10] The original psalm and centuries later, the crucifixion account, *both* talk of a hostile crowd, the stripping of clothing from the Victim, the dividing of clothing, mockery, the piercing of the hands and feet, the gloating over His agony, the jibing at His trust in God, the cynical suggestions to let God deliver Him, the thirst, the wagging of heads, and finally the cry of abandonment.[11]

Jesus was not, however, the only one who had quoted from this psalm. In the rabbinic literature we are told that when Esther had become queen, according to Rabbi Levi, she was forced to enter into "the chamber of the idols," at which point "the divine Presence *left* her." Esther then reportedly exclaimed: "My God, My God, why hast thou forsaken me."[12] Like Jesus, Esther's experience that the "divine Presence" had left her, moved her to cry out in abandonment in the very same words, the words of the psalm. But would it have been in those exact words?

As we have previously seen, the common language spoken by first-century Jews would have been Aramaic. Yet when it came to the Scriptures they were always read and studied in Hebrew (for the basic reason that they were originally written in Hebrew). So, was Jesus' cry in Hebrew or Aramaic? If in Hebrew, then it is fairly reasonable to assume that He was quoting from the psalm. But if His cry was in Aramaic, then it would be equally reasonable to assume that He used some words that just *happened* to be in a psalm. The problem is that if you examine the saying at hand, it is actually a mixture of *both* Aramaic and Hebrew! Mark gives it as: "Eloi [My God], Eloi, lama [why] sabachthani [forsaken me]?" whilst Matthew prefers: "Eli, Eli, lema sabachthani?"[13] The word *sabachthani* is Aramaic in both Gospels. The *Eloi* of Mark is close to the Aramaic, whilst the *Eli* of Matthew resembles Hebrew. Conversely, the *lama* of Mark is likely to be Hebrew, and the *lema* of Matthew is Aramaic. Not only is each Gospel writer presenting a mixed language quote, but each writer is opposite to the other. How did such confusion arise?

---

[10] Tertullian, *Against Marcion* 3.19, ANF 3:337.

[11] Compare Psa 22:1-21 to Mark 15:22-37 and Matt 27:31-50. Interestingly, the ninth hour was the Jewish ritual time for afternoon prayer; a time that Jesus chose to quote from a Psalm. Also see John Bligh, "Christ's Death Cry," *The Heythrop Journal* 1, 2 (1960): 143.

[12] *Babylonian Talmud Megillah* 15b. Also see a similar parallel in *Midrash on Psalm* 22:2.

[13] For an examination of the Hebrew/Aramaic sources of the wording of this saying, see Raymond E. Brown, *The Death of the Messiah: From Gethsemane to the Grave* Vol. II (New York: Doubleday, 1994), 1051-1056.

224 TAUGHT BY GOD

It is possible that an original mixed Aramaic-Hebrew quote was recorded by tradition. Jesus did not after all have to speak in strictly one language. But I think there is a simpler and neater answer. First, we need to remember that there were different dialects of the standard language. For example, as we have seen, Jesus would have spoken a Galilean dialect of Aramaic. Some scholars have thus concluded that the *Eli* of Matthew is the spoken or colloquial Aramaic, whilst *Eloi* is classical or formal. Secondly, it needs to be pointed out that what we have before us in the Gospels is not the Aramaic itself in Aramaic letters, but rather the Aramaic in Greek letters. In technical language, what we have is a transliteration of an Aramaic quote in Greek. The obvious difficulty being that a "transliteration of Semitic vowels and consonants was not an exact procedure."[14]

To illustrate the point, if you took three people and asked them to transliterate the Coptic word for holy, *ethowab*, into English letters, you would get three different words. One may give it as *efouab*, another as *ethouab*, and the last as *ethowab*, each depending on how the word sounded to them. In other words, transliteration is not as strict as language; it is more fluid and is highly dependent on the translator. This "element of uncertainty"[15] thus needs to be taken into account. Possibly, then, one may suggest that Jesus' cry of abandonment may have been originally in a Galilean dialect of Aramaic, but its transliteration into Greek introduced a few Hebrew sounding words.

We now return to the query: If the Scriptures were written and read in Hebrew, and if Jesus was citing from the Scriptures, then should He not have done so in Hebrew? What we are really asking is whether Jesus was in fact quoting from the psalm, since He used Aramaic and not Hebrew. In the first place, it is feasible that an Aramaic translation of the Hebrew Scriptures existed.[16] Also, Jesus may have Himself translated the psalm to Aramaic "on-the-fly." Lastly, even if Jesus spoke in Hebrew, His hearers may have understood His words in their natural Aramaic. This would be similar to somebody quoting in a foreign language that you are familiar with, yet are not as fluent in. For instance, though you heard a sentence in French, in your mind you might understand it in English. We may then conclude with Raymond E. Brown that in all likelihood Jesus cried out citing the psalm in Aramaic:

---

[14] Raymond E. Brown, *The Death of the Messiah*, Vol. II, 1052.

[15] F. W. Buckler, "Eli, Eli, Lama Sabachthani?", *The American Journal of Semitic Languages and Literatures* 55, 4 (1938): 379.

[16] *11QTargum of Job* shows that there were Aramaic translations of the Scriptures even before Jesus.

...there is no convincing reason that He could not have spoken them in Aramaic; and no matter what language He used, there is good reason to think that an early Aramaic-speaking Christian community might have preserved them in Aramaic.[17]

But whether it is Aramaic, Hebrew, or a mixture of the two, we still are left with a difficult problem. When Jesus cried out "My God, My God...," the immediate reaction of the crowd was: "Look, He is calling for Elijah!" What does Elijah have to do with this cry of abandonment?

THE ELIJAH PROBLEM

Why would anyone think that Jesus was calling out for Elijah, when He quite clearly, in a loud voice, called out for God?[18] And for that matter, how did a seeming call for Elijah relate to giving Jesus wine?

> Jesus cried out with a loud voice, saying, "*Eloi*, Eloi, lama sabachthani?"... Some of those who stood by, when they heard that, said, "Look, He is calling for *Elijah*!" Then someone ran and filled a sponge full of sour *wine*, put it on a reed, and offered it to Him to drink, saying, "Let Him alone; let us see if Elijah will come to take Him down."[19]

Any reader who is unfamiliar with Aramaic does not sense any real or immediate obstacle. When reading this text in Greek, English, or any other language, *Eloi* (and Matthew's *Eli*) the word for God, looks to be quite similar to the Greek *Elias*, or English *Elijah*. And since they look the same in written form, the reader unfamiliar with Aramaic would point out that the crowd obviously misheard or misunderstood what Jesus said. In fact this is what non-Jewish hearers of Mark's Gospel have been doing ever since. The only catch is that though *Eloi* (God) and *Elias* (Elijah) may look the same, they certainly do not sound the same. A first-century Jew could never make this mistake for he or she could not possibly confuse two words that were so different. Some scholars have thus suggested that Matthew changed the word from *Eloi* to *Eli* to explain why the crowd became confused.[20] But even

---

[17] Raymond E. Brown, *The Death of the Messiah*, Vol. II, 1053.

[18] For a further study on the Elijah misunderstanding see, Mark F. Whitters, "Why Did the Bystanders Think Jesus Called upon Elijah before He Died (Mark 15:34-36)? The Markan Position," *The Harvard Theological Review* 95, 1 (2002): 119-124.

[19] Mark 15:34-36.

[20] Joachim Jeremias, "Elijah," in *TDNT* 2.935 n. 62. Jeremias claims that *Eli* is the original

then, Matthew's *Eli*, though perhaps more similar to *Elias*, would still be difficult to confuse for an early Jew.[21] It is thus forgivable for us as non-Semitic readers to mistakenly see the link from to *Eloi* to *Elias*. But the Jewish hearers of Jesus could not possibly make this same mistake, and so we must ask: Why did the bystanders think that Jesus was calling out for Elijah? Scholars have proposed a number of solutions, some realistic, some fantasy.[22]

One proposal is that the saying was not heard in a closed or controlled environment. And thus, though ordinarily the two words would not be confused, in the open chaotic environment of Golgotha where three simultaneous crucifixions were underway, where the crucified would have been screaming out in agony, they certainly could be.[23] If we then factor in that the "Galilean dialect did not enjoy a reputation for clearly articulate speech,"[24] and that Jesus was a Galilean, then it becomes even more sustainable that Jesus was misunderstood by His non-Galilean mockers (for the crucifixion was in Jerusalem and not Galilee). In this way Matthew and Mark may not have been puzzled themselves (since they were Jews who were accustomed to the Galilean dialect), but may have included this misunderstanding of the crowd since it historically occurred. This is of course entirely plausible, though perhaps not historically verifiable.[25]

The most realistic possibility is, however, that the confusion lies not in the name of Elijah, but in Elijah himself. To see this we need to look centuries earlier to the death of Elijah, or the lack thereof:

> Then it happened, as they [Elijah and Elisha] continued on and talked, that suddenly a chariot of fire appeared with horses of fire, and separated the two of them; and Elijah went up by a whirlwind *into* heaven.[26]

Ever since that fated day, Elijah had been a consistent figure in the eschatological expectation of Israel. God had revealed through the prophet

---

word that Jesus spoke, and that it could be easily taken as a contraction of *Elias*.

[21] See F. J. Matera, *The Kingship of Jesus: Composition and Theology in Mark 15* (Chico: Scholars Press, 1982), 30-31.

[22] Some scholars have claimed that it was the Romans who were confused, in that they only caught *Eli* from all of Jesus' words. Or that perhaps they heard *helios*, the sun god, hence they gave Jesus wine to revive Him till the sun returned to save Him (as the land was darkened).

[23] R. H. Gundry, *Mark: A Commentary on His Apology for the Cross* (Cambridge: Wm. B. Eerdmans, 1993), 967.

[24] Frank Zimmermann, "The Last Words of Jesus," *Journal of Biblical Literature* 66, 4 (1947): 466.

[25] Kent Brower, "Elijah in the Markan Passion Narrative," *Journal for the Study of the New Testament* 5, 18 (1983): 86.

[26] 2 Kgs 2:11.

Malachi that Elijah would return: "I will send you Elijah the prophet before the coming of the great and dreadful day of the Lord."[27] He would return as a forerunner, as one who would anoint and reveal the Messiah at the end times. We should also bear in mind that this was not the first time in the Gospels that the person of Elijah had caused confusion.[28]

These points leave us with two options. Either the crowds heard *Elias* (Elijah), and looked to these expectations of Elijah in revealing the Messiah. Or else, they heard *Eloi* (God), and since Elijah was to be sent by God to anoint the Messiah, simply took the call for God to mean: "God, send Elijah for Me." In both cases, it is the fact that Elijah will anoint the Messiah that is relevant, especially if we consider that Jesus was crucified as the "false" Messiah. Accordingly by saying, "let us see if Elijah will come to save Him,"[29] the bystanders were effectively mocking: "Yes, God has forsaken You, for He has not and will not send Elijah to manifest You as the Messiah." Put in a different way, to the bystanders Jesus could not be the righteous Man or Messiah of God; else Elijah on the account of God would have come to His aid as was expected.

Immediately after this, something then moved someone in the crowd to offer Jesus sour wine. Many have sought to show the link between the taunts of the crowd and the giving of the wine. I think, at least in this case, the simplest answer is the best: "the offer of a drink of wine at this moment is simply the final term in a long series of mocking and rejection motifs."[30] But why wine? The Romans, it would seem, had a long custom of offering wine to "the one crucified in order to reanimate him."[31] This may have served to numb the pain of the suffering, or, perhaps on the other hand, it may have been given to revive a fainting man. One may suggest that given the mockery of Jesus concerning Elijah, it would certainly be plausible that the wine was given to prolong Jesus' life in order to taunt Him further that Elijah still had not come. In any event, though the crowd was right in noting that Elijah had not come, they were radically mistaken as to *why* he did not come.

[27] Mal 4:5.
[28] Mark 9:9-13, Matt 17:9-13. Also see Tadros Y. Malaty, *The Gospel According to St. Mark*, 286.
[29] Matt 27:49.
[30] Kent Brower, "Elijah in the Markan Passion Narrative," 91.
[31] Gerard Rosse, *The Cry of Jesus on the Cross: A Biblical and Theological Study*, tr. Stephen Wentworth Arndt (New York: Paulist Press, 1987), 18. Also see R. H. Gundry, *Mark*, 968.

A Theology of Abandonment

If Jesus called not for Elijah but for God, then this saying becomes all the more difficult. In what manner can the Son of God be forsaken by God? Inconceivably, how can God abandon God?

Faced with such a saying most scholars have sought to do away with its difficulty by either underplaying Jesus' divinity, or else overplaying His humanity. Or, as is often the case, they have simply introduced void imaginings into reality. In this vein nearly every possibility and combination of these possibilities has been offered. Some claim that Jesus was speaking metaphorically, others that His divinity at this point had separated from His humanity, and others still, that He had in fact despaired and lost faith.[32] Some more creative scholars have suggested that Jesus cited the beginning of the twenty-second psalm in the hope that His hearers would know its joyous end, or that, perhaps, He continued to pray the rest of the psalm in a low voice.[33] On the other hand, some naively assert that Jesus never actually said those shocking words. Rather Jesus is imagined to have said: "My God I bequeath to You..." or worse still: "My God why have You praised Me?"[34]

It would be futile to consider the viability of most of these artistic suggestions. Instead only two will be examined, one for it is popularity, the other for its seeming probability.

The first is rather drastically mistaken: that Jesus despaired and lost faith. If Jesus had lost hope then why did He call out "*My* God"? And more significantly, why cry out with a citation from a psalm? In the words of a noted scholar: "Jesus is praying, and so He cannot have lost hope; calling God 'My God' implies trust."[35] One would hardly cry out to God with the words of a psalm, if one did not still hold hope in that God. Rather, as John Chrysostom has clearly seen, even "to His last breath He honors God."[36] What Jesus is questioning is not the existence, nor the power, nor the ability, but the seeming silence of the One addressed as "My God." Standing before this unrelenting silence Jesus "is so isolated and estranged that He no longer uses 'Father' language but speaks as the humblest servant."[37] For the first

---

[32] F. W. Buckler, "Eli, Eli, Lama Sabachthani?", 378.

[33] Fred Smith, "The Strangest 'word' of Jesus," *The Expository Times* 44 (1933): 260.

[34] Rabbi Dan Cohn-Sherbok, "Jesus' Cry on the Cross: An Alternative View," *The Expository Times* 93 (1982): 216. Looking to such different meanings has led scholars to a variety of conclusions, for example see L. Paul Trudinger, "'Eli, Eli, Lama Sabachthani?' A Cry of Dereliction? Or Victory?", *Journal of the Evangelical Theological Society* 17 (1974): 235-238.

[35] Raymond E. Brown, *The Death of the Messiah*, Vol. II, 1049.

[36] John Chrysostom, *The Gospel of Matthew*, Homily 88.1, PG 58:776; NPNF 1 10:521.

[37] Raymond E. Brown, *The Death of the Messiah*, Vol. II, 1051. Also see R. H. Gundry,

time in His life Jesus addresses God not as Father but as "My God." Yet even then all He "brings out by His cry is the silence of God..."[38]

Another suggestion is that Jesus had not only the first line of the twenty-second psalm in mind but also its joyous conclusion, and thus He did not really feel abandoned. Whilst I agree that it upsets the saying to divorce it from its context in the psalm, I would also suggest that is far worse to overlook or suppress the gravity of the saying by *only* looking at the pleasant ending of the psalm. In other words, instead of only examining the saying in terms of its original situation in the psalm, it is "more proper to interpret the words of the psalm here in the sense of the situation of Jesus."[39] Though the psalm ends in hope and thanksgiving, it was not this that Jesus quoted:

> ...Jesus echoed not the latter part of the psalm but its opening, and to read into these few tortured words an exegesis of the whole psalm is to turn upside down the effect...[of] this powerful and enigmatic cry of agony.[40]

If we also consider that Jesus quoted in Aramaic and not Hebrew, and that Matthew and Mark neglected to mention that Jesus meant or said anything more than the one line, then it becomes all the more difficult to sustain such a notion. Thus whilst the context of the psalm is important, it is necessary to interpret this saying of Jesus in *His* situation, rather than in the situation of the Psalmist. This is not to deny an undeniable prophecy, but rather to read it in the life of Jesus.

But what then is the situation of Jesus? As we have seen time and time again, Jesus understood Himself to be not only in a unique relationship to God as His only Son, but also as sharing the divinity of the One He called Father. In fact He shared it so fully that He could daringly claim: "I and My Father are one."[41] Yet, at the very same time Jesus now was declaring that He had been abandoned by His God. Is the Father then separated from the Son? Is their communion broken, even if it be for a single moment? These are painful questions. And for this reason many have preferred not to answer them. But though painful, such questions *need* to be answered, for at their core is the very real meaning of who Jesus is.

Though this saying of Jesus is certainly permeated with mystery throughout, we will seek out its meaning by considering two questions:

Mark, 966.

[38] Jean-Claude Sagne, "The Cry of Jesus on the Cross," *Concilium* 169 (1983): 56.

[39] Jurgen Moltmann, *The Crucified God* (Minneapolis: Fortress Press, 1993), 150.

[40] R. T. France, *The Gospel of Mark: A Commentary on the Greek Text* (Cambridge: Wm. B. Eerdmans, 2002), 652.

[41] John 10:33.

Why has Jesus been abandoned by the Father? And, *how* would it be possible for such an abandonment to take place?

The first question looks back to the beginning of humanity. Man from the time of Adam *fell*, and with him the entire creation. Followed to its finality, to its ultimate end, sin "when it is finished"[42] leaves man in a state of separation from God—in a word, abandoned. As the esteemed Cyril of Alexandria put it: "We had become accursed through Adam's transgression and had fallen into the trap of death, *abandoned* by God."[43] Clearly, it should be noted, the abandonment rests upon the sin of man and not the neglect of God. For it was man that took those tragic and catastrophic steps away from God, the result of which is abandonment. But man though abandoned, was not forgotten.

Place next to this the words of Gregory of Nazianzus, who famously encapsulated three centuries of Christian thought in a single and most pregnant formulation: "*that which He [Jesus] has not assumed He has not healed...*"[44] In other words, whatever has not been united to the limitless, infinite, perfect, divine Son of God, cannot be made perfect, infinite, limitless.[45] For want of a better phrase, this may be termed the *assumptive principle*. That which has not been "touched" or "assumed" by the divine cannot be saved. And thus if Jesus did not take to Himself flesh, and become a real man, then humanity could not be saved. For a man cannot save a man; nor can flesh be sanctified unless touched by God. If Jesus did not assume a real mind, body, emotions, or what have you, then these cannot be healed. And consequently humanity would still remain in its deplorable condition.

Essentially, if the epitome, finality, and ultimate consequence of the fall, is separation from God, effectively the abandonment of humanity by God, then in order to bring man back into union with God, to overcome that separation and abandonment, Jesus would need to take upon Himself the *abandonment of humanity*. The limitless Son of God, in Cyril of Alexandria's estimation, would need to indescribably become the abandoned:

> He had to submit to the abandonment that our human nature had suf-
> fered... Then, living like *one of the abandoned* and also participating like us
> in flesh and blood, He says: "Why have you abandoned me?"[46]

[42] David H.C. Read, "Expository Problems: The Cry of Dereliction," *The Expository Times* 68 (1957): 262.

[43] Cyril of Alexandria, *On the Unity of Christ* (New York: SVS Press, 1995), 105.

[44] Gregory of Nazianzus, *To Cledonius the Priest*, NPNF 2 7:440.

[45] This does not in any way blur the distinction between man and God, but simply is indicative of the *energies* of God that are "communicated" through the Incarnation.

[46] Cyril of Alexandria, cited from Gerard Rosse, *The Cry of Jesus on the Cross*, 73-74. Also

He who was united to the Father from before all ages would need to become the forsaken so that He could "undo our abandonment by His obedience and complete submission."[47] For only then could our abandonment be assumed, sanctified, and restored into life united with God.[48] Here, however, we need to take care. Cyril of Alexandria, the ever-present guardian of Christology, is quick to qualify that it would be foolish, "blasphemy, and a proof of complete madness" to leap from this to the claim that the cry of abandonment came from the humanity of Jesus which was abandoned by His divinity.[49] Rather, as we shall soon see, the divinity of Jesus was in an inseparable union with His humanity. To be clear, the cry was of abandonment by the Father, and not a somewhat schizophrenic declaration of the separation of the natures in Jesus.[50]

After having seen *why* Jesus was required to become the abandoned, we now come to our second question: *How* could such an abandonment be possible? How could Jesus, the Son of God, be forsaken by His Father?

To answer these questions we must follow in the footsteps of an Alexandrian master. The great Cyril was aware of the difficulties in understanding the relationship of the humanity and the divinity of Jesus. So he employed a number of analogies, his favorite being that of the soul and the body.[51] If you were to look at the relationship of the two you would undoubtedly find a number of things to be true: (1) The soul is a *distinct* reality to the body; (2) both exist in a *union* without compromising either reality; and (3) the union of these two realities is a *single subject*, the human being.

---

see Origen, *Commentary of Matthew* 135, GCS 38.2:279; Augustine, *On the Grace of the New Testament*, FC 20:68.

[47] Cyril of Alexandria, *On the Unity of Christ*, 105.

[48] For completeness we should briefly note that mystics such as John of the Cross have described periods known as the "dark night of the soul" where the believer no longer feels the presence of God, but through struggle, may ascend beyond emotion into union with God. For example see John of the Cross, *Dark Night of the Soul* (New York: Riverhead Books, 2002). More recently, see the published letters of Mother Theresa of Calcutta, which describe a similar experience, *Come Be My Light: The Private Writings of the "Saint of Calcutta"* (New York: Doubleday, 2007). This mystical experience of abandonment has often been related to the cry of Jesus on the Cross. Though valid in part, we should remember Jesus' crucifixion was not simply a "mystical trial," it was the very real abandonment of Jesus by God.

[49] Cyril of Alexandria, *On the Unity of Christ*, 106.

[50] It should be noted that the incorrect notion of the cry deriving from the divinity separating from the humanity was put forward by Eusebius of Caesarea, Epiphanius, and even Hilary of Poitiers: "The cry to God in truth is the voice of a body departing, having declared the separation of the Word of God from itself" (*On Matthew* 33.6, SC 258:254). Needless to say this was correctly and forcefully rejected by the Alexandrian Fathers, even though it continued in some varying forms in later Scholasticism.

[51] Cyril of Alexandria, *Scholia on the Incarnation* 8, SCA 300-301.

If you were to then take the analogy a step further, you would find that this union of soul and body in the one human being would produce a number of interesting results: (1) A purely *physical* event (of the body) can actually affect the soul, for example pain may cause depression; (2) a purely *psychic* event (of the soul) can also affect the body, for example sorrow can cause physical tears;[52] and therefore by the union of the soul and the body, (3) the body and soul can experience things that they could not have unless they were united. The one thing that therefore becomes strikingly clear is that a human person cannot do a *purely* physical act nor a purely psychic act, for every act of the person involves the soul and body together. Therefore it would be a body-soul act. For instance if a child by the name of Jimmy were to have headache, we could hardly say: "Jimmy's head has a headache." For, properly speaking, it is not the head that suffers, but Jimmy who suffers from a headache. It then is fairly clear that Jimmy suffers in his body, and because the body is united to the soul to form the one person of Jimmy, Jimmy suffers. And thus it would be comical to claim that only Jimmy's body suffers, as if his body were a separate entity to the person Jimmy.

Similar to the body and soul analogy, we may understand that Jesus' divinity and humanity are two different natures. But when they come together in union they constitute a *new condition* without compromising the integrity of either nature.[53] And thus there is no purely divine act after the union, nor a purely human act. Every act is that of the God-enfleshed, the *one* Person of Jesus Christ:

> ...the one and only Christ is not two fold, even though He is understood as compounded out of two different elements in an indivisible unity, just as man is understood as consisting of soul and body...we must maintain that both the manly as well as the Godly sayings were uttered by *one Subject*.[54]

It is now that Cyril's brilliance becomes all too clear. Just as the soul is able to experience new things (for example anguish) when united to the

---

[52] Or to take the matter further, physical symptoms (such as pain, nausea, and even neurological deficits) which cannot be attributed to physical causes, are often the result of psychological factors—a disease process known as *conversion disorder*, or severely *somatoform disorder*. Obviously this is a pathological process and thus is not as accurate as the analogy of sorrow producing tears, but nevertheless it reveals the vulnerable link between the psyche and the body.

[53] We should be careful to point out that the union of divinity and humanity does not create a *new hybrid or mixed nature*, else each nature would cease to be what it was before the union. And thus Jesus would not be fully God and fully man. Rather, the union brings about a *new condition*, or a new spectrum of possibilities in the one Incarnate Person of Jesus.

[54] Cyril of Alexandria, *Third Letter to Nestorius* 8, SCA 271.

body (which is in pain), or the body new things (for example tears) when united to the soul (which is sorrowful), the same may be said of Jesus. What was impossible before the union becomes possible after it. The divinity is now able to experience the human condition in the one Person of Jesus:

> So it is we say that He both suffered and rose again, not meaning that the Word of God suffered in His own nature... but in so far as that which had become His own body suffered, then He Himself is said to suffer these things, for our sake, because the *Impassible One was in the suffering body*.[55]

If you like, the flesh allows the Son of God a new condition of expression. Just as the soul cannot feel pain, but once united to its body, it can; as God He cannot possibly suffer, but once united to His human nature, He can. And thus God-enfleshed can experience pain, suffering, anguish, tears, and even death.[56] Or as Melito of Sardis so shockingly put it: "God has been murdered."[57] Not as God, nor merely as a man, but as the one God-enfleshed Person of Jesus.

Returning then to our original question of how God the Son may be abandoned, we may suggest with great resolve: As God, the Son cannot possibly be abandoned, for He is in perfect union with the Father. But by uniting to His humanity, in the Person of Jesus, the Son may experience abandonment in His flesh. And thus though God cannot be abandoned, God-enfleshed certainly can be, and was. Consequently, *if Jesus in order to heal our abandonment had to become the abandoned, then He did so as God-enfleshed!* It is here that we must be vigorously clear. Jesus in no way was being metaphorical. The Son of God-become-man was literally and genuinely abandoned (in every sense of the word) on the cross by the One He called Father. He was left hanging, abandoned by man, nature, and God. He felt within Him the severing of an indissoluble bond. This was no illusion, nor exaggeration of speech; it was an exclamation of an incomprehensible truth.

But the end was not here. Remember what was not possible before the Incarnation, became possible after it. Therefore the power of Jesus' divinity emanates through His humanity. By assuming the human condition, by becoming "one of the abandoned," by enduring unspeakable loneliness and anguish, and by tasting separation from God in a way that we can never imagine nor describe, Jesus assumed, overcame, and sanctified our

---

[55] Cyril of Alexandria, *Second Letter to Nestorius* 5, SCA 262.

[56] Ambrose, *On the Christian Faith* 2.7.56, NPNF 2 10:230.

[57] Melito of Sardis, *On Pascha* 96; See *On Pascha and Fragments: Texts and Translations*, ed. S. G. Hall (Oxford: Clarendon Press, 1979), 57.

abandonment. He brought together an impossible chasm, bringing man once more into unity with God. The cry of abandonment on the cross is then "not a reproach against God, but the *explosion* of suffering in love."[58]

This is made radically clear when it dawns that this abandonment was in perfect obedience to the Father: "Abba, Father, all things are possible for You. Take this cup away from Me; nevertheless, *not what I will*, but what You will."[59] What seems to be an indescribable division in the life of God is in actual fact the declaration of unity. The cry reveals "absolute Innocence in absolute abandonment—yet out of that abyss there comes the ultimate word of reconciliation and of peace."[60] The Son in sacrificing His will for the Father, in willingly submitting Himself to an agonizing torture unknown to humanity, was in fact proclaiming "the loss of God for the love of God."[61] In His moment of complete and utter abandonment Jesus identifies Himself with the will of His Forsaker, and in doing so reveals the love of God for man, the very revelation of the Father Himself. Jesus, the Abandoned, living entirely and acutely for the sake of revealing God's love to man is then the Icon of the Invisible: He reveals the Word of the Father for man. By emptying Himself, He momentarily grants humanity a glimpse into the intimate life of God. By becoming the Abandoned, Jesus takes the place of *Isaiah's* forsaken widow of old. He takes the place of barren humanity, He assumes her utter rejection and hopeless abandon, and returns to her the teaching and gift of Himself—the Word of God:

> O you afflicted one,
> Tossed with tempest, and not comforted…
> All your children shall be *taught by God*,
> And great shall be the peace of your children.[62]

Let no one then imagine that this is a cry of despair. It is nothing less than the very real abandonment that in weeping anguish clings with the force of the universe to the seemingly absent hands of the Father. It is this cry, this glorious theology of abandonment, this ineffable glimpse into the intimate life of the suffering and loving God, which marks the very content of what it means to be *taught by God*. It is the untainted and unequivocal

---

[58] Jean-Claude Sagne, "The Cry of Jesus on the Cross," 58.

[59] Mark 14:36. John Chrysostom pointedly notes that calling out "My God…" in fact "shows how He is of *one mind* with the Father who had begotten Him." See his *The Gospel of Matthew*, Homily 88.1, PG 58:776; NPNF 1 10:521.

[60] David H.C. Read, "Expository Problems: The Cry of Dereliction," 262.

[61] Gerard Rosse, *The Cry of Jesus on the Cross*, 67.

[62] Isa 54:11-13.

word of Jesus. How else, only moments later, could the centurion standing at the foot of the cross, and with him conciliated humanity, but respond: "Truly this Man was the Son of God!"

ABBREVIATIONS:

ANF   A. Roberts and J. Donaldson, eds. Ante-Nicene Fathers. 10 vols. Buffalo, N.Y.: Christian Literature, 1885–1896. Reprint, Grand Rapids, Mich.: Eerdmans, 1951–1956. Reprint, Peabody, Mass.: Hendrickson, 1994.

CCL   Corpus Christianorum. Series Latina. Turnhout, Belgium: Brepols, 1953-.

EHG   St. Ambrose of Milan. Exposition of the Holy Gospel According to Saint Luke with Fragments on the Prophecy of Isaias. Translated by T. Tomkinson. Etna, Calif.: Center for Traditionalist Orthodox Studies, 1998.

FC   Fathers of the Church: A New Translation. Washington, D.C.: Catholic University of America Press, 1947-.

GCS   Die griechischen christlichen Schriftsteller der ersten Jahrhunderte. Berlin: Akademie- Verlag, 1897-.

LFC   A Library of the Fathers of the Holy Catholic Church Anterior to the Division of East and West. Translated by Members of the English Church. 44 vols. Oxford: John Henry Parker, 1800-1881.

NPNF   P. Schaff et al., eds. A Select Library of the Nicene and Post-Nicene Fathers of the Christian Church. 2 series (14 vols. each). Buffalo, N.Y.: Christian Literature, 1887–1894. Reprint, Grand Rapids, Mich.: Eerdmans, 1952–1956. Reprint, Peabody, Mass.: Hendrickson, 1994.

PG   J.-P. Migne, ed. Patrologiae cursus completus. Series Graeca. 166 vols. Paris: Migne, 1857–1886.

PL   J.-P. Migne, ed. Patrologiae cursus completus. Series Latina. 221 vols. Paris: Migne, 1844–1864.

SC   H. de Lubac, J. Daniélou et al., eds. Sources Chrétiennes. Paris: Éditions du Cerf, 1941-.

SCA   John McGuckin. Saint Cyril of Alexandria and the Christological Controversy. New York: SVS Press, 2001.

Bibliography:

Alexander of Alexandria. *Epistles on the Arian Heresy.* ANF 6.

Alfayev, Hilarion. *St. Symeon the New Theologian and Orthodox Tradition.* Oxford: Oxford University Press, 2000.

Allison, Dale C. "Q 12:51-53 and Mark 9:11-13 and the Messianic Woes." In *Authenticating the Words of Jesus.* ed. Bruce Chilton and Craig A. Evans. Leiden: Brill, 2002.

_____. *The End of the Ages has Come: An Early Interpretation of the Passion and Resurrection of Jesus.* Philadelphia: Fortress Press, 1985.

Ambrose of Milan. *Exposition of the Gospel of Luke.* EHG.

_____. *On the Christian Faith.* NPNF 2 10.

Amphilochius. *My Father is Greater than I.* PG 83.

Amram, David Werner. *The Jewish Law of Divorce According to the Bible and Talmud.* Philadelphia: Edward Stern & Co., 1896.

Andersen, Oivind. "Oral Tradition." In *Jesus and the Oral Gospel Tradition.* ed. Wansbrough. Sheffield: Academic Press, 1991.

Anonymous. *Incomplete Work on Matthew.* PG 56.

Athanasius of Alexandria. *Discourses Against the Arians.* NPNF 2 4.

_____. *Homilia de Semente.* PG 28.

_____. *Life of St. Anthony.* FC 15.

_____. *To the Bishops of Egypt.* NPNF 2 4.

Augustine of Hippo. *Explanation of the Psalm* CCL 40.

_____. *Harmony of the Gospels.* NPNF 1 6.

_____. *On the Grace of the New Testament,* FC 20.

_____. *On Faith and the Creed.* NPNF 1 3.

_____. *On the Psalms.* NPNF 1 8,

_____. *On the Trinity.* NPNF 1 3.

_____. *Our Lord's Sermon on the Mount.* NPNF 1 6.

_____. *Sermons on New Testament Lessons.* NPNF 1 6.

_____. *Tractates on John.* NPNF 1 7.

Aune, David E. "The Problem of the Messianic Secret." *Novum Testamentum* 11 (1969): 1-31.

Baeck, Leo. *Judaism and Christianity.* tr. Walter Kaufman. Philadelphia: Jewish Publication Society, 1958.

Bailey, Kenneth E. "Informal Controlled Oral Tradition and the Synoptic Gospels." *Asia Journal of Theology* 5(1): 34-54.

_____. *Jesus Through Middle Eastern Eyes: Cultural Studies in the Gospels.* Illinois: Intervarsity Press, 2008.

_____. *Through Peasant Eyes.* Grand Rapids: Wm. B. Eerdmans, 1980.

Banks, Robert. *Jesus and the Law in the Synoptic Tradition.* Cambridge: Cambridge University Press, 2005.

Basil the Great. *To the Caesareans.* NPNF 2 8.

Beasley-Murray, G. R. *Jesus and the Kingdom of God.* Grand Rapids: Wm. B. Eerdmans, 1986.

Berkey, R. F. "Eggizen, Phthanein, and Realised Eschatology." *Journal of Biblical Literature* 82 (1963): 177-187.

Black, M. "Not Peace but a Sword." In *Jesus and the Politics of His Day.* ed. E. Bammel and C. F. D. Moule. Cambridge: Cambridge University Press, 1984.

Blevins, James L. *The Messianic Secret in Markan Research, 1901-1976.* Washington, University Press of America, 1981.

Bligh, John. "Christ's Death Cry." *The Heythrop Journal* 1, 2 (1960): 142-146.

Blinzler, Josef. *The Trial of Jesus: The Jewish and Roman Proceedings Against Jesus Christ.* Westminster: Newman, 1959.

Booth, R. P. *Jesus and the Laws of Purity: Tradition History and Legal History in Mark 7.* Sheffield: JSOT, 1986.

Borgen, P. "God's Agent in the Fourth Gospel." In *Religions in Antiquity.* Leiden: Brill, 1968.

Bouteneff, Peter C. *Beginnings: Ancient Christian Readings of the Biblical Creation Narratives.* Grand Rapids: Baker Academic, 2008.

Brandon, S. G. F. *Jesus and the Zealots.* Manchester: Scribners, 1967.

Brower, Kent. "Elijah in the Markan Passion Narrative." *Journal for the Study of the New Testament* 5, 18 (1983): 85-101.

Brown, Raymond E. *Jesus God and Man: Modern Biblical Reflections.* London: Geoffrey Chapman, 1968.

_____. *An Introduction to New Testament Christology.* New York: Paulist Press, 1994.

_____. *The Death of the Messiah: From Gethsemane to the Grave.* 2 Volumes. New York: Doubleday, 1994.

_____. *The Gospel According to John.* 2 Volumes. New York: Doubleday, 1970.

Brown, Schuyler. "The Matthean Community and the Gentile Mission." *Novum Testamentum* 22, 3 (1980): 193-220.

———. "The Secret of the Kingdom of God." *Journal of Biblical Literature* 92, 1 (1973): 60-74.

Bruce, F. F. *The Hard Sayings of Jesus.* Illinois: Intervarsity Press, 1983.

Buckler, F. W. "Eli, Eli, Lama Sabachthani?" *The American Journal of Semitic Languages and Literatures* 55, 4 (1938): 378-391.

Budge, E. A. W. *Coptic Homilies in the Dialect of Upper Egypt.* London: British Museum, 1910.

Bulgakov, Sergius. *The Lamb of God.* Grand Rapids: Wm. B. Eerdmans, 2008.

Burkill, T. A. *Mysterious Revelation: An Examination of the Philosophy of St. Mark's Gospel.* New York: Cornell University Press, 1963.

———. "The Historical Development of the Story of the Syrophoenician Woman (Mark VII: 24-31)." *Novum Testamentum* 9, 3 (1967): 161-177.

———. "The Syrophoenician Woman: The Congruence of Mark 7:24-31." *Zeitschrift für die Neutesamentliche Wissenschaft* 57 (1966): 23-37.

Byrne, Brendan. *'Sons of God'—'Seed of Abraham.'* Rome: Biblical Institute Press, 1979.

Caird and Hurst. *New Testament Theology.* Oxford: Oxford University Press, 1995.

Caird, G. B. *The Language and the Imagery of the Bible.* London: Gerald Duckworth & Co., 1980.

Cameron, P. S. *Violence and the Kingdom: The Interpretation of Matthew 11:12.* Bern: Peter Lang, 1988.

Carson, D. A. "Do the Prophets and the Law Quit Prophesying before John?" In *The Gospels and the Scriptures of Israel.* ed. Craig A. Evans and W. Richard Stegnar. Sheffield: Sheffield Academic Press, 1994.

Casey, P. M. *From Jewish Prophet to Gentile God: The Origins and Development of New Testament Christology.* Louisville: Westminster John Knox, 1991.

Cassian, John. *Conferences.* NPNF 2 11.

Charlesworth, James H. *Jesus within Judaism: New Light from Exciting Archaeological Discoveries.* London: SPCK, 1989.

Chromatius. *Tractate on Matthew.* CCL 9a.

Chrysostom, John. *The Second Epistle to Timothy.* NPNF 1 13.

———. *The Gospel of John.* NPNF 1 14.

———. *The Gospel of Matthew.* PG 57; NPNF 1 10.

Claude-Larchet, Jean. *Mental Disorders & Spiritual Healing: Teachings from the Early Christian East*. San Rafael: Sophia Perennis, 2005.

Clement of Alexandria. *Who is the Rich Man that Shall Be Saved*. ANF 2.

_____. *The Stromata*. ANF 2.

Cohn-Sherbok, Rabbi Dan. "Jesus' Cry on the Cross: An Alternative View." *The Expository Times* 93 (1982): 215-217.

Collins, Adela Yarbro. "Mark and His Readers: The Son of God among Greeks and Romans." *The Harvard Theological Review* 93, 2 (2000): 85-100.

_____. "Mark and His Readers: The Son of God among Jews." *The Harvard Theological Review* 92, 4 (1999): 393-408.

Cyprian. *Treatises on the Lord's Prayer*. CCL 3a; ANF 5.

Cyril of Alexandria. *Commentary on Luke*. CGSL.

_____. *Commentary on John*. LFC 48.

_____. *Fragment*. MKGK.

_____. *On the Unity of Christ*. New York: SVS Press, 1995.

_____. *Scholia on the Incarnation*. SCA.

_____. *Second Letter to Nestorius*. SCA.

_____. *Third Letter to Nestorius*. SCA.

Cullmann, Oscar. *Salvation in History*. New York: Harper & Row, 1967.

_____. *The Christology of the New Testament*. London: SCM Press, 1959.

_____. *The State in the New Testament*. London: SCM Press, 1957.

Dalman, Gustaf. *Jesus-Jeshua: Studies in the Gospels*. New York: Macmillan, 1929.

_____. *The Words of Jesus*. Edinburgh: T & T Clark, 1909.

Danker, Frederick W. "Luke 16:16: An Opposition Logion." *Journal of Biblical Literature* 77, 3 (1958): 231-243.

Daube, David. *The New Testament and Rabbinic Judaism*. London: The Athlone Press, 1956.

Davies, W. D. *The Setting of the Sermon on the Mount*. Cambridge: Cambridge University Press, 1964.

Davies, W. D. and Allison, Dale C. *The Gospel According to Saint Matthew*. 3 Volumes. Edinburgh: T & T Clark, 1991.

Davis, Stephen T. "Was Jesus Mad, Bad, or God?" In *The Incarnation*. ed. Stephen T. Davis, Daniel Kendall, Gerald O'Collins. New York: Oxford University Press, 2002.

Derrett, J. Duncan M. "Korban, ho estin doron." *New Testament Studies* 16 (1970): 364-68.

_____. "Law in the New Testament: The Syro-Phoenician Woman and the Centurion of Capernaum." *Novum Testamentum* 15, 3 (1973): 161-186.

DeCantanzaro, C. J. *Symeon the New Theologian: The Discourses.* New York: Paulist Press, 1980.

Didymus the Blind. *Fragments on John 17. JKGK.*

Dodd, C. H. *The Interpretation of the Fourth Gospel.* Cambridge: Cambridge University Press, 1953.

_____. *The Parables of the Kingdom.* Glasgow: Collins, 1978.

Dorotheos of Gaza. *Discourses and Sayings.* tr. Eric P. Wheeler. Michigan: Cistercian Publications, 1977.

Du Toit, A. B. "Hyperbolical Contrasts: A Neglected Aspect of Paul's Style." In *A South African Perspective on the New Testament.* ed. J. H. Petzer and P. J. Martin. Leiden: Brill, 1986.

Dufton, Francis. "The Syrophoenician Woman and Her Dogs." *Expository Times* 100 (1989): 417.

Dunn, James D. G. *Christology in the Making: A New Testament Inquiry into the Origins of the Doctrine of the Incarnation.* London: SCM Press, 1980.

_____. "Demon Possession and Exorcism in the New Testament." In *The Christ and the Spirit.* 2 Volumes. Grand Rapids: Wm. B. Eerdmans, 1998.

_____. "Jesus and Purity: An Ongoing Debate." *New Testament Studies* 48 (2002): 449-467.

_____. *Jesus Remembered.* Grand Rapids: Wm. B. Eerdmans, 2003.

_____. "The Messianic Secret in Mark." In *The Messianic Secret.* ed. Christopher Tuckett. Philadelphia: Fortress Press, 1983.

_____. *The Parting of the Ways: Between Christianity and Judaism and their Significance for the Character of Christianity.* London: SCM Press & Philadelphia: Trinity Press International, 1991.

_____. "The Tradition." In *The Historical Jesus in Recent Research.* ed. James D. G. Dunn and Scot McKnight. Indiana: Eisenbrauns, 2005.

Easton, Burton Scott. "The Beelzebul Sections." *Journal of Biblical Literature* 32, 1 (1913): 57-73.

Edersheim, Alfred. *The Life and Times of Jesus the Messiah.* Grand Rapids: Wm. B. Eerdmans, 1953.

_____. *The Temple: Its Ministry and Services as they were at the Time of Jesus Christ.* London: James Clarke & Co, 1959.

Ephrem the Syrian. *Commentary on Tatian's Diatesseron. JSSS* 2.

Epiphanius the Latin. *Interpretation of the Gospels. PL Supp* 3.

Evans, Craig A. "Authenticating the Words of Jesus." In *Authenticating the Words of Jesus*. ed. Bruce Chilton and Craig A. Evans. Leiden: Brill, 2002.

Evans, Owen E. "Expository Problems: The Unforgivable Sin." *The Expository Times* 68 (1957): 240-244.

Evdokimov, Paul. *The Sacrament of Love: The Nuptial Mystery in the Light of the Orthodox Tradition*. New York: SVS Press, 2001.

Fanous, Daniel. *The Person of the Christ: The Earthly Context of the Savior*. Boston: Regina Orthodox Press, 2008.

Fitzmyer, Joseph A. *A Christological Catechism: New Testament Answers*. New York: Paulist Press, 1991.

_____. *The Gospel According to Luke*. 2 Volumes. New York: Doubleday, 1985-1986.

Florovsky, Georges. *Bible, Church, Tradition: An Eastern Orthodox View*. Massachusetts: Nordland Publishing Co, 1972.

Flusser, David. *Jesus*. Jerusalem: Magnes Press, 1998.

France, R. T. *The Gospel of Mark: A Commentary on the Greek Text*. Cambridge: Wm. B. Eerdmans, 2002.

Friedlander, Gerald. *The Jewish Sources of the Sermon on the Mount*. New York: Ktav Publishing House, 1969.

Fuller, R. H. *The Foundations of New Testament Christology*. New York: Scribner, 1965.

Lewis, John. *Christianity and the Social Revolution*. London: Victor Gallanez, 1935.

Gaston, Lloyd. *No Stone On Another: Studies in the Significance of the Fall of Jerusalem in the Synoptic Gospels*. Leiden: Brill, 1970.

Gillet, Lev. *Communion in the Messiah: Studies in the Relationship between Judaism and Christianity*. London: Lutterworth Press, 1942.

Gregory of Nazianzus. *On the Holy Lights*. NPNF 2 7.

_____. *Oration on Holy Baptism*. NPNF 2 7.

_____. *Orations*. NPNF 2 7.

_____. *To Cledonius the Priest*, NPNF 2 7.

Gregory the Great. *Forty Gospel Homilies*. PL 76.

_____. *Letter 39 to Eulogius*. NPNF 2 13.

Gundry, R. H. *Mark: A Commentary on His Apology for the Cross*. Cambridge: Wm. B. Eerdmans, 1993.

Hahn, Ferdinand. *The Titles of Jesus in Christology: Their History in Early Christianity*. Cambridge: James Clarke & Co., 2002.

Hart, J. "Corban." *Jewish Quarterly Review* 19 (1907): 615-50.

Harvey, A. E. *Jesus and the Constraints of History.* London: Duckworth, 1982.

Hasler, J. Ireland. "The Incident of the Syrophoenician Woman." *Expository Times* 45 (1934): 459-461.

Hawkin, D. J. "The Incomprehension of the Disciples in the Markan Redaction." *Journal of Biblical Literature* 91 (1972), 491-500.

Hay, Lewis S. "Mark's Use of the Messianic Secret." *Journal of the American Academy of Religion* 35, 1 (1967): 16-27.

Head, Peter M. *Christology and the Synoptic Problem: An Argument for Markan Priority.* Cambridge: Cambridge University Press, 1997.

Heinemann, J. "The Background of Jesus' Prayer in the Jewish Liturgical Tradition." In *The Lord's Prayer and Jewish Liturgy.* ed. J. J. Petuchowski and M. Brocke. London: Burns & Oates, 1978.

Hendrickx, Herman. *The Sermon on the Mount.* London: Geoffrey Chapman, 1984.

Hengel, Martin. "Jesus, the Messiah of Israel." In *Studies in Early Christology.* Edinburgh: T & T Clark, 1995.

————. *The Son of God: The Origin of Christology and the History of Jewish-Hellenistic Religion.* London: SCM Press, 1976.

————. *The Charismatic Leader and His Followers.* Edinburgh: T. & T. Clark, 1981.

————. *Was Jesus a Revolutionist?* tr. William Klassen. Philadelphia: Fortress Press, 1971.

Hiers, Richard H. *The Historical Jesus and the Kingdom of God.* Gainesville: University of Florida Press, 1973.

Hilary of Poitiers. *On Matthew.* SC 254.

Hooker, Morna D. "The Prohibition of Foreign Missions." *The Expository Times* 82 (1971): 361-365.

Hopkins, Gerard Manley. *The Major Works.* Oxford: Oxford University Press, 2002.

Horsley, Richard A. *Jesus and the Spiral of Violence: Popular Jewish Resistance in Roman Palestine.* Minneapolis: Fortress Press, 1993.

Hurtado, Larry W. *How on Earth Did Jesus Become a God? Historical Questions about Earliest Devotion to Jesus.* Grand Rapids: Wm. B. Eerdmans, 2005.

Instone-Brewer, David. *Divorce and Remarriage in the Bible: The Social and Literary Context.* Grand Rapids: Wm. B. Eerdmans Publishing Co., 2002.

Iranaeus. *Against Heresies.* ANF 1.

Jeremias, Joachim. "Elijah." In *TDNT* 2.

_____. *Jesus' Promise to the Nations*. London: SCM Press, 1958.

_____. *New Testament Theology: The Proclamation of Jesus*. London: SCM Press, 1971.

_____. *The Proclamation of Jesus*. London: SCM Press, 1971.

Jerome. *Commentary on Matthew*. CCL 77.

_____. *Letter to Amandus*. NPNF 2 6.

_____. *Letter to Eustochium*. NPNF 2 6.

John of Damascus. *An Exact Exposition of the Orthodox Faith*. NPNF 2 9.

_____. *Sacra Paralleia*. PG 96.

John of the Cross. *Dark Night of the Soul*. New York: Riverhead Books, 2002.

De Jonge, M. *Jesus, the Servant Messiah*. New Haven: Yale University Press, 1991.

Justin the Martyr. *Dialogue with Trypho*. ANF 1.

Kasper, Walter. *Jesus the Christ*. New York: Paulist Press, 1976.

Kazen, T. *Jesus and Purity Halakhah: Was Jesus Indifferent to Impurity?* Stockholm: Almqvist & Wiksell, 2002.

Kelly, Henry Ansgar. *Satan: A Biography*. Cambridge: Cambridge University Press, 2006.

_____. *The Devil, Demonology, and Witchcraft*. Oregon: Wipf & Stock, 2004.

Kesich, Vesilin. *The Gospel Image of Christ*. New York: SVS Press, 1991.

Kinukawa, Hisako. *Women and Jesus in Mark: A Japanese Feminist Perspective*. New York: Orbis Books, 1994.

Klausner, Joseph. *Jesus of Nazareth: His Life, Times, and Teaching*. New York: Macmillan Company, 1949.

_____. *The Messianic Idea in Israel: From Its Beginning to the Completion of the Mishnah*. New York: The Macmillan Company, 1955.

Kloppenborg, John. "Alms, Debt and Divorce: Jesus' Ethics in their Mediterranean Context." *Toronto Journal of Theology* 6 (1990): 182-200.

Kümmel, W. G. *Promise and Fulfillment: The Eschatological Message of Jesus*. London: SCM Press, 1957.

Ladd, George E. *The Presence of the Future: The Eschatology of Biblical Realism*. Grand Rapids: Wm. B. Eerdmans, 1974.

Lampe. G. W. H. "The Two Swords." In *Jesus and the Politics of His Day*. ed. E. Bammel and C. F. D. Moule. Cambridge: Cambridge University Press, 1984.

Lane, W. L. *The Gospel of Mark*. Grand Rapids: Wm. B. Eerdmans, 1974.

Leeuw, Gerardus van der. *Religion in Essence and Manifestation: A Study in Phenomenolgy*. tr. J. E Turner. 2 Volumes. Gloucester: Peter Smith, 1967.

Lewis, C. S. *Mere Christianity*. London: Collins, 1952.

Llewelyn, Stephen. "The Traditionsgeschichte of Matt. 11:12-13, Par. Luke 16:16." *Novum Testamentum* 36, 4 (1994): 330-349.

Loader, William R. G. *Jesus' Attitude towards the Law: A Study of the Gospels*. Cambridge: Wm. B. Eerdmans, 2002.

Luz, Ulrich. "The Secrecy Motif and the Marcan Christology." *The Messianic Secret*. ed. Christopher Tuckett. Philadelphia: Fortress Press, 1983.

Macarius the Great of Egypt. *Saint Macarius the Spirit Bearer*. tr. Tim Vivian. New York: SVS Press, 2004.

Malaty, Tadros Y. *The Gospel According to St. Mark*. Alexandria: St. George Church, 2003.

Manson, T. W. *Only to the House of Israel? Jesus and the Non-Jews*. Philadelphia: Fortress Press, 1964.

_____. "Realized Eschatology and the Messianic Secret." In *Studies in the Gospels: Essays in Memory of R. H. Lightfoot*. Oxford: Basil Blackwell, 1955.

_____. *The Sayings of Jesus*. London: SCM Press, 1954.

_____. *The Teaching of Jesus: Studies of Its Form and Content*. Cambridge: Cambridge University Press, 1945.

Marcus, Joel. "Mark 14:61: 'Are You the Messiah-Son-of-God?'" *Novum Testamentum* 31 (1989): 125-141.

_____. "The Beelzebul Controversy and the Eschatologies of Jesus." In *Authenticating the Activities of Jesus*. ed. Bruce Chilton and Craig A. Evans. Leiden: Brill, 2002.

Marshall, I. Howard. *The Origins of New Testament Christology*. Leicester: Apollos, 1990.

Matera, F. J. *The Kingship of Jesus: Composition and Theology in Mark 15*. Chico: Scholars Press, 1982.

McKelvey, R. J. *The New Temple: The Church in the New Testament*. Oxford: Oxford University Press, 1969.

Meier, John P. *A Marginal Jew: Rethinking the Historical Jesus*. 3 Volumes. New York: Doubleday, 2001.

_____. "Reflections on Jesus-of-History Research Today." In *Jesus' Jewishness: Exploring the Place of Jesus in Early Judaism*. ed. James H. Charlesworth. New York: Crossroad Publishing Company, 1996.

_____. "The Historical Jesus and the Historical Law: Some Problems with the Problem." *The Catholic Biblical Quarterly* 65, 1 (2003): 52-79.

Melito of Sardis. *On Pascha and Fragments: Texts and Translations*. ed. S. G. Hall. Oxford: Clarendon Press, 1979.

Meyendorff, John. *Marriage: An Orthodox Perspective.* New York: SVS Press, 1975.

Meyer, Ben F. *The Aims of Jesus.* London: SCM Press, 1979.

Moltmann, Jurgen. *The Crucified God.* Minneapolis: Fortress Press, 1993.

Montefiore, C. G. *Some Elements of the Religious Teaching of Jesus.* London: Macmillan, 1910.

Neusner, Jacob. *A Rabbi Talks with Jesus: An Intermillenial Interfaith Exchange.* New York: Doubleday, 1993.

_____. *From Politics to Piety: The Emergence of Pharisaic Judaism.* New Jersey: Prentice-Hall, 1973.

_____. *The Idea of Purity in Ancient Judaism.* Leiden: Brill, 1973.

Noel, Conrad. *Jesus the Heretic.* London: J.M. Dent, 1939.

Notley, R. Steven. "The Kingdom of Heaven Forcefully Advances." In *The Interpretation of Scripture in Early Judaism and Christianity.* ed. Craig A. Evans. Sheffield: Sheffield Academic Press, 2000.

Origen . *Commentary on Matthew,* GCS 38.

_____. *Fragment.* GCS 41.

_____. *On Prayer.* GCS 3.

Pagels, Elaine. *The Origin of Satan.* New York: Random House, 1995.

_____. "The Social History of Satan, the 'Intimate Enemy': A Preliminary Sketch." *The Harvard Theological Review* 84, 2 (1991): 105-128.

Pelikan, Jaroslav. *Jesus Through the Centuries: His Place in the History of Culture.* New Haven: Yale University Press, 1985.

Perrin, Norman. *Rediscovering the Teaching of Jesus.* New York: Harper & Row Publishers, 1976.

_____. *The Kingdom of God in the Teaching of Jesus.* London: SCM Press, 1963.

_____. *Jesus and the Language of the Kingdom.* Philadelphia: Fortress Press, 1976.

Pitre, Brant. *Jesus, the Tribulation, and the End of the Exile.* Grand Rapids: Baker Academic, 2005.

Räisänen, Heikki. "The 'Messianic Secret' in Mark's Gospel." In *The Messianic Secret.* ed. Christopher Tuckett. Philadelphia: Fortress Press, 1983.

Read, David H. C. "Expository Problems: The Cry of Dereliction." *The Expository Times* 68 (1957): 260-262.

Rhoads, David. "Jesus and the Syrophoenician Woman in Mark: A Narrative-Critical Study." *Journal of the American Academy of Religion* 62, 2 (1994): 343-375.

Riches, John. *Jesus and the Transformation of Judaism*. London: Darton, Longman & Todd, 1980.

Ridderbos, Herman N. *The Gospel According to John: A Theological Commentary*. tr. John Vriend. Cambridge: Wm. B. Eerdmans, 1997.

Rosse, Gerard. *The Cry of Jesus on the Cross: A Biblical and Theological Study*. tr. Stephen Wentworth Arndt. New York: Paulist Press, 1987.

Rowland, Christopher. *Christian Origins*. London: SPCK, 2002.

Royster, Bishop Dmitri. *The Kingdom of God: The Sermon on the Mount*. New York: SVS Press, 1992.

Russell, Jeffrey Burton. *Satan: The Early Christian Tradition*. Ithaca: Cornell University Press, 1982.

_____. *The Devil: Perceptions of Evil from Antiquity to Primitive Christianity*. Ithaca: Cornell University Press, 1977.

Sagne, Jean-Claude. "The Cry of Jesus on the Cross." *Concilium* 169 (1983): 52-58.

Salibi, Dionysius bar. *A Response to the Arabs*. tr. Joseph P. Amar. Belgium: Peeters Publishers, 2005.

Sanders, E. P. *Jesus and Judaism*. London, SCM Press, 1985.

_____. "Jesus and the First Table of the Jewish Law." In *The Historical Jesus in Recent Research*. ed. James D. G. Dunn and Scot McKnight. Indiana: Eisenbrauns, 2005.

_____. *Jewish Law from Jesus to the Mishnah*. London: SCM Press, 1990.

_____. *The Historical Figure of Jesus*. London: Penguin Books, 1993.

Schlier, Heinrich. "daktylos." *TDNT* 2 (1964).

Schmemann, Alexander. *The Eucharist: Sacrament of the Kingdom*. tr. Paul Kachur. New York: SVS Press, 2003.

Schurer, Emil. *The History of the Jewish People in the Age of Jesus Christ (175 BC-135 AD)*. ed. Geza Vermes and Fergus Miller. 2 Volumes. Edinburgh: T. & T. Clark, 1973.

Schweitzer, Albert. *The Quest of the Historical Jesus*. tr. W. Montgomery. London: SCM Press, 2000.

Schweizer, Eduard. *Jesus Christ: The Man from Nazareth and the Exalted Lord*. London: SCM Press, 1989.

_____. "The Question of the Messianic Secret in Mark." In *The Messianic Secret*. ed. Christopher Tuckett. Philadelphia: Fortress Press, 1983.

Severus of Antioch. *Cathedral Sermons*. Homily 98, PO 25.

Sigal, Phillip. "Aspects of Mark pointing to Matthean priority." In *New Synoptic Studies: The Cambridge Gospel Conference and Beyond.* ed. William R. Farmer. Macon: Mercer University Press, 1983.

Smith, Fred. "The Strangest 'word' of Jesus." *The Expository Times* 44 (1933): 259-261.

Socrates Scholastcius. *Ecclesiastical History.* NPNF 2 2.

Stylianopoulos, Theodore G. *The New Testament: An Orthodox Perspective.* 1 Volume. Massachusetts: Holy Cross Orthodox Press, 1997.

Taylor, Joan E. *The Immerser: John the Baptist within Second Temple Judaism.* Grand Rapids: Wm. B. Eerdmans, 1997.

Taylor, Vincent. *Jesus and His Sacrifice: A Study of the Passion-Sayings in the Gospels.* London: Macmillan & Co., 1939.

_____. *The Names of Jesus.* London: Macmillan, 1953.

Tertullian. *Against Marcion.* ANF 3.

_____. *Against Praxeas.* ANF 3.

_____. *Prescription Against the Heretics.* ANF 2.

Theodore of Heraclea. *Fragment.* MKGK.

Theissen, Gerd. *The Gospels in Context: Social and Political History in the Synoptic Tradition.* tr. Linda A. Maloney. Minneapolis: Fortress Press, 1991.

_____. *The Miracle Stories of the Early Christian Tradition.* Edinburgh: T & T Clark, 1983.

Theissen, Gerd. and Merz, Annette. *The Historical Jesus: A Comprehensive Guide.* London: SCM Press, 1998.

Theresa of Calcutta, Mother. *Come Be My Light: The Private Writings of the "Saint of Calcutta."* ed. Brian Kolodiejchuk. New York: Doubleday, 2007.

Thiering, B. E. "Are the 'Violent Men' False Teachers?" *Novum Testamentum* 21, 4 (1979): 293-297.

Trudinger, L. Paul. "'Eli, Eli, Lama Sabachthani?' A Cry of Dereliction? Or Victory?" *Journal of the Evangelical Theological Society* 17 (1974): 235-238.

Tuckett, Christopher. *Q and the History of Early Christianity.* Edinburgh: T & T Clark, 1996.

_____. "The Problem of the Messianic Secret." In *The Messianic Secret.* ed. Christopher Tuckett. Philadelphia: Fortress Press, 1983.

Van Der Loos, H. *The Miracles of Jesus.* Leiden: Brill, 1968.

Vermes, Geza. *Jesus in His Jewish Context.* Minneapolis: Fortress Press, 2003.

_____. *Jesus the Jew: A Historian's Reading of the Gospels.* London: SCM Press, 1983.

_____. "Jesus the Jew." In *Jesus' Jewishness: Exploring the Place of Jesus within Early Judaism*. ed. James H. Charlesworth. New York: Crossroad Publishing Company, 1996.

_____. *The Authentic Gospel of Jesus*. London: Penguin Books, 2004.

_____. *The Religion of Jesus the Jew*. London: SCM Press, 1993.

Ward, Benedicta. *The Desert Fathers: Sayings of the Early Christian Monks*. London: Penguin Classics, 2003.

Whitacre, R. A. *John*. Illinois: InterVarsity Press, 1999.

Whitters, Mark F. "Why Did the Bystanders Think Jesus Called upon Elijah before He Died (Mark 15:34-36)? The Markan Position." *The Harvard Theological Review* 95, 1 (2002): 119-124.

Willis, Wendell. *The Kingdom of God in 20th-Century Interpretation*. Massachusetts: Hendrickson Publishers, 1987.

Wilson, S. G. *The Gentiles and the Gentile Mission in Luke-Acts*. Cambridge: Cambridge University Press, 1973.

Witherington, B. *Christology of Jesus*. Minneapolis: Fortress Press, 1990.

_____. *John's Wisdom: A Commentary on the Fourth Gospel*. Louisville: Westminster John Knox Press, 1995.

_____. "Matthew 5:32 and 19:9—Exception or Exceptional Situation?" *New Testament Studies* 31 (1985): 571-576.

Wrede, William. *The Messianic Secret*. tr. J. C. G. Greig. London: James Clarke & Co, 1971.

Wright, N. T. "Jesus and the Identity of God." *Ex Auditu* 14 (1998): 42-56.

_____. *Jesus and the Victory of God*. Minneapolis: Fortress Press, 1996.

_____. "Jesus' Self-Understanding." In *The Incarnation*. ed. S. T. Davis. Oxford: OUP, 2002.

_____. *The New Testament and the People of God*. Minneapolis: Fortress Press, 1992.

Young, Brad H. *Jesus the Jewish Theologian*. Massachusetts: Hendrickson Publishers, 1995.

Zeitlin, Irving M. *Jesus and the Judaism of His Time*. Cambridge: Polity Press, 1988.

Zeitlin, S. "Korban." *Jewish Quarterly Review* 33 (1962): 160-63.

Zimmermann, Frank. "The Last Words of Jesus." *Journal of Biblical Literature* 66, 4 (1947): 465-466.

CPSIA information can be obtained at www.ICGtesting.com
Printed in the USA
BVOW030838150713

325733BV00002B/63/P